EXTRAORDINARY POWERS IN HUMANS

BY PANE ANDOV

Note for Librarians: A cataloguing record for this book is available from Library and Archives Canada at www.collectionscanada.ca/amicus/index-e.html
ISBN 1-4251-3017-8

Offices in Canada, USA, Ireland and UK

Book sales for North America and international:
Trafford Publishing, 6E–2333 Government St.,
Victoria, BC V8T 4P4 CANADA
phone 250 383 6864 (toll-free 1 888 232 4444)
fax 250 383 6804; email to orders@trafford.com
Book sales in Europe:
Trafford Publishing (UK) Limited, 9 Park End Street, 2nd Floor
Oxford, UK OX1 1HH UNITED KINGDOM
phone +44 (0)1865 722 113 (local rate 0845 230 9601)
facsimile +44 (0)1865 722 868; info.uk@trafford.com
Order online at:
trafford.com/07-1086

10 9 8 7 6 5 4 3 2 1

Dedicated to all humanity in true search of ourselves: who are we, where have we come from, what are we doing here, and where are we going. Deepest respects to everyone, over there, who will continue this work and make this knowledge more complete, by adding new revelations and discovering new ways that will improve our understanding of our true nature, our place in the Universe and our obligations to it...

PREFACE

"Extraordinary Powers in Humans" is a non-fiction book, which actually offers guidance to every one who wants to discover and develop his or her extraordinary psychic abilities. It is a powerful manual which contains a huge amount of theoretical and practical data concerning meditation, Kundalini energy, astral projection, remote viewing, telepathy, aura, clairvoyance, psychometry, psychokinesis and much more.

Basically, the book is not limited in time since it stretches from the ancient Yoga systems to the advanced and modern UFO phenomenon. Figuring out the purpose of existence, the human is somewhere in the middle. That is why *"Extraordinary Powers in Humans"* can be considered unique, because it contains so many subjects that fit in one great unity. In fact, the author describes the human evolution as a systematic process, up to the top point on the scale of the universe, the way he sees it.

Anyway, *"Extraordinary Powers in Humans"* has the potential to change someone's way of life, one's perception of reality, to develop extraordinary skills and offer him/her a chance to discover the purpose of incarnation here on Earth. Thus, to achieve all that, the book is written in a form of a special manual that leads one from the basics of the spiritual science to the point of discovering the most hidden spiritual secrets, which at the end leads to self-realization. For the same purpose, the book is divided in six major sections that contain a huge amount of theoretical and practical data leading the reader deep inside the world of the paranormal.

Stylistically viewed, the book starts with the introduction to the spiritual science by dealing with the basics of the meditation. To achieve that goal, the author offers the reader a clear perspective what meditation is, what can be achieved through it and how to meditate.

Once the disciple is able to meditate as deep as the ocean, the disciple will certainly discover presence of something very powerful in one's self with the passage of time. That powerful thing is known as Kundalini energy that exists in every human, but mostly in a latent state. In fact, this mighty force is the source of all the extraordinary powers in a human being. Thus, the second section deals with all the data connected to the Kundalini energy, which on the other hand is the most important

4

thing for everybody who wants to develop his or her mental skills. Therefore, a detailed explanation of how the Kundalini energy circulates in all of the energetic centers known as chakras follows, which is crucial for people to understand their true nature and to realize that they possess psychic abilities, which if awaken and cultivated can be very powerful.

Furthermore, a huge amount of data about astral projection with techniques for achieving the "out of the body" experience can be found in the third section of the book. Because of the complexity and variety of this phenomenon, which drags many other subjects in it that need to be clearly understood, this ability is explained in details (perhaps the most of all the others).

The forth section of *"Extraordinary Powers in Humans"*, gives the reader a complete perspective of how it feels to be present on the astral plane seen from the author's personal long years of experience. The author's eighteen carefully chosen "out of the body" experiences show a clear picture what a human can encounter while on the astral plane, how to deal with it, where to go, etc. However, the dominant subject in the above-mentioned author's astral trips is his contact with alien species. It is an extraordinary section, filled with so much data that are so amazing as to often push the reader to the limits where he/she starts questioning his/her comprehending of the reality and what is truly going on.

Furthermore, *"Extraordinary Powers in Humans"* explains that each of the psychic abilities is connected with the human's third eye, which can be developed with a right training. Thus, the author gives seven stages of training using zener cards, letter cards and other tools, and as each stage is completed the training gets harder and harder. The training starts with the zener cards, which are also known as ESP cards and present the basics of the modern parapsychology. Although most of the humanity considers them only useful tools for ESP testing, they are much more than that. In addition, they are powerful tools, through which one can develop his/her third eye with the special training. However, in this section the author clearly explains that after mastering the fifth stage of this universal training, the spiritual student can choose which extraordinary ability to awake and develop. Partly in the previous and partly in the last section, the author gives a complete theoretical and practical guidance for achieving ESP, remote viewing, clairvoyance, aura observation, psychometry, telepathy and psychokinesis. *"Extraordinary Powers in Humans"* ends with the method that will induce the awakening of the powerful spiritual force, which will lead the person to his or her self-realization.

Anyhow, this book bears a special message that will be debated amongst true spiritual disciples for a long time. Throughout the whole book, the author clearly stands on a viewpoint that it takes major self-discipline, top determination and persistence beyond words to keep up with everyday hard training. One of the amazing dimensions of the *"Extraordinary Powers in Humans"* is that the author has presented the whole processes of mental skill development from the very beginning to the ending point, so that the disciple can achieve and develop hidden psychic powers only by following author's suggestions.

Anyway, the true message that this book contains goes deeper then developing psychic powers. In fact, it uses them only as a bridge to get "somewhere" in time and space, from where the true picture of the reality becomes visible. Those whose spirits are driven by the same mystical force as mine is and who find the book useful for their practice should pay tributes as I do to my beloved wife Svetlana for putting up with me all this time necessary to write the book. If it were not for her unconditional love and support as well as her taking care of the home and the family the book would have never been written.

Last, but not least many thanks to Mrs.Suzana Goceva Zdravkovska to whom I am deeply indebted for having read the manuscript carefully and given valuable suggestions for improving my English – without her help the book would have read much worse. Needless to say, all deficiencies and errors are mine. Have a good journey to that "somewhere". Who knows, perhaps we will meet there, someday.

June 2005

THE AUTHOR

Pane Andov was born in Skopje, Macedonia in 1973 and is a resident of Republic of Macedonia. Andov specialized in computer science and worked as a computer expert in Macedonian Telecom until recently. At the present, he is a chief editor of the magazine "The Sixth Sense" that covers topics related to meditation, Kundalini energy, astral projection, remote viewing, telepathy, aura, clairvoyance, psychometry, psychokinesis and much more.

At the age of fourteen, Andov became interested in Yoga and Buddhism. Inspired by all the incredible powers that yoga masters had

demonstrated as a result of long years of practicing meditation, he started figuring out the mystery of their way of life. He became attached to all of the human's psychic abilities, but particularly to the extraordinary ability called astral projection.

The idea that human's consciousness can leave the physical body and visit the other world gave him an impression that he had missed something important in his life. He felt hunger for the knowledge and he was determined to get it. Thus, Andov meditated six hours a day and started to discover his inner potentials. The new world that was opening in front of him made him realize that the reality was not what it seemed to be, but something completely different. At that time he became one of the best experts in the field of parapsychology in the region of Former Yugoslavia. Throughout the years, Andov had successfully demonstrated his paranormal abilities in front of thousands of people.

Today he is the master of Yoga and Parapsychology and lives an extraordinary life. In his spare time, Andov gives classes to hundreds of people who want to develop their extraordinary senses.

Chapter 1
INTRODUCTION TO THE SPIRITUAL SCIENCE

When the time is ripe, each of you will take your first steps on a long journey towards the spiritual dimensions that are your true home. I remember my first steps as if it were yesterday. So, for all of you who feel ready to begin the journey, I have chosen to introduce you to spiritual knowledge, the same way I had been introduced to a long time ago.

It was late September 1988 when my uncle Rudek finally returned from his long journey to the East. I desperately wanted to see him and so, the next day, went to pay him a visit. The moment he saw me on his doorstep, a smile lit up his face and we shook hands like two close people who had not seen each other for a very long time. He offered me a drink and, after fifteen minutes of small talk, abruptly changed the topic of the conversation, starting upon a most unusual subject.

"My dear nephew, he said, "I probably shouldn't tell you this because you're too young to fully comprehend it all, but I have seen so many astonishing things on my past travels that I really must tell you about them. You have reached the age at which you will begin to make choices, which will undoubtedly affect your future, so perhaps it wouldn't be too terrible if you heard about these things, which are probably amongst the most important in life."

I became silent, dumbfounded by what next this grand old man might talk of. After a long break, accompanied by further quietness, he exhaled deeply and began to speak:

"As you already know, I have spent these five last years of my life traveling all across Tibet, Nepal and India. Believe me, these places are a world apart from our own. People there do not live as we do. In fact, their approach to life is utterly different from our own because they live their lives by a wholly different philosophy, believing that a person's true self is embodied not in the physical body, but in a spirit originating from another world. Once the physical body becomes frail no longer suitable for life, the spirit departs and returns to the immaterial world.

Ordinarily, the spirit will return to this world, born once more in a process that repeats itself repeatedly. This progression, known as reincarnation, is one of the basic beliefs that make this approach to life so much different from our own."

I did not want to interrupt him, so I remained silent, still not sensing just where the conversation was headed, not quite knowing what exactly he was trying to tell me.

"You probably wonder why am I telling you this, but I have to start somewhere for you to understand me better. A spirit, which you can understand it like a life force, is the real essence of every living form in the Universe. It might sound unbelievable to you, but I have met Tibetan monks who are capable of separating the spirit from the physical body, visit the immaterial world and return back again."

"What did you say they were capable of"? – I could not restrain myself anymore and began wondering if my uncle was joking with me or if he had lost his mind over the years.

"Look, nephew, judging from the expression on your face, I know this is difficult for you, but please, let me finish. What do you think made me go to the East in the first place?"

"I don't know uncle, to look for a better job, I guess". -I really did not know the true reason for his stay there for so long and whenever I had asked my mother about him, I had never been given a straight answer.

"No, I'll tell you why. I have heard so many strange stories about extraordinary abilities, which apparently Tibetan lamas and yogis possess in Tibet and India. Anyway, the real answer is that I was on a spiritual quest.

Everybody, including your mother, considered me a ghost chaser because I went to the East to find out if those stories were true. They all thought I was a fool and that I would never find what I was looking for because those stories were pure fiction and they were not real, but, they were all wrong. They were all wrong, because I proved to myself I was not mindless and that the stories were true. I had visited so many Buddhist and Hindu Temples on my journey and I had understood that the ancient ways were still alive. I had been around many yogis and seen what they were capable of, traveled with unusual people who had so many strange stories to tell, but I spent most of the time with Tibetan lamas learning their ways. Besides all that, I had visited a few Yoga festivals across India which are very popular there and witnessed what we could call – way beyond ordinary things."

"What kind of things uncle"?

"Powers, my nephew, I'm talking about mental powers like telepathy, psychokinesis, ability to see the invisible, astral projection, levitation, ability not to feel any pain, aura observation, inner heating, super hearing and many more. All those mental powers can be developed and cultivated by every human with proper training, which usually lasts for more than ten years."

"Oh, come on uncle, just like a superman, huh? You are joking with me again, right?

"No. I see that you have inherited much from your mother. I swear that the things I'm telling you about are true and that I have seen them with my own eyes. I will prove to you that I am not telling any lies. Wait for me a minute and I will show you something that will convince you I'm not telling jokes to you."

He went to the other room and in a while he returned with so many photographs in his arm-hold, it seemed he could hardly carry them all.

"This is a part of the photos I managed to bring with me from the East. I will go to get us something to eat, meanwhile, feel free to see them all. Some of them are quite extraordinary, I know you will agree."

Most of the pictures showed my uncle with Tibetan lamas, Indian yogis and strangely dressed people, beautiful landscapes from Tibet, Himalayas and India were on some of them, but there were some unbelievable to my eyes. One of those photos showed an old Tibetan monk levitating in thin air about 1.5 feet above the ground. I kept looking at the space between him and the ground to notice some ropes or anything, still not believing what this picture meant. A very old lama who was in the legs crossed sitting position (aside his years) was giving the impression of one shining with strange vitality. The picture was very clear and judging from the look on his face, I could tell that the old man was in some kind of altered state of mind.

However, a skeptic awoke in me again and I started to look for some small anomaly that would prove to me the picture was a fake. Yet, there wasn't any, which increased my excitement thinking that perhaps there was a possibility my uncle was telling the truth. Five minutes later my uncle returned trying hard to hide the smile on his face.

"I see you'd found one of those extraordinary photos I was telling you about. So, what do you think?"

"Uncle, do you really expect me to believe this is not a fake?"

"The picture you are holding in your hands is an original my dear Pane. I was the one that took the picture and I swear to you that it is not a fake. You can believe whatever you like, but this old monk can really neutralize Earth's gravity only by using the power of his mind. In Tibet and India, this is called Yoga flying and beside the old lama you are looking at on the picture, I have met four other people who are capable of achieving the same. Luckily, I had managed to take the photographs of them all while they performed a levitation that was even greater triumph for me and unbreakable proof that this ability existed. I can assure you that to be a witness of such an event is much more exciting than to see the same phenomenon on the picture. It is like magic in front of your eyes and it is an experience you can never forget."

"How can that be possible?

"I'm not quite sure, but the Tibetan lamas told me that it had something to do with some powerful force hidden in every human. They believe that human can awake this hidden force with long years of practice of some kind of special meditation combined with strictly chosen breathing techniques."

"What is meditation uncle"?

"That is a very difficult question. As far as I managed to learn, it can be explained as a process in which the mind is diving so deep in its own essence until the true reality becomes visible. However, it is only a bridge that takes one into the depths of his or her own inner world until one reaches certain point from where the meditation as a process stops and the new conscious state takes over."

"What do you mean by new conscious state?"

"The meditation process is altered by super conscious state which offers the person numerous choices."

"I'm not with you uncle. Please, explain it to me in simple words".

"Once the super conscious state they call Samadhi takes over, infinite possibilities lie before it. In other words, one's spirit can choose what experience to induce. The closest I had come up with is that it is some kind of Trance in which the spirit can use certain mental powers like seeing the human aura, out of the body experience, telepathy, super hearing, bioenergy, clairvoyance, psychokinesis, ability to see without eyes and many more. What is even more interesting is that those mental powers are only the beginning of the spiritual evolution of humans. All this is nothing compared to the true spiritual experience which belongs to no experiences known to average people and only understandable to a spirit that has reached self-realization."

I could still remember the excitement on his face when he was speaking about those powers like he wanted them more than his own life. Every astonishing photo that my uncle showed me had even more astonishing story and I heard them all with great interest. After a few hours of unforgettable conversation, the time had come for me to go home. While I was at the door leaving, he told me that he had just one more thing to say to me: "There are two realities in life. The first one is the reality we take as normal and where everything is defined and explained and the other is the one that has a hidden dimension, where nothing is clearly defined and fully explained. Remember that you have the option of choosing the reality you want to live in. The first one is called physical reality and everything in it starts and ends in the dimensions of the physical world. The second one, known as spiritual reality, has no such limits because it goes beyond the physical world. Thus, you can come up with the simple conclusion that the second reality offers much more than the first one.

Believe me, I have not told you all this because you are my nephew, but because I have recognized great spiritual potential in you ever since you were a small boy, intelligence beyond the average level and most important of all - a pure of heart. Anyway, Pane, before you become one of those covered with the cocoon of the average lifestyle, please consider the other option. Allow your heart to tell you what the right choice is and if you choose to live in the spiritual reality I can teach you how to reach it. If not, forget we've ever had this conversation."

At the end my uncle smiled and I remember him saying:

"Don't worry, whichever you choose, you will always be my nephew and very close to my heart."

On my way back home, two things had been spinning in my head – confusion created by all the data my uncle revealed and indescribable sense that he was telling me the truth. I stayed awake all night long, because the conversation was endlessly repeating itself in my mind. Journey to the other world, physical flying, psychokinesis, telepathy, and ability to see without eyes - can all this be true? A strange desire for exploring was coming forward and I knew which reality I was going to choose. The months were passing by and despite the fact that I was only fourteen at the time, it did not take me long to understand that the Yoga was not a religion but a whole science. I realized that this incredible science was based on a huge and complex system, which could lead anybody to complete harmony of the mind, spirit and body.

The basic thing my uncle taught me was that if I wanted to discover and develop my inner potentials I would have to learn how to meditate. He clearly explained to me that there was not just one meditative technique in Yoga but that there were numerous techniques for meditation, depending on the goal, which needed to be achieved.

So, day after day, I started to learn all that my uncle considered was important for me to know about the states of the mind and control of the breathing process. It was hard at the beginning but my spirit was determined to discover the secrets of Yoga and Buddhism and like everyone who deeply believes in one's self I succeeded and learned how to meditate as deep as the ocean. Under my uncle's instructions I meditated six hours a day and started to discover my inner potentials. The new dimension that was opening in front of me made me realize that the reality was not what it seemed to be, but something quite different. I was going deeper into my own essence, increasingly each day driven by some unknown force.

My uncle was an excellent teacher and very soon I was feeling filled with mental strength. I felt hunger for the true knowledge and I was determined to get it. A desire to master all the psychic powers was so visible in me, but mostly I was attracted to the extraordinary ability called astral projection. The idea that one's consciousness could leave the physical body and visit the other world had given me the impression that I had wasted precious time of my life. A sense that perhaps I was too old to begin the training was pushing me to train harder and to absorb the teaching faster. Day by day I was becoming somebody else, somebody that I would've never become if I have made the first option my choice.

I never sensed the time passing by until two years later when my uncle told me that he had decided to leave Macedonia and return to Tibet. He said that he made a promise to the Tibetan lamas to return to their lamasery in order to follow the ways of Buddha. Fortunately, he taught me all that he knew about the spiritual reality, or at least he said that he did. At the end he told me that every human being had its own Karma and that he hoped ours would meet again some day. I knew that he was leaving for good, but I managed to stay calm and told him I hoped for the same, too. I had no need to express my gratitude for what he had done for me because he already knew. He had saved me in every way one could possibly be saved. After so many years our paths crossed just a few times for short. The very last time we saw each other tears rolled down on his face and he told me he was a happy man because the little boy once had been his student could be his teacher now.

14

Therefore, this book presents most of the theoretical and practical data I managed to collect during my walk along the spiritual path. From the bottom of my soul, I hope it will do some good to somebody else, too. I believe the true spiritual knowledge belongs to every life form in the Universe and not just to a single individual. Therefore, I honor all those of you who will help making the knowledge more complete by adding the pieces in the mosaic from your own experience and help in spreading it to everyone who feels ready to accept it. Good luck!

Subchapter 1.1
THE LAW OF KARMA

There are million of things that one has to learn about the spiritual science, so usually it is a slow process which takes very long. Among the first things that someone willing to walk along the spiritual path has to understand, is how the law of Karma works. Many times, the Karma would not allow fast spiritual jump. In a case like this one has to put big effort to clean previous Karma as much as possible by trying to fix the major mistakes made somewhere in the past, which also means a start of a new and more constructive life.

Karma is an extremely powerful law, and never forgets to even the scores, because it is based on a single simple rule - every present action in the Universe has its own reaction, which will come somewhere in the future. If during our life span we are spreading vibrations, which are filled with kindness and love, we will certainly encounter the same vibrations and the other way around in the future. Humans, with purified hearts and correct relationships with all those around them, those who do not hate and always tell the truth and can easily fulfill our days with joy and happiness in so many ways are considered persons that bring light and their auras radiate strong positive energy always.

Usually, a meditation practice of many years creates that kind of people. Perhaps the message concerning the Karma, given by one of the greatest wise men of all times - Milarepa, should better speak for itself:

"Life is short and the time of death unknown". Therefore, inter yourself into meditation and avoid acting negatively even if your life is in stake. Shortly, the whole purpose should be explained with these thoughts: "Act in a way that you will never have to embarrass yourself in the future, and hold strongly to that rule. If you act by that rule no matter how opposite the existing rules are, you can be sure that you will never let down the instructions that were once given by the highest Buddhas."

Despite the fact that it is invisible at first sight, the Karma is a natural law that runs all things. It is a result of moral acting or moral consequence of some act done for selfish reasons.

Usually, one is not aware of the Karma until he or she tries to follow some spiritual path. When that happens, almost instantly it clears up that there is some connection between the experiences manifested through the meditation process and the Karma. It is so obvious because without meditation, there is no sense of the inner self and without it there is no awareness of the existence of the Karma. A person who is not aware of the existence of Karma cannot prevent further accumulation of the bad Karma either.

The law of Karma is extremely powerful, so one should be very careful about the reactions on every newborn situation, because the result of that specific action will induce adequate reaction in the future. There exists a short period of time we call a present moment somewhere between our every reaction to the environmental influences. The awareness of the present moment in which one has a chance to react one way or another is possible only if constantly conscious about the inner self, or is more specific about his or her presence in space and in time. Without that inner awareness on daily basis, one does not pay too much attention to things that happen at present and usually makes moves without thinking what those moves will bring tomorrow. Why is it so?

- That is because one has lost the awareness about the relationship: him/herself-the environment. Someone might say: "What is this man talking about; we are always fully aware of our environment?" Yet, is that so?

Besides using meditation as a process, which can take us deep into ourselves, it can also help us reach deeper awareness of our environment. In time, that awareness will allow us to see that in fact there is always a duality: me and my environment. If I drove a car, it would be "me and the driving". If I were happy, it would be "my happiness and I". If I ran, it would be "me and the running". If I spoke to somebody, it would be "me and the conversation with that somebody". I can go on to infinity but it is always the same – "Me and my environment".

To better understand this simple duality, we have to see the present moment. Unfortunately, most of the time our minds are occupied with thoughts born out of our own current problems or expectations of the future, so there is small room for the mind to see the present moment. The truth is, that most of the time the mind will notice the present moment after it has already gone. Instead of the mind, which is supposed to be living in the present moment, here and now one becomes aware of the present moment in the form of a memory of a moment that had just passed by. From my point of view, that is a totally wrong approach to reality.

Therefore, my point is this: true reality could be seen in this short sequence of time, which we call "a present moment"; here and now, in this moment; in each next moment to come. Every situation is new. It gives us the opportunity to act as never before. Because of the nature's true reality, which is emptiness that contains the potential of all choices known in the Universe, our intelligence is searching for the best solution from the infinite number of options in that particular moment in space and time. If the choice is not forced or triggered by impatience but spontaneous like a natural product of the state of mind, which is in a deep inner harmony, you can be sure it is always the right one.

Everything that needs to be done is to move our consciousness here and now, in this particular moment. It might sound strange to all of you, but the whole secret of how to feel truly alive and capable of making the best choice in some particular moment nothing more and nothing less, lies there.

Once our consciousness moves to the present moment, it will stop reacting on instinct, because of anger, fear or jealousy and it will respond spontaneously and in peace. In other words, once we catch the present moment and attach our consciousness to it, we are already in the center of all the happenings and while still there, we can easily make the best move we feel is appropriate for that moment.

In time, that constructive consciousness will take us to the correct relationships with our environment, which at the end will surely prevent further accumulation of the bad Karma. Once the cold winds of our bad Karma stop blowing into our minds, a more pleasant environment will appear which will provide a clear inner sight that happens to be the main condition for the mind to dive into the depths of its own true essence.

Subchapter 1.2
LOTUS POSITION (PADMASANA)

The first step for a disciple who feels ready to begin the inner journey towards self-realization is learning to meditate. However, before we go deeper into the subject of meditation, students have to master at least one Yoga position, which will enable them to comfortably sit and meditate. The most respected position by yogis is *padmasana* because it helps them to reach the deepest level of meditation and to achieve the topmost harmony of the mind, body and spirit in a way that no other meditative position does.

In Sanskrit, the word padmasana means Lotus, which is a symbol of purity that rises above the environmental dirt. The same way the Lotus grows through the dirt and rises above towards sunlight, a yogi who meditates in padmasana climbs the stairs of the spiritual evolution towards his or her self-realization.

When you master the padmasana, you are in a position to maintain your physical body stable for a long time. Because of the fact that the mind and the body are connected and influence each other, the stability of the physical body will in time bring the stability of the mind. If the stability of the mind has been achieved, the first step towards the deep meditation has been completed.

The Lotus position can also provide the best control of the breathing rhythm, known as *pranayama* in Yoga, and practicing it, a yogi can gain a full control over the body, mind and spirit. Practicing special pranayama techniques, a yogi can absorb and use the *prana*, which is a free vital energy that floats everywhere. The circuit of prana circulates best when one sits in padmasana and its strength is the most powerful.

If from any good reason one is not capable of sitting in this position, some effort should be made to learn how to meditate by being seated in a simple position with both legs crossed and the backbone in straight line. However, that position will not bring the topmost stability of the mind, body and the spirit like padmasana does, which is crucial for achieving deep and progressive meditation. Thus, each true disciple who wants to learn meditating as deep as the ocean, needs to master padmasana position as the very first step that has to be undertaken. Here is how the exercise for achieving Lotus position goes:

Once you have been seated, spread your legs and keep them at the distance of approximately 40 to 50 centimeters. Then, try to bend your left leg in the knee and place your toe on the right thigh and heel on the groin of the left leg. If this happens to be difficult for you, to master this so called half-Lotus position, it will be of great help if you oppress the left knee with your left hand as much as you can toward the floor. Do this at least 70 times and then outstretch your left leg and give yourself a minute to relax. When you have finished with the left leg, try to bend your right leg in the knee and place your toe on the left thigh and heel on the groin of the right leg. Again, if this is hard for you, repeat the oppressing with your right hand on your right knee in the same way you have done with the left leg. After you have oppressed your right leg 70 times toward the floor, outstretch your right leg and give yourself some rest. You should do five or more series with both of your legs on daily basis and soon you will be very close to achieving the whole Lotus position. Do not be discouraged if one of your knees touches the floor easier and to do the same with the other one is much harder and acquires much more effort. That is completely normal because human's body structure is usually asymmetrical. In time you will no longer feel any tension in bending both legs and by that time comes, you will know that you are ready for the complete Lotus. Then get your legs together, bring your hands beside the waist and take the sitting posture.

It is very important to keep your backbone erect and your sight straight. When you feel the stability and relaxation which padmasana provides, start to breathe deep but slowly and allow yourself to dive into the depths of your consciousness. In time, you will reach a point from where you can achieve deep and progressive meditation.

Subchapter 1.3
MEDITATION

Almost everybody has heard of meditation. A process in which one dives into the depths of one's own essence is known as meditation. Simply said, meditation represents freedom of exploration of the altered states of consciousness. Meditation can be shallow as a soft relaxation or it can be deeper than the ocean floor, all depending on the person's ability to manipulate those states of consciousness.

There are so many achievements that meditation can provide but not all of them can be achieved by just one meditative method. The truth is that there are many meditative methods created to achieve different goals. However, no difference how high the variety of the meditation methods is, they all possess the same starting point – calm and focused consciousness.

I have met so many people who meditate everyday and I can freely underline that almost every person has an opinion about what mediation is all about. Perhaps it might be a simple result of so many meditative schools present all around the world. However, I have met only a few people who (in my opinion) are really masters of the meditation and are living fires of the spiritual knowledge.

Most of these schools have relatively one thing in common: the meditative teachers interpret the experience by their own point of view determined by their level of spiritual development. On the other hand, very often it does not take the disciple deeper than to middle levels of the mind accompanied by relatively deep state of relaxation.

It is simply because many of the meditative teachers focus their training only on the mind forgetting that one's true self is not the mind but the spirit. The only right approach to meditation is to be constantly aware that the only thing permanent in one is one's spirit and not the mind because over the years the physical body undergoes a change as well as the mind.

In each new incarnation a person takes, there is a new physical body born a baby, grows as a boy/girl, becomes a man/woman and is getting old until it becomes not suitable to be a spirit carrier any longer. Each stage of the transformation of the physical body is accompanied by a changeable mind, which depends on the age, thinking one way or another. Along with the coming of the next stage, the mind changes its point of view by recognizing having been mistaken about many things all that time and starts to build a new surface on which its new understanding of the world shall be placed.

However, the spirit always remains the same. Apart from the physical body and the mind, the spirit observes their changes and accumulates their experiences. Hidden deep inside, it remains silent until one starts to realize that the true essence is the spirit and not the mind or even the physical body.

Thus, to reach these depths in ourselves where our spirit is, we need something to take us there. That something is called meditation. Figuratively speaking, during meditation, there are obstacles that hold us from diving deeper because we have to pass so many things in our mind, until we reach the bottom of our inner world where our spirit lies. Sometimes, it is very difficult for a beginner to understand the nature of the meditation itself, because it does not exist physically. It appears to the beginner that meditation is based on individual experience, which can often be very subtle and difficult to explain, and to a certain point this is true. Therefore, the first step one usually takes is to focus on the mind with the intention to calm it down, but soon realizes that it is full of wild mental storms, which do not allow

taking control over them by force. Each time a disciple tries to take them by force they become stronger and even wilder that on the other hand distracts the meditation even more.

The solution for this problem is simple. Do not fight them! Simply, shut them off! Do not pay attention to them any longer and in a while, when their opponent is gone they will be gone, too. When the annoying thoughts disappear, your mind will become clear and in position to dive deeper on your quest to find and join your spirit.

The only thing that can help you gain true experience on your meditative quest is to search deep down for the goodness in your heart. Always keep in mind that the spirit can be found only in a glowing surface that radiates from someone's pure heart and nowhere else. Thus, there is no secret formula or some secret psychic move to help you get there, but only a deep quest guided by the impulses of cosmic love, which comes straight from your heart. Following this simple rule will enable you to always know you are diving in the right direction, so the secret lies in the by-pass of your mind. Just jump over it, as if it did not exist and dive deeper and deeper until the Inner Light becomes visible. This is what true spiritual meditation is all about. In time, your deep search for the spirit will find it and that reunion will change you forever. Once this has been achieved, you will never be the same as before. No longer will you be ruled by your lower nature, but will become a being of a higher rank on the scale of nature. You will know who you are; you will be at peace; you will breathe in every single being and all the beings will breathe in you. You will be united with all of them. This kind of spiritual evolution can be achieved only by right meditation.

As I said before, meditation is a great thing, which can help us achieve so many other things. The Yoga is full of different meditative techniques designed to achieve certain goals. Yet, as a long practitioner of Yoga meditation, I have determined many techniques that are and some are not suitable for a modern person.

For that purpose, I have chosen to present two ·meditative methods in this book, which I'm completely sure, are suitable for anybody who lives a modern lifestyle. These are:

-DEEP PEACE MEDITATION
-ENERGY ABSORBING MEDITATION

The first meditation method can teach you how to reach inner peace and how to develop your inner awareness. In time and with constant practice this inner peace will come out to the surface and it will remain there, which will bring you a more constructive life by constantly providing you with a higher level of spiritual consciousness. The method itself is a solid background or base for all the further meditation experiences. Once you fully master this method, you will be ready for the majority of the other meditation techniques.

The second meditation method teaches you how to increase your bioenergy level by absorbing a huge amount of free energy from the natural bio-field, which exists all around you. In time and with practice you will indispensably feel that everything is moved by energy that flows everywhere, in everybody and in everything. The method itself is a solid preparation for the time when a real awakening of the powerful Kundalini energy will take place. The usage of this meditation method can easily awake some other psychic abilities among which the feeling of the surrounding natural bio-field is just a beginning.

Subchapter 1.4
DEEP PEACE MEDITATION

Sit in Lotus position and relax. Close your eyes and start to breathe slowly but deep. Take your breath down to the lower part of your abdomen, keep it there for a while and then slowly but gently send it back up on its way out. Always keep in mind that the amount of the absorbed prana is related to your control of the breathing process, so do not inhale and exhale shortly through your nose, use it only as a bridge which takes your breath directly to your abdomen instead. Remember that your abdomen has to run the whole process, not your nose.

The best rhythm for this meditative method is 4:2:4. You would probably find it difficult to get used to it in the beginning, but with little persistence and practice, you will surely master it. Five minutes of breathing in this rhythm will calm your mind and your body should become more relaxed. When you feel that you have managed to pull that off, release the control of the breathing process and let it take its own natural rhythm.

Next thing that you should do is to become aware of what is going on in your mind. Shortly after you have achieved that kind of awareness, you will notice that your mind is full of inner storms, tensions and all kinds of mental conflicts. The stronger you concentrate on them intending to calm them down or even neutralize them, the stronger and more intensive they will become. To calm all this manifestations in your mind you must build correct relationships with them. That can be done in a very simple and effective way. Start observing the thoughts that appear in your mind with the eye of a witness.

Do not play with them or even try to analyze them, just observe them. Watch how they form and pass in their silent way, and maintain the perspective that does not have at least one crossing point with them. After a while, you will feel the source they come from. At that moment you would be able to clearly see how shortly after they took form, they started to regroup themselves into chains of thoughts. One idea will pull at least few other ideas to the surface of your mind as a logical response to the first one, until some other idea with completely different context does not appear in your mind and again induces manifestation of other ones related to that one.

These thought chains will constantly be coming from the depths of your mind to the surface always taking different shapes on their way up. Therefore, your task is to monitor the changes that your thought chains are going through from the moment they appear in your mind to the moment they are gone and altered by other ones. Sooner or later, if you continue to observe these thought chains manifesting one after another still from the perspective of the silent witness somewhere in your mind, you will notice that they will reduce and after a while they will slowly start disappearing. This is a completely normal effect because you are not playing their game anymore and you are no longer attached to them emotionally. If you continue to maintain this concentration your brain patterns will soon change and that will lead you to an altered state of your consciousness.

In the end, the last thought chain will disappear from your inner sight and you will find yourself in a completely new situation. Your consciousness will be moved directly to the present moment. Once your consciousness finds itself in the present moment, it will instantly discover that it is empty. Still, the emptiness that your consciousness will see in that present moment will not be a complete emptiness, but it will contain potential of all known shapes in the Universe. It might sound strange, but if you manage to get this far, your consciousness will constantly be aware of this fact.

You will see that in the emptiness in which your consciousness is present, a hidden reality is becoming visible for you. It might seem as if you are being pushed into the pure reality and you will experience your consciousness sliding from moment to moment as never before. This experience will make it clear that reality has a characteristic of sliding from moment to moment.

When this moment comes, all you have to do next is to attach your consciousness directly to that present moment and you will find that you are remaining in the pure reality all the time, by sliding from that moment to the next one. The feeling will be so vivid and so amazing that your whole being will float in the Inner Light. The best part is that your consciousness will not fly on the wings of the illusion created from the shadows of your past and your expectations for the future.

You will be here and now, and that's the starting point for every advanced meditation. In this stage of deep meditation you will understand that there is no need for you to completely attach and waste yourself on thousands of tiny, unimportant everyday problems, but you will decide that sometimes it is for the best to leave them solve themselves in their own natural way. If you believe in the laws of nature and that all things happen because of the Karma you should be able to understand what my point is.

Once you have succeeded to reach this state of consciousness, the environmental influences will not touch you the same way they have before. All the problems, doubts, fears and negative feelings will remain only as bigger or smaller storms on the surface. Deep down and where the peace is, you will be safe.

The world will manifest itself on the surface and you will see these manifestations in a way as if you were watching a show. You will be aware of them, but they will not be able to reach you. That awareness will bring you inner peace and the longer your consciousness remains in deep meditation, the faster it will become present in you, all the time, day and night. After an hour, maybe more return the physical body to the normal state and end the meditation.

In time, this meditation method will help you see the simple truth that your calm mind which thinks straight is to solve your problems, not your nervousness, fear, desire or hope. A calm mind that thinks straight always reacts spontaneously and in peace, which is the most important thing for making the right choice in some particular moment. Once you have become fully aware of the present moment knowing its potentials, you will be the master of yourself and you will always react the best way to the challenges of the next moment. The longer you keep sliding from moment to moment, the longer you will stay in true reality constantly aware of your presence in time and space. This method is very similar to something known as Zen in the East and is very practical for every modern person.

However, if you want to reach top experience, which this meditation provides, you have to understand the truth:

"Without the control of the breathing there is no peace. Without peace, there is no concentration and no depth. Without depth there is no meditation and without meditation there is no consciousness of what the things really are like."

Subchapter 1.5
ENERGY ABSORBING MEDITATION

Everything around us floats in energy. The problem is, people are usually not aware of the presence of the huge ocean of bioenergy that lies so close, and even if they are, they have to spend some time until they learn how to absorb the energy from it.

By absorbing the energy from this huge ocean that lies in the etheric plane, we do not take the energy from somebody else. After the absorbing process, a tiny loss of energy will appear in the global Earth bio-field, but almost instantly, that loss will be filled up with the energy that comes from space. So, everything is moved by energy. Energy flows everywhere, in everyone and in everything. We are all part of it. It flows through us and connects us in a special way.

The more energy we possess, the stronger we are and more capable of dealing with all the hard tasks that life brings. A method of meditation that is created for energy absorption from the environmental bioenergy field could be described as follows:

It is for the best if you practice this meditation method at night and in complete darkness. The absence of light will provide you with the best visualization ability, which is the most important thing about this exercise. The best time for it is 04:00AM because the prana is the strongest in that period of the day and the environmental disturbances are greatly reduced. You will achieve best results with this exercise if you sit in the lotus position. Calm your mind and body for at least half an hour of meditation, described in the previous method. When you reach the state of deep inner peace, you need to become aware of your natural bioenergy that runs in your etheric body.

Keep your eyes closed and focus on your hands. Feel the charging of a bio-power in them. Stretch your arms forward then start moving them slowly and in identical movements in the direction where your hands should intercept each other. When the distance of 10 centimeters between the two hands has been reached, stop. Feel the two-way energy circuit between the hands and follow the energy that flows from your left hand to the right hand, and opposite. Concentrate the best you can to find the middle point where those two energies meet. Now include your inner eye in that middle point and visualize a creation of a little blue-white energy ball. The bigger the amount of bioenergy that flows from both hands guided to the point where the intercept of the two energies will occur, the bigger the ball will grow.

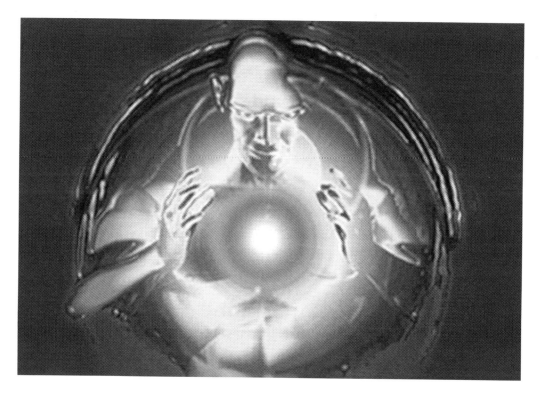

When the shiny energy ball reaches the size of 7 centimeters, just increase the distance between the two hands and allow more space for further growing. When the psi-ball reaches the size of 10 centimeters put the other energy barrier around it. This energy should rotate around the surface of the ball, and its color should be green-white. As soon as you have created the protective barrier, the blue-white bioenergy is sealed and protected from vaporizing into the natural bio-field. Then, remove your hands and let the psi-ball levitate close to your body. If you have done everything right, you should feel the strong pulsating energy that comes from the etheric ball and it should be very easy for you to control it without your hands. Give the mental command and push the energy ball away from you. Send it about 3 meters away from you and then stop it there. Then release the psi-ball from your control and let it levitate on its own. The moment you have set the energy ball free, you will feel a strange change in your room.

Note: *Sometimes when the energy in the psi-ball is too strong, it can be felt like gentle magnetism in the hair or on the skin. There is also a possibility that some of you will experience strong zooming sound in your ears. The effect of the zooming sound is because you have made a change in the energy level of the natural bio-field which has spontaneously triggered a minimal amount of Kundalini rising. In other words, the connection that you have established with the natural bio-field has tickled the asleep and latent energy in your etheric body, and when that happens, almost always it is followed by strong zooming sound. If that effect appears, do not be afraid, it is completely normal and will pass in ten to twenty seconds. The energy will hit the energy centers in your etheric body and starting there it will leave your energy system by joining the natural bio-field. As soon as that happens, the zooming sound will disappear.*

The next thing you should do is to lock your mind again on the energy ball. Using your hands, start to pull the psi-ball back to you. When you have pulled the etheric ball to a meter distance from your physical body, stop and give it strong magnetic power. Take off the protective green-white shield and allow the absorption to follow. Visualize as the psi-ball starts to pull and absorb more energy from all around you and becomes bigger. When it reaches above 2 meters in diameter, cut off the magnetic force of the psi-ball. Put the protective shield on again, and do not allow the loss of the bioenergy.

When you have done that, simply visualize yourself walking into it, with your etheric body. If that happens to be difficult for you, just concentrate and imagine you are walking into the psi-ball physically, which will produce the same effect. Put yourself into it 100 %. If you have successfully projected your etheric double in the energy ball, the first thing that you should experience is a levitating effect along with the feeling of no weight. It will feel like floating in the liquid of pure energy.

Perhaps, in the beginning, you will experience the effect of biolocation of your consciousness, but in time and with practice, you will sure master it. When you find yourself floating in the energy ball, open yourself completely and allow the full penetration of the bioenergy directly into every single atom of your etheric body.

That way, all the energy centers will absorb the maximum level of prana energy. When you are absolutely positive you have managed to absorb all the energy from the psi-ball, just step out of it and return to your physical body. With your eyes still closed, use your inner eye to push the energy ball as far as possible. Then just release the green-white protective shield and shut down the psi-ball. After completing this meditation method, you will feel relaxed, fresh and filled with energy.

Once in a week energy absorption from the natural bioenergy field is enough and it will enable you to feel more vital, healthier and more in the mood that will help you in all the things every day brings. In time, your bioenergy will be increased to the level that will allow you to help someone by making healing changes. Use your bio-potential wisely and only for everybody's well being.

Chapter 2
KUNDALINI YOGA

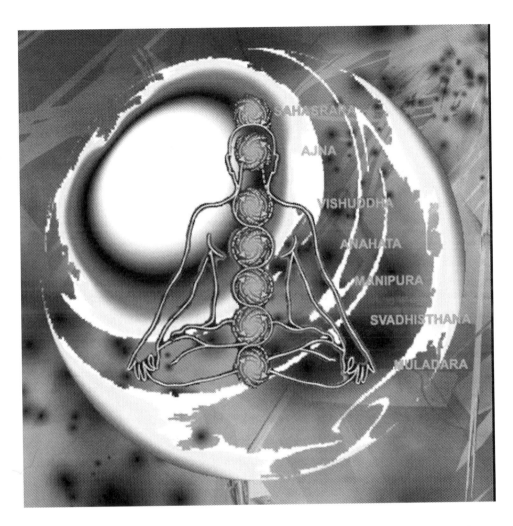

The Kundalini Yoga system is one of the oldest systems of Yoga. Accordingly to the meaning, this system of Yoga studies all aspects of the vital cosmic force in humans known as Kundalini energy. This powerful inner force lies hidden in everybody and once awaken it changes one's consciousness in a way like no other thing does. While it is in a latent state people are more or less conscious about their deeper nature, but when this mighty force becomes active, it causes spiritual evolution allowing them to experience altered states of their consciousness.

Physiologically, when this Kundalini energy becomes active, it climbs up through the spinal cord directly to one's head with the main purpose to cause certain changes in the brain activity. It is amazing what Kundalini does to the human body. It has been proven that when it reaches the brain it brings the bioelectrical power supply to the brain cells, which are usually out of function. It actually hits the whole area of the brain but influences mostly the cells that are connected to the psychic abilities of the mind. Still, this is only a part of what Kundalini does, because its main purpose is to bring the spiritual evolution to people by showing them their true nature.

However, before we go deeper into the system of Kundalini Yoga, we need to understand what yogic term prana and pranayama means. In Sanskrit, the word prana means "The breath of life force". This life force is in fact vital etheric energy that flows freely across the whole etheric plane. Through the process of breathing, we all take this vital energy in and out, and without it, we would not be able to live, because besides food and water, it provides us with vitality essential to our existence.

Kundalini Yoga is clearly teaching us that there is a strong connection between the rhythm of breathing and the mind. Since ancient times, the yogis have been aware of this fact and they have developed a system of techniques for controlling the prana through the breathing process known as pranayama. Today, knowing that the mind and the body are in tight connection and influence each other, we can get a clear picture of the importance of controlling the way we breathe. We all consume prana through the air we breathe, which in fact is oxygen we inhale and carbon dioxide we exhale, but when we practice the pranayama we are in position to increase the amount of the prana and to distribute it into our energetic system.

The pranayama contains hundreds of breathing rhythms depending on the goal that needs to be achieved. Thus, in a single pranayama technique the time required for taking the breath, holding it into the abdomen and exhaling it is defined by the purpose of the practice.

For a further understanding of Kundalini Yoga teaching, we have to accept the fact that besides our physical body we possess other bodies, which are subtler by nature. The existence of one of these bodies has been scientifically proven in 1939 by the invention of the Kirlian photography. A former Soviet Union couple, who proved that in and around the physical body there is a hidden energetic body visible as radiance, which emanates in many colors, developed this invention.

Technically, a Kirlian photography involves the transferring of a high frequency charge through a metal plate attached to a Polaroid film camera base. The fingertips are lightly placed on the film encased in a light-tight bag, and an electric exposure is made. Sixty seconds later, after the film develops, the Kirlian photograph is complete and the subject's energy field is revealed.

The energy field that exists around every living thing is not physically visible unless one possesses an open third eye, because its structure is of etheric substance. The bottom line is, the etheric energy field mainly consists of protective shield, energy centers called chakras and a vast net of energy channels known as nadis.

According to some ancient Yoga scripts all these chakras are whirlpools of prana energy that keeps the human alive. It has been estimated that one's etheric body possesses 72,000 nadis or energy channels, 77 main energy centers connected with all the nadis, 7 of which are primary.

These 7 primary chakras represent the basic structure of the Cosmos starting from the state of highest density, touchable and material to the state of subtlety, untouchable and immaterial. They also represent a path of human evolution, which goes from the organic darkness and unconsciousness to a cosmic consciousness, which radiates.

Each one of these primary chakras has its own level of vibration determined by the current state of the Kundalini energy. These seven chakras play the leading roles in the process of Kundalini rising and with the primary energy channel known as *Sushumna nadi* and the two secondary energy channels *Ida nadi* and *Pingala nadi*, they make the powerful energy stream that Kundalini energy runs through.

These centers have touch points in human's physical body along the spinal cord. It is well known that in this spinal cord, there is a cerebrospinal fluid and when Kundalini energy awakes in the lowest chakra helped by the pranayama, this fluid starts agitating. On its way up the spinal cord during the rising process, the Kundalini takes this cerebrospinal fluid along, straight to the brain, changing the states of consciousness in the same time. That's why before the great awakening happens; Kundalini Yoga strongly suggests fully prepared person's inner self if one is to take the heat of the Kundalini rising, which induces a mighty wave of many psychic effects.

Thus, the Kundalini will be canalized directly to its last destination with no side effects only if one's spirit is ready, purified and focused in the right direction. It is well known that at first one is better not to experiment with this powerful force on his/her own, except if forced to, as for example when the Kundalini awakes unintentionally and without one's will. In that case, an immediate search for a guru or at least an advanced and experienced student in this subject is recommended. It would be very foolish for anyone inexperienced to start playing with this dangerous force. The energy system is certainly not prepared to take the heat of the rising and the Kundalini can easily strike some chakra with all its strength, the result of which can sometimes be very dangerous.

To those who find themselves in a position with the active Kundalini energy, which causes altered states of their consciousness, and there is not any guru or even advanced Kundalini Yoga student in their neighborhood, my advice would be:

First and basic – do not panic. Panic makes the situation worse. Your fear will intensify the effects Kundalini brings and they will take their own course, which will be completely out of your control. So, no matter how bad the situation looks at first, act cool as if the things happening to you were nothing that could hurt you and it would be a piece of cake to control them.

If you conquer your fears, you have gained the first step towards gaining control over this strong force. Make the best effort to calm your mind. Calm and stable mind can help you a lot to deal with this wild and powerful force.

Lie down or sit in some of the meditative positions. It is better to keep your backbone erect and your breathing deep and relaxed. If you feel that Kundalini energy is forcing its way up with great speed and strength, do not fight it- let it pass. Do not pay any attention to the strong zooming sound you hear because it is completely normal and it appears almost in each rising of the Kundalini.

Without any exceptions, do not try to move your physical body in the moments when Kundalini climbs up. If you do not panic, if you keep your mind calm and if you do not move, it will be gone in a short while. When the zooming sound is off, and you have felt that the energy has left your body through the top point of your head, the Kundalini has gone - then you can move and get up.

It is essential to understand that this powerful force, which produces a terrifying zooming sound and runs straight up along your spinal cord is your own energy and not some alien force. If you accept this truth, you will do just fine.

The feeling of some alien force that wants to conquer and destroy you is common case in the unintentional awakening of Kundalini, but the truth is that it is your own bullet shooting at you. Everything you keep in your inner locker, the Kundalini force brings out. If peace dominates your spirit, the Kundalini force will flow smoothly on its way out through your head and the opposite.

When this happens to be the case, try to concentrate on love, peace and friendship. Clear your mind from all the negative thoughts and feelings and think absolutely positive in every way.

If you act by these friendly suggestions, your chances to deal with unintentional awakening of this eternal life force are much bigger, than if you panic and you are overtaken by your fear. The Kundalini effects will withdraw and you will continue with you normal life in a few days.

If these effects do not disappear and the manifestations induced by the Kundalini rising remain longer, or even if rising repeats itself many times during a day, I suggest an immediate search for someone who is expert in the field to help you in your further dealing with it.

Luckily, the unintentional awakening of Kundalini force happens rarely. I hope no one will need this, but the same thing happened to my wife, so I assume it is important to be mentioned. According to the Kundalini Yoga, it takes twelve years of hard training to become capable and ready to lift this powerful inner force. However, it is true that one walking along the spiritual path can take giant steps forward only after the awakening of the Kundalini energy happens, so to fear this inner latent force is a totally wrong approach. The best way to master this inner energy is to find a good guru who will guide you through the secrets of Kundalini Yoga.

If you manage to find one, then you certainly are considered happy because the guru will take care of all the danger points along your long years of training. The guru will monitor all the stages of your spiritual development and he will safely guide you to the awakening of your Kundalini energy. However, to find a good, wise and experienced guru usually is a chance of one in a million, so many of you will have to take the other way which is far harder and not the safest one.

Anyway, the Kundalini Yoga is primarily for the strongest that are determined to find the purpose of their own existence. If the nature loves you, it will provide you the way to reach what you are after. When your Karma is ready, the nature will start the process of awakening of the Kundalini force on its own. There is nothing mystical about this; it is just a simple fact of how the nature works.

When the Kundalini has been awaken and is in full power, you become a fire of a living knowledge, a user of incredible mental powers and driver of your own destiny.

The law of Karma cannot touch you anymore, because you are above it, and the people that meet you, recognize divine incarnation in you. All the horizons of this and other worlds are open in your consciousness and you can move wherever you want with your higher bodies. Your eyes will always shine with wisdom, your heart will always bring the message of love and your deeds will always be full of compassion and friendship. With all respect for other systems of Yoga, I believe that the Kundalini Yoga offers the most. However, before we go further into explaining different subjects in the spiritual science, let us take a close look at the seven primary chakras.

Subchapter 2.1
MULADHARA

In Sanskrit, *Muladhara* means: "base". It is the first chakra in the spiritual evolution of humans. This chakra is located in the base of the spine and corresponds to the pelvic plexus. It lies between the origin of the reproductive organ and anus and it is a point where Sushumna, Ida and Pingala nadis meet.

The Kundalini energy is usually symbolized with a three and a half time coiled female serpent, asleep or in a latent state in Muladhara chakra. The most important aspect of this chakra is being a shelter where the mighty Kundalini sleeps. According to the Tantric traditions the three coils of the serpent represent the three major aspects of nature: Sattva–harmony, Rajas-action and Tamas-inertia, while the half coil itself symbolizes the transcendental consciousness. Although the Kundalini Yoga and the Tantra have their differences, they both symbolize the latent power in humans in the shape of a sleeping goddess Kundalini Shakti as incarnation in the human body, which possesses potential to bring the ultimate light or darkness to the spirit.

It is known that Muladhara chakra releases the main vital energy, which is responsible for the body reproduction and, it plays the major role in the transformation process of these sexual forces into the spiritual potentials as well. During the moments of sexual ecstasy, the Muladhara chakra increases its activity, so the orgasm can be used as a fire starter for the Kundalini. To the best of my knowledge, the orgasm has been used as a jump board for awakening of this mighty force through the sexual act of the love couple in some Temples across northern India even these days.

However, although it is the lowest center in human's spiritual evolution, the significance of the Muladhara chakra is very important and should be treated with great respect. The awakening of this primeval force is the beginning of the human evolution because mostly, the whole process starts here in Muladhara chakra.

Usually, it takes years of deep meditation, all kinds of pranayama exercises, and many physical exercises known as asanas, but most of all a purified, creative and quiet life to complete the awakening process of all of the 7 primary chakras. The process of awakening the main chakras is a completely different matter from the awakening of Kundalini energy and it lasts until all of the chakras become active.

If pulsating feeling appears in the physical point where the Muladhara is located, it is usually a clear sign that awakening of this center is close, even active to some level. Still, the Muladhara chakra possesses a high level of activity in humans whose sexual life is active. However, in no uncertain terms it has to be understood that active Muladhara chakra does not necessarily mean an active Kundalini energy. In fact, the parallel awakening of these two different processes almost never happens.

The awakening and rising of the Kundalini is strictly an individual matter, but the greatest masters of the Kundalini Yoga always advise aspirants to awake their primary chakras before starting to work with this powerful force. It rarely happens but is fully possible, that Kundalini could be asleep in some higher chakra than Muladhara. In that case, it surely is a result of long and hard efforts in the past incarnations. Actually, it means, a start of climbing up of the awaken Kundalini from the chakra that was asleep in the previous incarnation. Yet, it is a case of one in a thousand, and most of the humanity must achieve the awakening of the Kundalini in the Muladhara chakra.

Subchapter 2.2
SVADHISTHANA

The second chakra is *Svadhisthana*. In Sanskrit, the word Svadhisthana means: "one's own self". In the human body, this chakra corresponds to the hypogastric plexus in the genital region and it is very close to the location of the Muladhara no matter whether a male or female is concerned. It controls the liquid factor of the body associated with the taste and the reproductive glands – the testicles in males and ovaries in females. This center is connected with the subconscious mind, the collective unconsciousness and long forgotten genetic memories. When Svadhisthana chakra becomes active, the consciousness of the disciple is hit by a tornado of a million psychic manifestations, which usually possess dark character. When this happens, disciples must deal with all those mental conflicts that are the product of the collected negative Karma, which sometimes can be generated even from their past lives.

Therefore, in time when Svadhisthana chakra awakes, the debts of Karma come out in a "full glory". For that reason, besides a deep meditation, the Kundalini Yoga points out on following the moral doctrine that contains many rules for the right relationship of the disciples with the world around them. Only if the disciple's mind is focused on the highest spiritual goal and tends to purify itself, the disciple can smoothly pass along the path within the mental storms that contain all sorts of psychic impressions. These previously repressed psychic impressions in the depths of the unconsciousness for a very long time swim freely on the surface of the consciousness now. The huge spectrum of those manifestations can often cause disturbances in the meditative process, but that is a stage of development that each truthful disciple walking along the path of self-realization must go through. In other words, the second chakra represents a center in which one's consciousness cleans itself from the dark Karma, which on the other hand will create the right conditions for awakening the next higher chakra. The disciple, even in this stage of the spiritual growth, feels the guilt in his or her consciousness for every immoral thing done, no matter whether the wrong thing appeared in deeds, words or thoughts.

Physiologically, like all the other chakras Svadhisthana pulsates when irritated, starts to awake or it is fully active. According to the oldest Sanskrit scripts, in ancient times, the primary home of the latent Kundalini Shakti was in Svadhisthana and not in Muladhara as it usually is the case today. A fall of the spiritual evolution of humans by alien interaction of some other civilization, which had come from the stars in the time of Earth's global flood, is clearly mentioned in those scripts.

However, so many things are vague about our distant past that sometimes a human has to take the facts open-minded no matter how contradictory the facts are. Sometimes, our history records present contradictory facts in order to search for true facts that really happened thousands of years ago. To the best of my knowledge, that interaction really happened and it is the main reason for the Kundalini Shakti's sleeping in the Muladhara nowadays that had been the highest animal chakra in those days.

Subchapter 2.3
MANIPURA

The third center is the *Manipura* chakra, which in Sanskrit means "City of Jewels". This chakra is located in the solar plexus area, right behind the hoof. Physiologically, it coordinates the digestive processes and the activity of the organs situated in the abdomen. The pranic energy is very strong in this center and in the East it is also known as the center of inner heat, where the chi energy can be driven out of the physical body.

The Chinese masters of martial arts consider this center very important because according to them the source of the powerful energy they call "chi" lies there.

According to witnesses, by using this chakra they can focus their energy to one point in their bodies and become resistant to a sword thrust in that particular place, and similar things. Speaking of martial arts, as far as I know, the Shaolin monks are the top masters of using the energy that comes from this center.

On the other hand, the usage of the Manipura chakra on The Himalayas is almost a common thing. Many have witnessed the abilities of the lamas and yogis who usually meditate sitting in the snow, dressed only in thin robes: through the process of their meditation they release the heat that comes from their own physical bodies and melt the snow around them. Despite the fact that they are half-naked and exposed to temperatures way below zero, they look as if experiencing overheating.

However, while the level of the spiritual evolution in a human is in Muladhara and Svadhisthana chakra, the disciple's consciousness can easily fall into many emotional traps hidden in the lower nature. Only after the disciple's consciousness has evaluated these two chakras and experienced purification in Manipura chakra, these emotional traps are easy to detect and avoid. Therefore, we must treat this chakra with great respect because it holds our personal power, will and control.

Subchapter 2.4
ANAHATA

A center that corresponds to the heart plexus is known as *Anahata* chakra. Physiologically, it controls the circulatory, respiratory and immunity systems. Spiritually, this center is special because it is the residence of the human soul. Here in Anahata chakra the purification of the emotions transforms the individual into a more subtle being and one loses the hard connection with the material world. In Sanskrit, the word Anahata means "incessant". The name is a symbol for the incessant connection of the human soul with the cosmic love like the one of the primeval forces in the Universe. When this center is activated, a human becomes the fire of the cosmic love. From now on, unselfishness dominates one's deeds and he or she gives everything without expecting anything in return.

It is sufficiently enough for a person to know that some good deed is done, and one does not look for a reward or gratitude for it. What one feels in his/her spiritual heart is a feeling of unlimited love as never before. It is as if a light is coming out from the center of Anahata chakra, which makes one to feel overjoyed. If Anahata is awake, the disciple surely experiences the phenomenon of amplifying the strength of the thoughts. The stronger the thoughts become, the more the disciple becomes aware of a vast ocean of thoughts that exists everywhere around him or her.

One of the tasks of the Anahata chakra is to send each thought born in the consciousness directly to that vast ocean of thoughts. If the disciple's thoughts are purified, noble and divine, they will cause an identical thought vibration in every similar mind throughout the whole Universe.

Wherever these individuals go, they always bring luck, love, and peace and pain relief along. With the unconditional love that radiates from their spiritual hearts, they have acquired the ability to heal. They project their spiritual energy into the part of the body where the pain is present and induce the healing changes. In the time of Kundalini rising, when the energy passes through the Anahata chakra, the heart of the yogis open in full glory and start to shine in all directions.

This chakra is also known as "Unstruck Note", because unstruck sound is the sound of silence. In this spiritual "silence", which is the underlying sound of the Universe, a disciple passes the gateway to higher consciousness.

Subchapter 2.5
VISHUDDHA

The fifth center located in the base of the throat that corresponds with the carotid plexus is known as *Vishuddha* chakra. In Sanskrit, the word "Vishuddha" means purification, so it is considered a purifying center. All of the smallest anomalies and impurities remained from the lower chakras will be purified here.

It is well known that when this center is active, it extracts special nectar that influences many psychophysical processes in the human body. With the help of this nectar, it is possible for a yogi to achieve neutralization of the inner and outer venom.

On various Festivals in some parts of India, the yogis drink a very strong venom and stay alive and in the mood as if drinking pure water. If an average person drank just a smaller amount of the poison that these yogis drank, he/she would be dead in less than a minute. About this ability, yogis usually say that it is strictly connected with the control of the nectar that Vishuddha extracts with the help of a special Kriya method. They also underline the fact that by using this nectar they are capable to survive without any food and water much longer than an average person is. It is interesting that almost every yogi who demonstrates this ability is seated in padmasana. They explain padmasana as a sitting position that prevents energy leakage from the physical body. At the same time, it allows them to accumulate a huge amount of pranic energy and with the strength of their minds to always keep their body processes controlled.

However, the fact is that they force all the processes in their physical bodies to a minimum, which analytically speaking means a need of a supreme control of the nerve system. The body of the yogi is in a self-induced hibernation state, and helped by the Vishuddha chakra (which extracts the energetic food); the yogi can stay alive much longer that it is publicly known.

Another characteristic of Vishuddha is the legendary elixir of youth. When Kundalini flows through this center, it distributes a great amount of regenerative power throughout the whole physical body. Each cell in the body is exposed to a process of regeneration and the phenomenon of getting younger is strongly visible. The roles of Vishuddha chakra are many, but the primary is the purification of the mind. So, thanks to the level of the clear mind, reached by the help of active Vishuddha chakra, a yogi can focus all the mental strength into one mantra and accumulate a great pranic force in it.

Subchapter 2.6
AJNA

The sixth center is called *Ajna* chakra and is a special center in human. It is located in the middle of the forehead at the pineal gland, and from the outside, it is marked as a point between the eyebrows.

This chakra is also known as a third eye or command center because it controls all processes in the human body including the senses. In Sanskrit, Ajna means "Command" and that explains the specialty of this chakra: "High level of spiritual development in which the yogi's mind can communicate with the mind of other person, and control it if necessary."

A psychically awaken person can observe the events that take place on an astral plane or even higher with this chakra. All paranormal abilities, which an individual latently possesses like: telepathy, telekinesis, astral projection, levitation, materialization, ability to see aura and many more are possible only if Ajna chakra is functional. The level of consciousness is so high in this center that the yogi starts to see the hidden essence of all visible appearances. The yogi's perception starts to change its focus and the yogi starts to see the light aura around all life forms. With the use of the Ajna chakra power, the yogi can easily read other people's thoughts and intentions, make telekinetic influence on them, heal them, etc.

Therefore, when the third eye in one is open, the spirit is free to walk to other worlds. That kind of person is always fully conscious on an astral plane and enjoys the privilege of using the best performance the astral body can offer. In contrast to the average astral traveler, this kind of person is capable of taking long astral trips into deep space, and his/her stay there can be estimated between a few hours to a few days.

However, when the mighty Kundalini reaches this chakra, it comes to a point where the three powerful streams Sushumna, Ida and Pingala nadi join again in one big stream of consciousness which goes straight to the highest chakra.

Yet, despite the fact that the yogi's consciousness is expanded beyond limits, the journey with the Kundalini Shakti is still not over because the final battle with the yogi's own Ego remains to be won in the highest chakra. If the yogi succeeds to win there, the Nirvana will be his/her.

WARNING:

The true disciple must always be very cautious when some chakra becomes active. This especially concerns Ajna chakra because when this center becomes active, an explosion of all kinds of psychic experiences accompanied with unusual symptoms that sometimes are difficult to be explained emerges. In most cases when Ajna chakra starts to manifest its true nature one starts to gain psychic powers like astral projection, telepathy, telekinesis, ability to heal, super hearing, etc.

Therefore, when that happens, the disciple has to be very careful because there is a good chance to become blinded by the shine of those psychic powers, as much as to start feeling a strong urge to use them for selfish reasons. To avoid the seductive nature of mental powers the disciple has to focus on his or her spiritual heart with the intention to remain modest and on the right path.

Usually, most of the disciples fail this test and start to feed their own Ego. When these abilities manifest themselves, the Ego is the first thing that comes out from the shadow and creates an illusion of greatness. Thus, the disciples start to think of themselves as of beings of a higher rank and see other people as beings of a lower rank. Worst of all, they cannot resist the desire to demonstrate their abilities wherever they go. That is a totally wrong path and it will jeopardize their further spiritual evolution. In time, the lack of spiritual consciousness will surely bring the extinguishing of the active chakra, which will automatically withdraw the gained psychic powers. When this happens, the disciples will remain to swim in their own stupidity with absolutely no chance for further spiritual development. To avoid all these deviations from the right path, the disciple's heart should be very modest and always aware of the potential risk, which the psychic abilities hide. There is nothing wrong with the psychic powers; this book's primary purpose is to develop them, but only when used for constructive purposes and when it is absolutely necessary.

Therefore, a piece of advice for a disciple:

When at a certain level of your psychic development your mind becomes very strong and starts to manifest paranormal abilities, you must always keep the flame of the cosmic love lit. This inner flame will save you from not taking the dark path and it will safely guide you towards the light.

Subchapter 2.7
SAHASRARA

Sahasrara is the seventh and the highest of all the chakras. Its location is in the aura above human's head, but its lower boundary still touches the physical body on the crown of the head. This chakra contains the vibrations of all other chakras and awakes only if the disciple is fully ready for it. Despite the fact that there is a global opinion about Ajna chakra being the home of the highest power, I believe that this is a wrong belief.

The greatest spiritual power lies in Sahasrara and not in Ajna chakra. The Sanskrit translation of the word Sahasrara explains everything - "Thousand-Petal Lotus".

In the Kundalini Yoga, each chakra is symbolized with its own number of petals, but Sahasrara has the most. The symbolic meaning for thousand petals of Sahasrara is the thousand spiritual powers in humans that lead them to the highest point of spiritual evolution. It leads the yogi to a power and knowledge beyond normal human understanding. This chakra is beyond all experiences because the spirit that observes the act of observing and the object of observing become one.

The consciousness is at the top level and faces maximum expansion. When Kundalini Shakti reaches this point of spiritual height, the consciousness of the yogi that has passed the three main energy channels, awaken all lower chakras and come to the door of Sahasrara explodes and disperses into a million pieces and rejoins again in one big

54

mighty unity. One consciousness fades away until it dies and a new purified and illuminated one is born. The Ego and all its manifestations are destroyed in the final battle and the yogi has been set free from the eternal circle of life and death. That is an experience of Nirvana. It is a state of the spirit that only a few - the most worthy ones will be lucky to experience during their lifetime.

A very interesting fact is that the nature of the Kundalini energy is bipolar but when it rises and reaches Sahasrara chakra it becomes mono polar or one complete unity. This unity of Kundalini born in Sahasrara chakra, in ancient India was called "The great joining of Shiva and Shakti". In the old scripts of Kundalini Yoga, Shiva and Shakti represent the male and female principle in humans. In Sahasrara, the ecstasy of the spirit is infinite and new horizons (greater than the ones opened when Kundalini was passing through the Ajna chakra); appear in front of the yogi. No word can describe this experience, which in fact, is the highest spiritual achievement. When this has been accomplished, the yogi has beaten the weal of Karma and now blissfully floats on the level of Nirvana. It is just then when the yogi is much higher than the Karma can reach. The yogi is finally free, because once the yogi's worthy spirit has touched the subtle energy of Nirvana's plane, he or she will never have to reincarnate again except if a decision has been made to help the global spiritual evolution of humankind.

According to a Yoga tradition, a spirit that has reached the Nirvana and taken a physical form again, comes from the love of humanity, so it is called an Avatar – The One, who brings the message of God. An Avatar always offers the path of cosmic love, peace and understanding. The Avatar's spiritual vision is always the same: "To help every living being to discover the path that will lead it to its true home".

However, most of the effects that appear when Kundalini energy passes through Sahasrara are beyond the analytical mind because they are present much higher on the planes than the physical, and only those who have experienced them can understand them. Perhaps the best association for this experience is what some yogi said once: "The light that radiates from the Sahasrara chakra stretches in all directions where the third eye can reach".

Subchapter 2.8
INTRODUCTION TO PSI POWERS

In the first Chapter, I explained how meditation process works and gave you two practical methods you could use in everyday life. In the second Chapter I explained the nature of Kundalini energy and its manifestations when it passes through the main seven chakras, seen from mine own seventeen years of experience in practicing Kundalini Yoga. If you have understood the first two Chapters, you are fully prepared for all the further subjects that this book will present to you.

In the following chapters, I will explain some of the psychic powers that people latently possess. Again, from mine own experience with those unbelievable abilities I will try to show you how to awake, develop and fully make use of them in your life. I will give a lot of theoretical and practical data, so everyone that wants to take an adventure in exploring the latent potentials can do it by this book, which in fact is a manual. Therefore, I have done my best to put a huge and complex subject in a simple dimension understandable for everyone concerning the awakening, developing and using these psychic powers.

Anyhow, the things that follow come as a result of a very long practice and hard years of training of special techniques that are tightly related to these parapsychological powers:

-Astral projection
-Remote viewing
-ESP and Clairvoyance
-Telepathy
-Psychometria
-Aura observing
-Psychokinesis

As far as Kundalini energy is concerned, by the end of the book you will find a special method for awakening and rising of this mighty force described, but I strongly suggest avoiding it before you have achieved everything described in this book.

Chapter 3
ASTRAL PROJECTION

Astral projection known as a special kind of "Out of the body experience" is a phenomenon that rapidly gained popularity over the last two decades. Today, this extraordinary phenomenon is a part of major researches in many scientific institutes throughout the world. Very promising discoveries have been achieved, that are creating a pleasant environment for further research of this wonderful ability called astral projection.

More and more scientists agree with the fact that every human being has a center in the brain that allows him to induce the "out of the

body" experience, but in only a handful of people this center is highly developed. The truth is that even in this small percentage of those who possess the ability to willingly induce an "out of the body" experience, only a few ones have a fully operational center for astral projection.

What exactly astral projection is? Perhaps you have heard the term from your friends, read in some book or somewhere on the Internet, or even had your own "out of the body" experience.

Anyhow, this phenomenon has many definitions but one of the simplest would be: "A process where your consciousness in your astral body separates from your physical body by your own will and projects on an astral plane is called "astral projection". The astral projection can be clearly defined in two categories:

- SPONTANEUS (part conscious) ASTRAL PROJECTION
- INTENTIONAL (fully conscious) ASTRAL PROJECTION

In the spontaneous astral projection, the astral body usually separates from the physical body through the state of normal sleep, during a clinic death, in states caused by alcohol, drugs or anesthetic overdose. In cases like these, we talk about automatic, spontaneous and not intentional astral projection. The level of clearness of the astral sight in these cases can vary among people, but it is usually foggy and causes certain anomalies in the movement coordination of the astral body. Mostly, this anomaly of the astral sight is a product of one's unconscious awakening on the astral plane and one's disability to remain there longer.

Just the opposite of the spontaneous astral projection, when intentional astral projecting takes place, the individual enters the astral plane willingly and fully conscious. One is fully awake and conscious in his/her astral body; one sees his/her physical body lying down on the bed, he or she is free to move everywhere and do everything. With the intentional "out of the body" experience one can explore higher worlds that are new to him or her, communicate telepathically with other astral beings, move with great speed, easily pass through physical objects and walls, travel in space and time and much more.

Note: Because of the complexity and variety of this phenomenon that drags so many other subjects along that the true spiritual walker needs to understand, this ability will be explained the most.

Subchapter 3.1
ASTRAL BODY

Every life form in the Universe possesses an astral body, but it seems to be an infinite area to cover. That is why we have to hold our attention mostly on topics, which concern humans. So, before we go deeper into the subject of the astral projection we have to understand what the astral body is and what kind of characteristics it possesses.

The astral body is one of the subtle bodies of a human and by appearance is a precise transparent copy of the physical body. Its structure is made of astral substance that vibrates on higher frequency than the physical matter. That makes the astral body invisible to the physical sight but it can be physically seen if the astral creature chooses to materialize itself, or one possesses the ability to see the "invisible" that comes from the fully opened third eye. It shouldn't be mistaken for a human soul, because as the physical body is just a soul carrier for the physical world, the astral body is also a soul carrier for the astral world as a different layer of the Universe.

From all the knowledge that humankind succeeded to collect so far, the Universe consists of at least seven energy layers or planes that possess different levels of density and different speed of vibration. In Buddhism the process of self-realization that in the end ends with the Nirvana, is in fact a journey through all those planes from the lowest to the highest, in which the human soul is united with the cosmic soul.

However, today with the help of the astral projection new horizons open in front of us, which give us an opportunity to get closer of answering the eternal question about life and death. Furthermore, death takes a new shape in our understanding because we are beginning to realize that it is only a transition of the soul into another plane of existence.

By learning how to project the astral body on an astral plane, we learn many things about our deeper nature or should I better say our true self and its origin, and forget many things imprinted on us by the society from the very day we took the physical body. I believe that in time, astral traveling will make us different because we will start to understand that physical plane is only a part of the major reality that we are connected to. In fact, there are many things that are part of the reality that is invisible to us, yet still real as much as everything else in the physical world.

Therefore, an astral projection allows us to consciously leave our physical bodies and step into the astral plane. When we do that, we are in our astral body that possesses totally different characteristics and performances than our physical body. Opposite from the physical body, which is exposed to a high gravitational force, the astral body is capable of neutralizing this force only by simple conscious command.

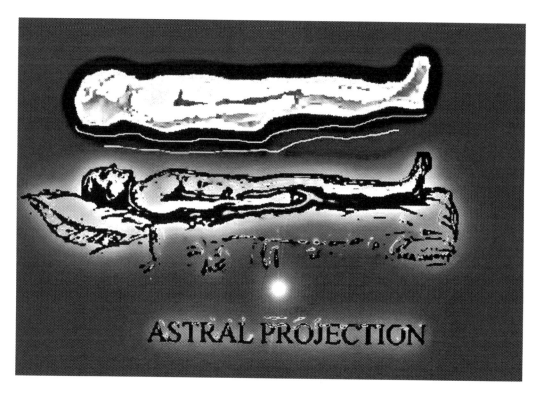

Levitating around physical bodies, going outside, flying over oceans and continents, traveling great distances in high speed, exploring the deep space and looking what's happening in other levels of the astral plane and much more is possible when one succeeds to willingly project one's consciousness in the astral body.

The astral body cannot be stopped by any physical blockade and can easily walk through walls and similar things. It cannot hurt itself or at least in most of the cases. It hears much better than the physical body, it sees much better, and if trained well can visually perceive objects from all sides at once.

While the astral traveler is out of the physical body, he or she communicates telepathically. That means that if one wants to communicate with some other entity in the astral plane or higher, the individual does not have to move his/her limbs, be heard, he/she communicates naturally by creating images in his/her consciousness, which have imprinted emotions. So for example, if Japanese and American astral travelers meet on the astral plane, they will understand each other with absolutely no problem, despite the fact that they probably do not know the language of the other.

The astral body can easily change shape if the individual wants it to, and there are many creatures that like playing games with newcomers on the astral plane by changing the form of their astral bodies into something very terrifying. Usually the newcomer starts to run like hell, not understanding that the astral plane is just as his/her as anybody's out there. However, my personal opinion about changing the shape of the astral body is that very rarely someone has the true reason to do that.

Anyway, it also has the ability of becoming invisible for other astral creatures if it does not want to be noticed, or materialize before physical beings if it wants to be seen. That is very useful for someone when it comes in contact with aggressive astral creatures or it wants to transmit a clear message to someone who is on the physical plane. Thus, from any good sense perspective, the astral body is so much superior from the physical body. But knowing everything about what the astral body can do, doesn't necessarily mean that when someone steps consciously into the astral plane for the first time he or she has all the "arsenals" of the astral body for immediate use.

In practice, every beginner has to spend a few months only to learn how to control the astral body, which is of crucial importance for him/her to stay longer on the astral plane. You can figure out that it takes much longer for one to learn the advanced movements of the astral body.

For example, the astral sight is very complicated and it needs some time to be fully developed. It is not a rare case for the beginner to see very poorly, when out of the body, or even to see with absence of colors.

That is because the astral vision is still foggy and should be developed. It has not been used for quite long and now it needs some time to clear up and return to its normal. In time, the astral traveler can easily use the sight through walls observing one object from all sides, perceiving the light aura around every astral being and similar things.

Practically, for further developing of the astral vision, many methods are used. Personally, I think that the one with the zener cards is the best. However, for every one who is on the spiritual quest, the mastering of the astral body is the first step that one takes towards a huge immaterial territory in search for his or her true home.

Subchapter 3.2

ACCEPTABILITY OF THE ASTRAL PROJECTION IN THE SOCIETY

Spontaneous "out of the body" experiences are relatively common cases of many people. People that have experienced a spontaneous astral projection but don't know anything about it or even have not heard about anything similar from their friends are confused from what happened to them and do not dare speak to other people about it. It is just because they are convinced the experience they have had is not in the dimension of the normal things, and if they spoke about it, people would start laughing at them or even worse, they would think there was something wrong with them. That wrong approach is commonly forced opinion by people who lacking of expertise are convinced that astral projection is impossible to achieve and even if it is, they treat it as abnormal or even dangerous thing. This should explain it for the best why it is not a miracle having so many people silent about their experiences. It is a fault of the society itself. Fortunately, the changes of opinions in different generations result with gaining advantage of astral projection over the line that splits society opinions, slowly but surely.

Yet, what happens if the environment is strictly against astral projection? – Many years ago I personally had that kind of problem when people around me found out that I was working on a field of the astral projection. To tell you the truth, they strongly resisted that subject in the beginning.

Then, for the first time in my life I discovered how scared people are of anything unknown to them, of what they cannot touch and measure, then measure again, pack in a box and put it in a locker. It took me two years of hard training to gain some visible results. When people began to see some of the amazing stuff that I was able to perform, they accepted me again, but, this time they treated me with lots of respect and some of them were even scared of me.

As years went by, my psychic powers became stronger and I found myself in a strange situation. The stories about a boy, who had strange abilities, spread very fast through Skopje and people with all kinds of "out of the body" experiences started to ring my doorbell asking for explanation or meaning. Some of them even practiced with me.

As time was passing by, I was more and more in a position to see things that no one else around me could see, so I felt uncomfortable to speak about them. Imagine a situation like this: during the previous night, you had traveled with your astral body at great speed across our solar system and beyond. In the morning, you go to work and while drinking your morning coffee you hear all kinds of stories about electricity, cars, machines, love rumors etc. Everybody was able to tell their story but me. Despite the fact that I have always been very talkative and had great knowledge of almost every segment of life, I have never spoken about things I really wanted to. Eight years later, I simply started to keep everything that I was experiencing to myself, and even stopped speaking about my paranormal experiences with my best friends. I did that because I was fully aware that no one, not even my closest friends would understand and believe what I was experiencing in the astral plane.

Many people came to me asking if I wanted to participate in TV shows and present my abilities in public. I stopped speaking about my paranormal powers long time ago, but people still remembered me by my demonstrations I once had made and they were still coming occasionally. Seventeen years passed by and I realized that if I did not release the knowledge I had acquired, it would probably die with me. That is why I decided to write a book and share it with the rest of humanity. Therefore, my advice for every new astral traveler is:

Do not pay attention to what people say about your desire to explore the astral world. The society is always afraid of something that is unknown or different from the standard stream. If you feel (deep in your heart) that you are ready for the astral world, just keep on walking. In time, you will become much stronger and you will show them that the astral world is just as real as everything else in this world.

Subchapter 3.3
THE BEGINNER AND THE ENVIRONMENT

Absence of noise is a very important factor, essential for successful astral projection, especially for someone who is on the start line. A trained person can easily astrally project in the room with many people and noise, but for a beginner the best would be to find a quiet place to practice in peace and silence.

The best thing for a person is to turn off the mobile phone and every physical object that can cause any disturbance while practicing. Before even trying to astrally project, he or she should settle accounts with him/herself that the next forty or sixty minutes belong only to him/her and nobody else.

Once a student has begun the astral projection exercise, the advisable thing should be not to move anymore until he has finished. If the student moves just an inch he will jeopardize the entire exercise and the chances for astral projection to happen are very tiny, even tinier if somebody rings your doorbell or the phone rings. To avoid all these disturbances, the best thing to do would be to try to project the astral body around four o'clock in the morning. That is the time with the lowest frequency of people, the pranic energy is strongest and the chances for astral projections are the biggest, but it is not to be taken as a strict rule. If the body is deeply relaxed, and the mind fully concentrated, astral projection is possible in every period of the day. I know a man who goes on astral trips mostly through the daylight. He simply puts down his Venetian blinds to achieve a pleasant dim light ambient in his room, leaves his physical body and stays on the astral plane for hours. Perhaps he does it because he usually works night shifts.

However, in the beginning, it is important for the student to work alone. The main reason for this is to avoid the presence of another aura that happens when somebody else is present in the same room. Despite the fact that it serves as a protective shield for much negative psychic energy, which comes from the surrounding space, the aura also plays a major role in the process of astral projection. So, the beginner will succeed with the astral projection only if he or she manages to achieve a high level of openness to the environment, or in other words, if one manages to take off his/her aura shield.

For most of our life, we are not aware of the aura that surrounds our bodies but that does not necessarily mean that it does not exist. Every day of our life we are being constantly exposed to negative influences and without this protective shield we would be sitting ducks for many psychic forces with no guard at all.

Every parent knows how strange little babies act, when somebody they do not recognize, looks at them. That's because the aura is still not fully developed around the baby's body and the protective shield is still not functional. In time, as the aura around the baby becomes stronger the protective shield becomes stronger too. What I'm trying to say is that some other person's presence no matter how close this person is, makes the aura to keep certain defense mechanisms by default and it would not provide the perfect conditions for the astral body to leave the physical body. It will keep a few defensive mechanisms, and that will not be enough for a successful astral separation. But, if in the beginning a student is alone, in deep peace with a strong will to leave the physical body, the aura will sense that there is no danger around and will fully open allowing him/her to enter the astral plane.

Subchapter 3.4
CONNECTION BETWEEN A.P. AND DREAMS

Great emotional outbalance when dreaming, can easily change the structure of a dream itself. In most cases, this automatically leads the consciousness of the dreamer to an instant conclusion that he/she is dreaming. When this happens, the person is only a few moments aware of being in the middle of a dream. During these few moments, one has a chance to take an advantage of the situation and to awake on the astral plane because while dreaming one's soul is already in his or hers astral body. So, let us see what happens during these few moments while one becomes aware that he or she is dreaming:

-Instant physical awakening (*If his or her consciousness is not trained and very weak*)

-The dream is continuing as if nothing has happened and the awareness that he or she is dreaming is fading away (*If his or her consciousness is not trained and very weak*)

-Biolocation of his or her consciousness: A part of his or her consciousness is still in the dream and a part of it returns to the physical body. If one manages to stay awake somewhere in the middle, he/she will become conscious in the astral body that in most cases is very close to his/her physical body. (*Fully conscious state that can usually be induced if he or she is trained, but it can happen to him or her naturally because of the momentary strong and vital consciousness*)

-Disability of physical moving through which one's whole body is paralyzed but the consciousness is fully awake: The whole process is followed by a strong zooming sound as a result of the Kundalini energy rising. Although it is a creepy feeling, if the consciousness is not in panic it can easily slip out of the physical body. (*Fully conscious state that can usually be induced if he or she is trained, but it can happen to him or her naturally because of the momentary strong and vital consciousness or as a result*

67

of some extraordinary circumstances on the astral plane near his or her physical body)

-Instant awakening on an astral plane: Let us suppose that someone is dreaming of falling down from a very high building. In the moment of the falling down, one becomes aware that he or she is dreaming and that in fact he/she is on the astral plane, and cannot be hurt. As soon as that happens, one fully awakes in the astral body, the falling stops and he or she is free to explore the astral plane. (*Fully conscious state that can usually be induced if the individual is trained and very rarely happens spontaneously as a result of the instant astral awakening caused by strange circumstances in the dream*)

All of the above mentioned states of consciousness can happen to us during our dreaming time. Unfortunately, it is a big question whether our brain is programmed or not to remember such experiences. In fact, the achievement of the astral projection is not so hard, compared to the difficulty of remembering the things we have seen and heard while being conscious on the astral plane.

From one point of view, the memory we bring from the astral world can be compared to the memory of our dreams. The moment we awake physically, we remember the whole or at least the biggest part of the dream, but as minutes go by, the dream starts fading away from our memory until it is completely gone. That is why keeping the diary is so necessary.

Our brain is usually not programmed to keep and archive the data that we bring from the astral plane. When we dream we are already on the astral plane and when we wake up physically, the brain recognizes the experiences we have collected from there, as not important, not real, etc. Classified as unimportant data, the brain erases them from our active memory. Anyway, right exercises and keeping the diary can help us reprogram our brain to start registering these "out of the body" experiences or at least the events happening to us in our dreams on the same level it does with the experiences that happen to us in the physical reality.

This reprogramming of our brain is very important for a student who practices astral projection, because there are many methods for achieving the astral projection through the control of the dreams. Most of them are based on the programmed awareness about detecting the small anomalies that can be seen in a simple dream. Therefore, I will give you two simple dream control methods I have used so many times and I can freely say that they work almost always.

The first method tracks for some anomalies in your dream. For example: you dream you are walking in your room, but something is not right. The television is upside down, and one of the windows is broken. These anomalies are the main switches that can awake you on the astral plane because as soon as your consciousness detects them it will become clear to you that something is not right and that you are probably dreaming. In that instant, everything will change and some of the states I have mentioned above will happen to you. So, in those few moments that offer you a chance to awake in the astral world fully conscious, all you have to do is this - say to yourself: "I am (your name), I'm dreaming and I want to awake in the astral plane".

If you do this, in those few moments of awareness you will awake in your astral body and from there, you will be free to take an astral adventure.

The American shamans have developed the second method, which can awake your dreaming consciousness. It consists of making some effort to see your own hand while dreaming. When you manage to do that, you will become aware that you are dreaming, and during those few moments in which the astral portal is still open, you will have to put just some small effort to stay in the astral world. Where do you go from there, is your own choice.

Subchapter 3.5
SILVER CORD

According to the statistics, some astral travelers had seen some kind of connection between the astral and the physical body. These beliefs are actually based on the existence of live and vital elastic cord that connects these two bodies in the solar plexus area.

It is silver by color and when this cord tears apart, the physical death appears. Again, according to the testimony of these astral travelers, it has a characteristic of extending to infinity. The moment someone leaves the physical body, this silver cord is about a few centimeters big and as one increases the distance from the physical body, it outstretches and becomes thinner and thinner all the way until it disappears from one's astral sight after a few hundred meters.

However, it is my opinion generated from my own personal experience that this silver cord does not exist or at least it is not visible to me. If I consider the fact that I can perfectly observe everything on the astral plane including aura around every living thing that possesses soul and still am not able to see it after fifteen years of astral traveling, I can clearly say that there is no such thing as a silver cord. I apologize to everyone that does not share my opinion, but that is the way I see things. I cannot speak about something I have never seen and if somebody has spotted it, then it is a reality for him/her and I respect that.

Imagine there is really a silver cord, which can stretch out in light years. I have consulted other astral travelers whom I respect as experts in the field and they have mentioned they have never seen anything similar while they have been out of their physical bodies. Furthermore, it is true that some of the authors who cover the astral projection topics prefer to write that the silver cord exists. They say it is usually invisible for the astral sight and it is usually a result of their incompetence, or perhaps their fear of being discredited by the leading authors about the subject.

Most of the authors in the field have accepted the traditional opinion of existence of the silver cord, and usually do not have the appropriate experience to claim many things they cover in their books.

I remember the time when I was very young with about a hundred successfully done astral projections and greatly confused about still not having spotted the silver cord or anything similar to that. That was the time when my uncle went to Tibet and I was learning the secrets of esotery from my second teacher Velibor Rabljenovich.

I recall my first meeting with my friend and teacher Velibor Rabljenovich in 1993 when I came in touch with his incredible knowledge about astral projection. Despite the fact that he was only sixteen-year-old boy at the time, he was considered one of the leading parapsychological phenomena in the region of former Yugoslavia. His popularity spread very fast through the whole of Europe, especially in Germany after he had a meeting with Mr. Uri Geller in Israel where together they demonstrated their parapsychological abilities in front of many people. Velibor at that time was in top form, demonstrating with great easiness his best achievements in the field of clairvoyance, astral projection, telepathy and telekinesis. I have been lucky to learn from him for two years, and I am very grateful to him for training me to the point from where I could continue on my own. He had transferred the biggest part of his knowledge to me. As far as I recall, he was in Ohrid at the time, so I took the bus from Skopje to meet him. Until then, I had more than 100 successfully pulled off astral projections and I had never spotted anything like silver cord that connected my two bodies. I was confused, because in almost every literature I could lay my hands on the silver cord was mentioned. I started to explain to him that all that I had seen, had been transparent double surrounded by blue light and I had never seen any connections like silver cord or similar. He started laughing at me aloud and told me: "The silver cord my friend does not exist. I have traveled astrally a thousand times and I still have not seen any silver cord or anything similar. That has certainly been fabricated by people after fame and popularity."

That calmed me in a way you cannot imagine. All those years I thought I was doing something wrong. In time, I had learned that the actual connection between those two bodies existed, but on different basis. The connection is all about two impulses or codes, which are unique in the whole Universe. One code of the astral body matches only one code in the DNA of the physical body. Generally speaking, this connection is unique, complete and for the normal astral vision invisible. In time, when physical death appears, these codes separate. The first one that is in the DNA of the physical body dies along with the disintegration and the second one, the one in the astral body remains alive. If somewhere in the future, the

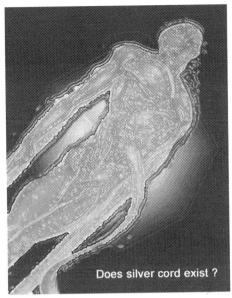

Does silver cord exist ?

same soul takes an incarnation again in a physical body, that same code will duplicate itself and the copy will be installed in the DNA of the new body. I believe you would agree that what nature does by itself is a completely amazing thing. Personally, I do not see anything mystic in it but one natural process, which is a part of a huge astral science we have just started to explore in the right way.

After the meeting with Velibor many things in my life changed. I found Velibor a sympathizer; teacher and a friend I can rely on about many things connected to astral projection, clairvoyance, telepathy, psychokinesis and much more. Anyway, he started to train me, and day-by-day, I was upgrading the basic knowledge that my uncle had given me. It took him two years to train me to a satisfactory level by using special techniques. Many times the training lasted more than six hours a day and most of that time I was blindfold, always concentrating on all the different things and objects that Velibor demanded from me. Two years later he left Macedonia and went to live in Serbia.

Many years passed since then and I have managed to master the astral science. I have left thousands of astral trips behind me. Even now, when I have reached the level that Velibor possessed, I still have not noticed anything similar to a silver cord, neither on my astral body, nor on any other creature on the astral plane no difference at all whether it is or is not in a possession of a physical carrier.

Subchapter 3.6
HOW LONG UNTIL THE FIRST ASTRAL PROJECTION

No one can tell you with any certainty how long will you have to practice before you achieve your first successful astral projection. It can be estimated from a few months to more than a year. Everything depends on you. The well-known relation stands here: "The percentage of talent needs the according percentage of training". If you possess 30% of natural talent, you will have to work it out 70%, and vice versa. Many things are connected with the genes that bring the natural gift to some people for better control of their astral body. Yet, it does not necessarily mean that if you do not have a high percentage of natural talent you will not become a great and experienced astral traveler. With practice and persistence, anything can be achieved.

The truth is, the more you want it the sooner you will get it. It is as simple as that, because the more you want it, the more it will push you to train harder and normally as a result you will accomplish it sooner. From my personal experience and from the experiences of other people who had mastered this extraordinary ability, the first time can be expected in about six months to a year. Usually this is considered an average time because the first thing someone willing to experience "out of the body" experience has to do is to train one's self to master a state of deep psycho-physical relaxation. When the shield of aura is off as a result of a deep psychophysical relaxation, the first step is accomplished.

The next thing is a question of will and belief. Without strong will, or should I say better, a big desire for leaving the physical body and a strong belief that he or she is capable of pulling that off, one can not achieve the astral projection. Therefore, after the deep relaxation, the next step is desire and belief. The stronger the desire for leaving the body is (accompanied by a solid belief that it can be done), the sooner the pulling forces between the astral and the physical body will weaken and provide ideal conditions for the consciousness in the astral body to slip out of the physical body.

However, the fastest way to experience an "out of the body" experience is by using the dream control method. As I said before, that is simple because while dreaming, you are already present on an astral plane and the only thing you have to do is become aware of yourself there. This method allows you to experience an "out of the body" experience much sooner, but without developing the skill of inducing Trance and to walk away from your physical body by your own will in any time and any place, you are just entertaining yourself. So, the right way is much harder, but it brings the best control of your astral body, which the dream control method cannot do.

By the way, a piece of advice for a beginner: Do not burden yourself with results, just keep on going. The harder you train the sooner the results will come. Always keep in mind that you (as much as every life-form in the Universe) possess an astral body stuck in your physical body by a magnetic field. The sooner you manage to weaken this magnetic field which is pulling your two bodies together, the sooner you will achieve your first successful astral projection.

Subchapter 3.7
RELAXATION TECHNIQUES

The modern way of life has brought a high-speed rhythm that totally exhausts people. Nervousness, psychic tension, stress, the feeling of tiredness, high blood pressure and heart anomalies are all the states that modern people encounter if they have not succeeded to prepare themselves for all kinds of attacks life brings. For everybody, no matter whether they work as workers, scientists, politicians, businessmen, doctors or students, the ability of relaxation is of great importance.

Every one irrelevant of the profession is asked for full concentration on his/her job, which means maximum use of physical and psychical efforts. That is why the moments of full relaxation are necessary for the body throughout the day to release the absorbed poison components from the organism. If the conditions allow it, it is better to find a quiet and peaceful place. Best results in relaxation can be achieved if you lie down in a flat horizontal position, which provides the flat line between the neck and the spine. The arms should be close to your side with the hands up and the legs should be about 30 centimeters apart. This position in the Yoga terms is called "Shavasana" and the maximum relaxation of the whole physical body can be achieved in it. Through the relaxation, your whole body will relax and all the nerve impulses will calm down. It is important that you remember not to move once you have started with the relaxation technique. In the beginning, the process of the breathing should be deep, slow and in a certain rhythm. Then, when you have felt that you have slipped into the deep, leave the breathing process and allow it to take its own natural rhythm. To succeed with the relaxation, you can use all sorts of visualizations or ideas that will take you to the state of calmness where you can forget everything that bothers you. Depending on the mood and imagination, in your thoughts you can take an imaginary trip to some place you like from the bottom of your heart, somewhere where you will be calm and happy.
Examples:

- You can imagine yourself swinging in a small boat that is so far from the shore and you try to hear the voices the wind brings. You fully enjoy lying in the boat and the feeling of swinging gives you even greater pleasure. Everything around you is so beautiful, you do not rush anywhere and you do not care where the boat will take you. You are fully free and left to the current of the waves. The nice smell that comes from the sea and the sound of the waves make you happy and in complete harmony.

- With the help of your imagination you can go to a wonderful huge forest. You feel every step you take, you hear the birds and you smell the fragrance of the trees and plants. The sun shines beautifully in the blue sky. Walking through the deep forest, you encounter a great waterfall. You sit on a rock and start watching the waterfall. The water is crystal-clear but nicely warm. You slip into the water and start to swim. You fully enjoy every movement that you make. The beautiful view combined with the sounds of the waterfall and forest life gives you a feeling that you are in paradise. You are completely alone with the nature.

- You find yourself walking on a wonderful ocean shore. You are enjoying yourself watching the sunset. Everything around you is in complete harmony. Rainbows appear up in the sky and the whole nature starts to vibrate with mystical vibrations. Great peace is overtaking control of your whole being. You feel so wonderfully that you think that you can stay there forever.

These calming relaxation techniques we practice through the day have refreshing influence on us and give us vitality to carry on with our daily duties. I would greatly advice everyone who has not mastered even one meditative technique to practice the above-mentioned ways of relaxation before sleep. A healthy dream can influence in a positive and recovering way, which is the opposite from the nightmares and bad dreams that influence in a negative and exhaustive way. *Why do we have bad dreams?* – Someone would ask.

An individual, who has fallen asleep with so many unsolved matters within him/herself and the environment, possesses thoughts like hatred, fear, jealousy, etc. So, after he or she falls asleep, his or her astral body will separate from the physical and it will go to the astral places where similar emotions can be found. Consequently, many manifestations of the lower nature will appear in his or her consciousness as nightmares and bad dreams.

On the other hand, the calming relaxation that has been done before the individual went to sleep will bring him or her complete relaxation of the muscular tissue and the nerve system.

It will clear the mind from all the negative thoughts as well, especially the ones that disturb the person a lot. All that will cause faster coming of the dream, and when it comes it will make the dreaming more peaceful, smoother and more constructive.

Once the consciousness in the astral body reaches the astral plane, despite the fact that it has left the physical unconsciously, it will go to the places where similar emotions exist and the manifestations of the positive and constructive nature will appear. The consciousness can more easily become aware of its presence on an astral plane from this kind of dreams than from dreams similar to nightmares. I think it will not be necessary to further explain the benefit that someone gets from the relaxation, starting with stress release, a great psychophysical health to developing latent or asleep potentials.

All of you who want to master the ability to astrally project on the astral plane, will be given a good exercise to help you reach a high level of deep and constructive relaxation, which is the main condition for achieving "out of the body" experience on your own will. This type of relaxation will bring you to the state of Trance where you can easily use your own force to heal yourself if necessary, or just canalize your inner energies. Normally, you have to exercise in a quiet and peaceful place with minimum environmental disturbances. It is not advisable to start the relaxation on a full stomach overloaded with huge amount of food or liquids. The cloths should be easy and comfortable. It is not smart to have any current air in the room, so you should open the windows five minutes before you start, and allow fresh prana to enter the room. You can put some good instrumental music to play while you exercise.

The best position for this purpose is Shavasana. This position is the most appropriate for yogis that are practicing Yoga Nidra. For all of you that have never heard about this system of Yoga, the direct translation of it would be "Yoga sleeping", but it is much more than that. This system is based on a connection with the inner consciousness, which is quite different from the normal sleep where the inner and the outer consciousness are absent. In other words, Yoga Nidra represents a system of exercises that allow the yogi to transfer the consciousness to his/her astral body and to take the journey deep in the immaterial world.

My purpose is exactly the same - to teach you how to visit the immaterial world with the help of this method of relaxation combined with one ancient Egyptian technique for astral projection. Here is how the method of relaxation goes:

When you have regulated all the above-mentioned steps and lied down in the position of Shavasana, start to breathe deep but gently. By "gently", I mean slow and deep rhythm, which will produce a stabilizing and refreshing effect on your whole body. Inhale the prana slowly and deeply, keep it for a while in your abdomen and then slowly exhale. The best rhythm for this exercise is 4:2:4. Once you have started your relaxation, do not open your mouth and use your nose only as a bridge that leads the prana in and out of the abdomen. If you have correctly pulled off the breathing rhythm, you will soon feel that something in your mind has changed and transferred your consciousness into a deeper level. Then, become aware of every part of your physical body. Do not change the rhythm of inhaling and exhaling; do not pay any attention to it. The breathing process will soon take its own rhythm that mostly suits your body.

It takes a while for a beginner to become aware of every small part of the body in a way the yogi is, but in time and with practice one will sharpen the ability to feel every miniature part of the physical body. The journey of the consciousness across the whole body starts with the toes of the right foot and ends with the top of the head. The most important thing is that you gain consciousness to feel your physical body becoming heavier.

The stronger the feeling of the heavier is, the deeper the relaxation will be. You should go systematically with the relaxation process starting with the biggest toe of your right foot. Feel it deep to the atomic level. Feel it becoming so heavy, much more than it normally weighs. Despite the heaviness in your biggest toe, you have to feel it so much more relaxed than before.

When you achieve that, you should continue with the next toe that is closest to it. The same procedure stands for every other small part of your body. When you are done with the toes, transfer your consciousness on your sole. Feel it becoming so much heavier and relaxed. Then focus your attention on your whole foot. After the completion of the whole foot, just repeat the same procedure with the lower parts of your right leg and go to your knee and thigh. In the end, you have to feel a total relaxation and many times increased weight in your whole right leg. Then feel the weight magnetically pulling you down to the floor.

If you have done it all, as it should be, you will experience the smooth energy flow in your right leg. The sensation of something pleasant that streams above and through your whole right leg will be so strong. Then repeat the same with the left leg. In the end, you will feel the same effects of total relaxation and heaviness that will provide the free flow of smooth energy in the whole left leg, as previously in the right leg. When you feel the energy flowing above and through the whole left leg, repeat the procedure with both legs at the same time.

When you have finished with both legs, you have to join the energies from them. It will feel strange but you will get used to it. The next step is the inner and the outer parts of your torso. Do not rush with the relaxation because it needs a great deal of concentration in the beginning to become aware of some parts of your physical body. Sometimes it is hard to become aware of some internal organ and to feel it, but in time and with practice you will eventually succeed. Once, the energies of the inner and outer parts of the torso mix with the energies of the two legs, it is the right time to transfer your consciousness to your right arm. The procedure is the same as everything done previously.

You start with the fingers, then with the whole hand, below elbow, elbow, above elbow and the shoulder. When you have succeeded to join the energy that flows through your right arm with the energies that circulate freely in your legs and torso, focus yourself on the left arm.

After the left arm has also been done, repeat the procedure with both arms at the same time. In the end, your whole body except for your neck and head will swim in free and pleasant energy. If the feeling of total relaxation and heaviness is also present, you will know that you are going towards the right direction for gaining the ultimate effect that this exercise provides.

Next, you continue with the same intensity with your neck and head. After finishing the neck, go to the mouth, tongue, teeth, throat, nose, cheeks, eye caves, eyes, forehead and hair, but try to remain much longer on the area of the brain and the top of the head. Especially pay attention to areas where the big, middle and the small part of the brain connect. To master the ability to feel the brain so precise, deep and sharp, much more time is needed than for all the other parts of the physical body, but give your best and in time you will do it. The moment your whole body starts swimming in powerful energy, you will know that you have completed the relaxation. The feeling of weightlessness will give you the sign that your brain patterns have changed from Alpha to Theta brain waves.

Note:

Easy achievement of the astral projection also means that one has mastered some way of reaching a total psychophysical relaxation. Almost instantly, when someone reaches deep level of relaxation and mental peace, he or she will start to feel the symptoms of the weight increase of his or her physical body.

The feeling of more weight is the first sign that his/her brain waves are changing the frequency from Beta (13-30Hz), to Alpha brain waves (8-12Hz). That actually means that his/her physical body has entered the state of deep sleep while the consciousness is fully awake.

For example, if you live in an apartment you will start hearing the conversations on floors below and above. If by any chance, any sharp sound appears it will strike you as a knife. That is because your senses are sharpened to their maximum. Yet, to achieve a fully conscious astral projection you must fall into Trance and your brain must start emitting the Theta brain waves (3-7Hz).

To reach a Theta state you should mentally concentrate on separation of your astral body with full capacity. That will change the brain patterns and it will allow you to leave your body and step into the astral world. In time, the frequent duration of the consciousness in the state of Theta will surely awake the Kundalini energy, which on the other hand will launch the consciousness even in higher planes from the astral plane – Delta brain waves (0,5-2Hz).

Your consciousness will be as sharp as a razor, the metabolism of your body will be at its minimum and you will feel the flow of vital energy. At this point, you have entered the state of Trance and your astral body is ready for the separation from your physical body. If you have done everything, as it should be, you will start to see with your eyes closed some foggy evaporation, which slowly leaves your physical body. Then focus your inner self on joining with that evaporation. That evaporation is in fact your astral body and when you join with it, you will feel half separated from your body. That moment is the proper time for you to start the technique that will lead you to a complete and conscious astral projection.

Subchapter 3.8
THE ASTRAL PROJECTION TEHNIQUE

The moment when you have joint with the foggy evaporation and the feeling that a part of your astral body is out, you are ready to start with the technique which will lead you to complete astral projection. The technique itself has been developed in ancient Egypt by one of the best masters of ancient Kabbalah. Until now, the technique has been considered a secret and usually given to the worthy disciples of Kabbalah in times of their initiation. I have been using this technique for many years and I can clearly conclude that it is probably one of the best techniques ever created with a purpose to induce an "out of the body" experience. In basic, this technique consists of seven segments or figures, which should be visualized one by one. Every figure has strictly chosen colors that influence the brain pattern and causes an extending of the consciousness. The benefit of this technique is that it will lead you from a deep and progressive relaxation to an altered state of consciousness or deep Trance wherefrom it will be very easy for you to leave your physical body and step into the territory of the astral world. If you want to succeed with astral projection it is very important for you to exercise this technique very slowly and fully focused. To complete the whole technique along with the relaxation that has to be done first, it usually takes about forty-five minutes to one hour. From the moment when you start with the relaxation to the end of the whole technique, it is also very important not to move at all. If you need to adjust yourself into a suitable lying position take five minutes, but once you start do not move an inch. Always keep in mind that this is a very important factor, which directly influences the success of the technique.

However, if you repeat this technique at least once a day and usually before you go to sleep, you will soon accomplish good results. In time it will provide you with an easy access to the astral world, wherefrom you will be in a position to visit strange places, make contact with astral creatures and explore space, go back in time, slip into the future and much more. Generally speaking, while your physical body is in a state of Trance thanks to this technique, your astral body will explore the mysteries of the astral world. So, let us see the seven figures.

Figure 1

WHITE DIAMOND

Figure 1 is a glowing white diamond with the sky blue sphere, which rotates in the center. The sphere rotates with a relatively fast rhythm emitting the sky blue light in the same way. Try to join with the rotating light inside your visualization slowly but fully focused. Open yourself completely to the blue light and become one with it. The moment when you have reached the point where you are rotating with the beam of light, enter the shiny sphere. Once you are in, vaporize your human contours and fully become a shiny blue sphere. Then after a few moments, feel and "see" the way you are starting to outstretch yourself into the diamond by taking the human form again. Your head must touch the top of the diamond, your hands must touch the two sideways and your heels must touch the bottom point of it. From that perspective, observe the blue sphere and the way it rotates in its own rhythm. In the same time, build a right attitude for yourself. Feel like a completely pure and innocent being. Become aware that all around you is a powerful diamond that vibrates like a strong field of pure energy. So, open yourself to that energy and allow it all to pass through you. If you visualize that perfectly, you will feel your senses becoming sharper and stronger. When you have achieved the visualization of all the things mentioned above, you are ready for the next figure.

Figure 2

GOLDEN SHINE

As you slowly go on to figure 2, you notice the brilliantly white light that comes from the center of the system. The road below you is made of a golden surface that shines and the traveling above it is at high speed. Do not forget that you are still in the interior of figure 1, so you use it as a vehicle to fly towards the white milky light that shines in the distance. Inside the visualization, try to sense the feeling of high-speed movement to perfection and the golden shine, which radiates from below. After a while, visualize the sound of a strong explosion on the surface of the white diamond, which causes the separation between the two of you. In that particular moment, feel the whole energy from the diamond and the sphere passing to you, which leaves the diamond completely out of energy. That causes the fall of the diamond directly on the golden road. After this is done, continue to fly above the golden road at about twenty meters altitude. On your way towards the brilliant light, you have to pass all the beautiful huge rings of dancing light. The rings are in many colors, but the rainbow dominates. You are passing through the rings in a great speed and the closer you are coming to the brilliant white light, the more you feel that you can see deeper and deeper in your inner essence. Perhaps the best association for this visualization can be found in the movie "A Space Odyssey 2001", in the moment when Dave Bowman enters the Monolith and when all sorts of light manifestations start to appear in front of him. After a while, you have come to the last point; there are no more rings to be passed and the golden road finally ends there. A major brilliant white sphere in front of you levitates. Then, stop in that position and wait until the sphere changes its color from white to golden. When that happens, move yourself again with high speed and enter the huge golden sphere. Suddenly in your visualization, you find yourself in a completely different place. The golden sphere has transported you directly above our atmosphere and from there, with the rest of the figures you will go further into space. If you have done all the steps previously mentioned, your visualization will become close to a real motion picture and you will feel weightless. In the same time, you will feel joy, calmness and unity with the whole Universe. Down below and not so much distant from you, there is our beautiful planet Earth. The planet's blue atmosphere shines beautifully and the whole sight in your visualization is incredible.

You feel joy and sensation as never before because everything around you breathes with peace and freedom. You feel free. Stay for a few minutes in that point of your visualization and then go on to the third figure of your journey.

Figure 3

COSMIC KEY

While you levitate above our planet and you feel like a free soul, it is time for you to continue your journey. Inside your visualization, you have to lift up the arms of your astral body, and to mentally convert to the creative forces of the Universe:

"Can I have the key of the astral kingdom through the force of the cosmic energy?"

Figure 3 is in fact the representation of that key. Way behind, you notice a strong white light and when you turn back to see what is happening behind you, the cosmic key is coming to you. The cosmic key shines with the color of the rainbow and gives you the calming feeling. Slowly it flies to your left hand and you have to open your hand to accept it. The very instant you touch it, a great light will come from it like a big flash and you will feel a great wave of energy that will pass through you. Then the key disappears from your left hand and you continue your journey in the direction of the Sun. On your way to the Sun you will have to pass by the planets Venus and Mercury to absorb even more energy in your astral body.

Figure 4

BLUE DISK

You slowly gain on planet Venus. In the distance close to the planet, you spot a little point of blue light, which comes from nowhere but moves towards you. The closer it gets to you, the more clearly you can see that the blue light comes from a big blue disk. The disk is in fact figure 4 of your visualization and it has the size of a hundred meters in diameter. On the surface of the disk, there is an engraving of the symbol of Venus. The symbol itself is also blue, but it contains a million tiny dots that glow more intensively. Your task is to join with those little blue shiny dots. So, as a part of your visualization, you become closer to the symbol and slowly start to fall into it. Open yourself to the life force that radiates from the symbol and join completely with it. You will simply know that you have done this right when you lose your human contours and you will feel a major stretching of your consciousness like water throughout the entire symbol. Next thing you should do is to visualize the way all the energy from the symbol flows directly into you. When you feel much stronger than before, you have entered the symbol of the blue disk. Then just regain your human contours and exit. Then again hang up your astral hands and mentally convert the creative forces of Universe: *"I have filled myself with the energy of the planet Venus."*

When you feel your whole cosmic being fully refreshed and full of new energy, go to the next figure of your inner journey.

Figure 5

YELLOW DISK

The engraving on the surface of figure 5 is in fact the symbol of the planet Mercury. It is the same size as the blue disk and it comes in a completely identical way when inside your visualization you come close to the planet Mercury. The difference is that this figure is yellow and the symbol engraved on the disk has a half moon in the upper part of the engraving. To join with the cosmic energy of the planet Mercury you have to come closer to the yellow disk and dive into the million tiny yellow light dots. When you have joined with its energy, leave the symbol and regain your human astral form.

Then you have to hang your astral hands up, and for a third time you convert to the creative forces of the Universe:

"I humbly kneel in front of the holy feet of Mercury."

When you feel even stronger than at the time when you have absorbed the energy from the blue disk, you can leave the planet Mercury and go further.

Figure 6

ASTRAL VEHICLE

On your way to the Sun on your right side from nowhere figure 6 materializes. It shines with the milky white light. The main purpose of this vehicle is intergalactic astral trips. Through the tree triangles, you can enter the vehicle. The wings of the vehicle start to swing and from the depths of your consciousness, the next picture appears.

Note: This vehicle is only for advanced users. In time, repeating the same technique over end over will cause an imprint in the astral matter. Once one becomes astrally stronger, he or she will truly see the same vehicle while performing the same technique and he or she can use it for long distance astral trips. A beginner does not have to enter it, at least for the first two years and in his/her visualization, he/she can just fly by, until starting to see the next figure.

Figure 7

ASTRAL WEAPONS

The last and at the same time the seventh figure is actually a presentation of the main astral weapons. They can protect you against many things that you can encounter in the astral world. The sword is for overcoming the personal fear, the stick is for protection from a strong light, the star is for basic protection and the cosmic cup is for protection of many things that do not have a touch point with the normal astral appearances. However, always remember that each of these weapons is designed basically for self-defense and never for attack. Every true astral traveler who sincerely wants to follow the path of the Universal wisdom must respect certain codex of rules.

91

Subchapter 3.9
AFTER THE TECHNIQUE

Once you are done with the technique, the separation process should start by itself. In most cases, you will experience something similar to a loss of gravity that pulls you up, and the next moment you will find yourself elevating in your astral body.

If you have succeeded to do this, you are ready to explore the astral plane. Do not distance much from your physical body, at least in the beginning, and try to pay attention to some details you will see in the astral plane. After the astral experience has ended and you have returned to your physical body, if possible check out the data you have brought from there for accuracy. What is to be done further will be explained later.

Usually, in the beginning the ability to visualize to perfection will be harder to achieve. In basic, to succeed with the technique, a total relaxation and sharpness of the consciousness are needed and if only one of them is missing you will not be able to visualize the seven symbols perfectly and achieve the astral projection. In practice, someone will have hard time to achieve good results with the relaxation exercise and someone will have difficulty in elaborating the technique that contains much visualization.

However, if the astral projection does not happen immediately after you have finished your technique, do not be disappointed. In any case, after putting some hard effort in the relaxation and the technique, you will be very close to achieving the astral projection.

The magnetic force between the physical and the astral body will certainly be much weaker and knowing this can help you to project your consciousness to your astral body that you can visualize as levitating above your physical. So, try to visualize that just one meter above your physical body, your transparent astral body levitates but unconsciously.

Start to project your consciousness into that transparent double, slowly but fully focused! To succeed with the transferring process, visualizing that you are physically there and bellow you lying on the bed is some other body that looks like you will help a lot. That will usually bring the effect of biolocation of your consciousness. A part of you will be up there and a part of you will remain down. When that happens, just start to maintain the visual perspective from above. Then just try to pull along the part of the consciousness that has been left below as best as you can. After achieving the transferring of your consciousness completely into the transparent double, you will lose the physical sense of having found out that you can see everything from above.

This astral projection method has achieved a high percentage of success with most of the students. Still, the beginner will have to make tremendous efforts of training at for least about six months, to master this technique to perfection. As I already mentioned before, the success primarily depends on the state of relaxation and the desire of the student to astrally project, so, the key of the success is in one's will. If the student possesses an iron will deep within, there is nothing to stop him/her from achieving it if the desire is sincere and strong.

If the technique is not suitable for someone, I will describe a few other techniques that are fully functional once they are elaborated.

Subchapter 3.10
PROJECTING THROUGH A MENTAL SCREEN

Here is also a good technique for someone who wants to master the astral projection ability. However, it is among the most difficult ones, because it demands huge mental effort of the mind to become completely empty. To achieve the best of result this technique should be performed after one is done with the relaxation and has reached a state of deep inner peace. Simply said, this technique requires stopping of the thinking process.

I'm not talking about thinking as if somebody isn't thinking, but about the strong command of the mind to delete, empty and neutralize everything that is born or streams on the mental screen of the consciousness.

Therefore, to succeed with this astral projection technique, your consciousness has to be transferred directly to the present moment in a way similar to the one described in the Deep peace meditation. The most important thing is that your consciousness has to become one big "NOTHING". To achieve this, your mind needs great strength because your thoughts are like bees and in the moment when it appears to you that you have succeeded to conquer them all, they will return a hundred times multiplied, stronger and much wiser. You will notice that your thoughts will do everything to embitter your effort to shut them off in one strike and to overcome the system of the consciousness. Therefore, the shutting down of your thinking system is possible only if you have completely understood the way the thinking process works. You must know how thoughts are being born, how they express themselves and how they disappear again in the depths of your consciousness.

If you understand all this, it will take only one strong command to delete all your thoughts. When I say a "strong command", I mean a command, which does not contain any "buts" or should I say objections. The truth is your mind will do whatever you let it do. If you issue the strong command, it will obey and your consciousness will become clear end totally empty. After you have remained in that state of emptiness for about ten seconds, you will notice that your consciousness is beginning to alter.

It is because our brain is usually programmed to receive the thought impulses that come in the form of words at first, and then it receives the impulses of images and emotions. If you have deleted the thinking process, the primary system of the mind (similar to a computer's Windows in case you delete some boot files) cannot load. By default, after the primary system fails to boot, the secondary system starts to load. Thus, another way of perception comes with the secondary system that allows the consciousness to see all sorts of images but mostly images from places that are far away.

When this starts to happen, your task is not to take any active contact with them but to just play the role of a silent witness. In the beginning, the images that will start appearing on your mental screen will be unclear and mostly black and white, but in time they will become more and more alive, clear and colorful.

To maintain the secondary system you must always play the role of a silent witness who observes everything but does not attach emotionally to anything. You must not think in words, not even once, because if you do, your brain will register the change of the brain pattern and it will switch on the normal regime of working that belongs to the primary system of the mind.

What does that mean? It means that the images coming as astral reflections from foreign places will vanish the very instant when you start thinking in words again, because your brain will automatically change this new frequency of working and will shut down all the centers responsible for the astral radiation. It will simply switch the nominal centers back on, and you will have to do the technique all over again.

Because of that, you must maintain the complete control of this method from the moment when you have shut down the thinking process to the moment of the complete astral projection. When images coming from the astral space become very clear and alive, everything you have to do is walk through one of them. The same moment you walk through one of these astral images you will find yourself in that place on the astral plane.

It is as if you are walking through the mirror and find yourself in another and strange dimension. Usually, experts in the remote viewing use this or similar technique with the purpose to visit places no difference how distant these places are from them.

However, to pull this off is more difficult than it sounds and only the most stubborn ones succeed. It takes the will of steel and determination beyond words.

Have you ever tried to force your mind to think strictly in images and not in words? Try it and soon you will notice that something strange is happening to your mind when you are doing that. Believe me, I have explored all kinds of consciousness states since I was fourteen, and I do think that the shutting down of the thought monologue is the place to look for solutions of many unknown things concerning the ability of human kind to astrally project.

Subchapter 3.11
PROJECTING THROUGH THE VISUALIZED DOOR

This is also a very good technique, which has some similarities with the previous one. I have used this technique many times and it works great. After a complete and total relaxation, try to make all your thoughts disappear. To achieve this you can trick your mind, which is very simple to perform. Try to visualize that there is a transparent sphere of glass in the center of your head, which is a source of strong light that produces heat.

Imagine your thoughts like flies that are attracted to the bright light that comes from the sphere. Do not do anything and just observe as the flies paste up and burn when they touch the surface of the glass. Wait until all of the flies are burnt from the heat of the sphere. When there is not a single one flying around it, remain still and wait a while longer to make sure that new ones are not coming and there has not been a fly left of the previous ones. Then, simply destroy the transparent sphere. In that state of emptiness, focus your mind on the next visualization. Imagine that you are locked in a room with walls of bricks.

There is a black door on one of the walls, which is the only way out. The door is locked and your task is to unlock it with the intention to walk through and enter the astral plane, but to unlock the door you must have a pyramid key, which fits the lock that has a pyramidal shape in the center of the door.

Next, visualize yourself materializing a pyramid key from your own astral energy, taking the key in your right hand and walking out from your physical body towards the door. Inside your visualization, once you achieve the perspective that you are standing in front of the door with the pyramid key in your right hand, put the key into the lock. The door starts to open and in that particular moment, in your visualization you will have to imagine a strong and sharp sound that comes from it. When the door is open, imagine yourself as slowly walking through the door and stepping into the astral plane. If you have done everything as you are supposed to, you will feel the loss of physical sense and you will find yourself standing in your astral body fully conscious.

Everything you have created in your visualization will disappear from your sight and in that moment you will realize that everything is back to normal except you, standing beside your physical body that lies on the bed. Then, if you are a beginner stay close to your body and if you are not, just go out of your room and have fun.

Subchapter 3.12

WHAT AFTER I HAVE LEFT MY PHYSICAL BODY?

The answer of this question lies in you. Generally speaking, the astral plane offers something to everybody. For many people the most accessible level of the astral plane is the one that shares the same space with the physical plane. By default, this level is the first people encounter as soon as they leave their physical bodies, but despite the fact that it is closest to the physical plane, this level is not the lowest of the astral plane that in fact possesses seven of them. Practice has shown that most people usually stay on this level and rarely touch the other ones unless they are well trained to.

Nevertheless, once in it, one is free to visit places of the physical Cosmos, places that are not accessible for him/her physically. Still, statistically speaking, despite the open opportunity, a very small percentage of astral travelers go to space towards the stars, so I can conclude that most of the people who are capable of astral traveling stick on Earthly explorations.

ASTRAL TRAVELING

However, the astral science is very deep and very complex to be learned and usually takes years before someone who travels across the astral plane can feel like walking in the backyard of his/her home. Despite the fact that the astral plane consists of seven levels, I am talking about an almost infinite area, which contains almost infinite number of places and even higher variety of life forms present in the material Universe. Thus, it is always difficult for a newcomer in the astral plane to adapt to the new reality that appears so much complex. Until the moment of leaving the physical body, one's primary problems have been to surmount the difficulty of leaving the physical body. Now, capable of doing this, one has found out that there are billions of things to be learned about getting along in the astral plane. This is the main reason for me to give a few friendly suggestions to a newcomer on the astral plane about further proper acts as soon as he/she manages to leave his/her physical body:

The most important thing is not to go far from your physical body. Observe your physical body from all sides and angles. If you have done that, you will find yourself in a strange situation. You will be completely awake and conscious and at the same time, you will watch yourself lying on the bed. In that moment, all the spheres will be broken. It will clear up that you are not just physical matter, but something more than just a combined structure of bones and flesh.

That acknowledgment will be imprinted in you so deep that you will never look upon yourself the same way as before. From now on, it will become clear to you that you are an intelligent life form residing only temporary here in this space and time and all at once your physical carrier is not suitable for you anymore, you will leave it and carry on.

Therefore, if in the beginning you stay close to or facing your physical body, it will surely cut many of your astral excursions. Nevertheless, you must always know that once you master the skill of controlling your astral body by straight watching your physical body without being pulled back in, you will have much bigger advantage than those who instantly leave the room like a bunch of headless chickens.

In practice, it turns out that the astral body first needs to get used to the vibrations of the astral plane. If you depart very far from your physical body, you will certainly have a more or less successful astral journey, but the consciousness will not be so strong and clear. On the contrary, if you remain close to your physical body in the first few astral projections by observing the details in your own room, you will have much stronger and clearer consciousness. However, one of the good things is that you can easily draw a distinction between the details of the things that are in your room and the details that are so far away.

It will be a good exercise for you to ask someone to write for you a word on a white sheet in big and bold letters. Ask him to put it on the top of the wardrobe in your room so that you can try to read it the next time you take a ride with your astral body. So, the next time you leave your physical body, read the word and slowly return in it, with no sudden movements in the returning process. Do not discourage yourself if you are not able to read the word correctly because the developing of the astral vision is still to come. Anyway, you will never misread the word when you become master of abandoning your physical body on your own will.

Nevertheless, in the beginning you will encounter many anomalies on the astral plane, which will be confusing for you, but in time with the developing of your astral sight those anomalies will disappear. Therefore, to solve all these little anomalies, you will have to practice other exercises for developing the ability of clairvoyance. The ability of clairvoyance is in fact the ability of clear astral vision, which will be further explained in this book.

Another good reason for you to stay close to your physical body during the first ten astral projections is the possibility of some transparent astral being's approach to you from somewhere. This astral being is in fact your guide through the astral plane. Despite the fact that the astral guide is always present on the astral plane, it is important to mention that he rarely shows himself. The statistics speak that in most cases he appears in the first ten astral projections and only if you stay close to your physical body patiently waiting for him.

If he appears to you, you must be very lucky because to learn directly from the astral guide is a rare privilege. In that case, everything you need to do is just follow his instructions. Once he introduces himself, know that each time you step into the astral plane he will appear to teach you all about the astral science and guide you to all of the seven levels of the astral plane. What is really important, do not ever contradict him because if you offend him or you start asking him about things that can gain you a selfish benefit, there is a good chance that you will become an unworthy student in his eyes and he will leave you. Just listen to his advice attentively and he will lead you to the final frontiers of the astral world. If you manage to reach the border where the astral and the mental plane connect, he will introduce you to another guide who will lead you through the higher world than the astral plane and that new guide will help you continue with your spiritual development.

Unfortunately, this happens rarely. More than 90% of all astral travelers have to learn the astral science slowly and on their own, so I will orient myself as if you were new and alone in the astral plane and you will have to learn how the things function on your own.

When you have acquired some starting experience, which usually takes about ten successfully astral projections, slowly and with full control of your astral body leave the room by passing through the wall, window or whatever. You will notice that you can easily move through hard objects with absolutely no difference how big the physical objects are.

Feel free to take an astral excursion. The way of your further procedure is up to you. You can walk, run, levitate, fly and much more. Everything you do in the astral plane is by your own choice but do not forget one thing - stay calm and fully focused with absolutely no emotional charge. Anyway, for a smooth ride through the astral plane you need calm and cool consciousness with no emotional charge. This rule must be respected at least in the beginning when you are still learning the basic things about the different ways of consciousness' reaction to different appearances present on the astral plane.

If you are too emotional, no matter whether your emotions move in a positive or negative direction, your astral excursion will be very short. The strong emotions you produce will cause instability to your consciousness, which on the other hand will result with great disturbance of your concentration. Losing your concentration for just a second or two in the beginning will end up your astral journey and push you back to your physical body almost instantly.

From another point of view, when we speak about emotions in the astral plane, there is also a possibility that you will be transported to lower or higher levels, depending on the nature of the emotional charge that you have expressed. Another major rule in the astral plane is: "The thoughts and the emotions are the driving force in the astral plane that will take you where you think or feel."

Thus, because of the potential risk present in some of the places that are in the lower levels of the astral plane, be very careful of what you think or what you feel while you are out of your body.

In general, you will find life wherever you go. If your thoughts are pure and noble, you will rarely pay a visit to the lower levels of the astral plane, which in fact is the worst part that a student must go through during his or her astral development. Still, eventually, every astral traveler encounters some negative entities. Yet, it is a standard procedure that every advanced student must go through and overcome.

In contrast to the lower levels of the astral plane, the higher ones have characteristics of great beauty. Everything you see there is so wonderful, almost incomparable to some beauty that can be seen here on Earth.

On the higher levels, life is so rich and you can see or contact all kinds of astral creatures if you want to. As far as human species are concerned, 90% that are present here do not possess a physical body any longer. In most of the cases, they leave their physical bodies for the last time after their physical death and arrive here where they stay for a longer or shorter period of time, which depends on their karmic debts or their level of spiritual development.

Although no one can determine the period of their stay here, usually their presence here varies from a few hours to a few hundred earthly years. This area of the astral plane has many inhabitants and is generally called "Higher Astral" or "The land of the eternal summer". Most of the people who have led a normal and good life can be found here. Here, the astral beings can enjoy the beautiful landscapes that are more wonderful than anything you can see on Earth, go for a walk by wonderful beaches, rivers, lakes, green regions, gardens, etc.

The fact that everything you can see here, no matter how beautiful it looks, is only a density of the astral matter that has been created by the astral inhabitants is also very important to be mentioned. An experienced astral eye can notice it by the aura, which surrounds the Land of the eternal summer. Let me explain how this is possible. For example: an average person was continuously dreaming about a nice and wonderful cabin on the beautiful ocean shore in his lifetime on Earth. This desire remained within until the very end of his physical life. After his physical death, he will surely come to the Land of the eternal summer if he has not done anything wrong, seriously wrong.

The power of his ideas and aspirations will help the astral matter to create the same ambient for him - a nice cabin on the beautiful ocean shore with wonderful and lively beaches. Despite the fact that it is an astral materialization, do not doubt the reality of everything you see there when you are on an astral trip. From some point of view, everything that can be seen there is just as real as anything here on Earth. One would ask: "How is that possible?" Well, astral plane is space where the simple thought can create or destroy a structure built of the astral substance. If you consider the fact that humans are usually attached to the physical habits, you will understand what I am talking about.

Astral travelers often see big cities in the astral plane that do not belong to Earth. They are as real as any city that can be seen here on Earth. Very often, a newcomer who has just left the physical body for the last time (with the character and expectations similar to those that have created the astral city) needs some time to understand that he or she no longer possesses the material body and is now in a completely different world.

Anyway, the choice after you astrally project and leave your physical body is all yours. Which road to take, depends on your own will, and nobody else's. Everybody is free to walk and function on his or her own in the physical world and the same applies to the astral world, too. However, the astral plane is so complex and difficult to explain that it usually takes years of learning to understand only the half of the things and the ways they really work. The way some things in the astral plane are is still an unfinished book, especially when a presence of intergalactic astral entities has been detected here on Earth. As far as I know, these intergalactic astral entities have a completely different life pattern and a completely different purpose to be here.

Nevertheless, I will try to explain all the things I have learnt about the way things in the astral plane function based on my own experience. All the things I will mention are generated from my personal diary and I hope it will be of great help to anyone who is astrally active and still possesses a physical body.

Subchapter 3.13
TECHNIQUE FOR ASTRAL TELEPORTATION

Note: This book is not designed just for beginners but also to be helpful to advanced spiritual disciples. Thus, before I go on explaining what can be seen in the astral plane from my own long years of experience, I will describe a technique that can be very helpful for those who want to go further with the exploration of other planes. However, it has to be clear that this technique is for advanced astral travelers only. To use this method, solid astral experience is required (at least 300 well realized astral excursions). Astral teleporting is one of the most useful abilities of the astral body because it provides quick traveling through space and time. When astral teleportation is in process, the consciousness is not experiencing the actual moving through time and space but only the change of the environment. The ambient is changing in the eyes of the astral traveler. In most cases, a blackout that lasts a few seconds is being caused between the two sites, but in the advanced stages this blackout is not present any more and the consciousness will experience only a blink of eye teleportation to another place. Anyway, after you have successfully projected your astral body, do not leave the room. Levitate at least 2 meters from your physical body and remain in that position. Look at your transparent astral body and try to see the aura that surrounds it. If you are an experienced astral traveler and if your astral vision is well trained it should not be difficult for you to feel and see the deeper levels of your astral body. Once you have managed to change the frequency of your astral vision and spotted the light of your aura, look deeper into yourself and search for the energy flow that runs through your astral transparent body.

With the right concentration and true effort you should be able to feel the energy that flows through you. Remember this: all you need is just patience and good concentration. The rest is a natural process. When you have discovered the energy stream, just focus to it and do not let go. The longer you keep your consciousness attached to the energy flow, the stronger it will become. At some point, you will feel that if you adapt your consciousness to the energy flow you will be able to flow with it. In this stage, you are capable of releasing the energy from your astral body. After you have reached the point where the energy flow becomes visible and your whole astral body starts to vibrate and glow, focus yourself on your astral arms. Feel as the strong energetic stream accumulated by all energy circuits starts to run through your transparent hands. Slowly stretch your astral arms in front of you and even slower, pull them back a little with the intention to join the astral hands.

Leave 30 centimeters of distance between the hands and do not join them any further. If you have done everything correctly by now, you should be able to see your astral body filled with light circuits that now circulate through your hands. Hundreds of tiny white-blue lights will start flowing through you. It is an incredible view, but hold your consciousness calm and under control. The effect of the closed energy flow will induce the feeling of strong magnetic pulling in your astral hands. Despite the strong force that will be forcing you to join your hands, remain in control and do not allow your hands to move for even a millimeter. I must say that everyone who feels and sees this entire running through his/her astral body will never forget the experience. Believe my words: the real experience is much higher than my efforts to describe the experience. I could only say that it is an experience beyond the experience because pure energy will flow through you and fill you with cosmic love to infinity. You will experience an infinite bliss flowing through you.

The next thing you should do is concentrate on the middle point between your astral hands. For an inexperienced astral walker to pull all this off is a very difficult task because his/her consciousness is not ready yet, so I must say again that this kind of consciousness requires major control of the astral body and lots of previous experience.

Change the direction of the white lights and redirect them through your hands straight to the middle point. Soon you will notice that the point where the energies join becomes a wonderful white-blue half-transparent ball of light. The more energy flows through your hands, the bigger the energy ball becomes. Do not stop to feed the energy ball and let it grow more. When it reaches the size of over 50 centimeters in diameter, the magnetic force between the hands of your astral body will become almost impossible to control. It will not surprise me at all, if your hands start vibrating and shaking very hard. In that moment, you must remain calm to a maximum and focused as best as you can. If you let go the control at this point and join your astral hands, the energy ball will vaporize and its energy charge will disappear into the natural bio-field. Then you will have to do it all over again, but I bet you will have to wait until your next out of the body experience.

Therefore, do not let go and ignore the strong pulling force between your hands. Try to release even more energy into the energy ball. Use your cosmic love to charge and you will not fail. Let the energy ball grow until it reaches the size where your whole astral body can fit in. If you manage to get this far, you will feel the presence of pure energy as never before in your life. This is the real astral energy that so many astral explorers are looking for. Then, concentrate on your aura and make a strong effort to stretch it until it fits into the inner wall of the energy ball. Just seal the outer border of your aura to the inner border of the energy ball. The moment you do that, you will lose your human contours and you will become a big shiny white-blue astral ball. Once you become an astral ball of energy, you will surely notice how illuminated your room becomes because of your light radiation. In that state you are fully ready to teleport. It will be enough to just concentrate on some place that you want to go and in the next second or two you will be there. Then, just unseal your aura from the energy ball, release the energy ball and take the normal form of your astral body back. If you want to, you can remain in the astral ball and go to other places. Have a nice astral trip!

Example: If you want to teleport close to our Sun, you should only focus to your strong wish to go there. In front of your astral sight, the image of your illuminated room will disappear and the image of the Cosmos with our Sun in it will appear. In a few seconds, you will experience a feeling as if you were passing through the mirror and you will be there. Then, just release your aura; free the energy ball or the transporter if you prefer; regain your normal astral body and carry on. To return to your own physical body, just concentrate on it and your room and after a while, depending on how far you are in the astral world, it will happen.

Note: Compared to the classical astral teleporting as a natural ability of the astral body, this method of teleporting brings so much more energy along. It must become clear to anyone interested in this subject that everything in the astral world is moved by energy, so with the help of the energy ball we can move faster and easier through space and time. Also, we can move more effectively through different levels of the astral and mental world and go through higher worlds that possess much higher cosmic nature if we are skilled enough. Nevertheless, I have personally designed this method of teleporting and used it so many times. I can not say that it does not bring potential risk of getting lost in time and space, so again, I do advise high level of precaution even when the astral traveler is well experienced in the field.

Chapter 4
ASTRAL EXPERIENCES FROM MY DIARY

I have had a clear access to the astral world for more than a decade and a half. The memories of all the strange places I have visited in the astral world are the most precious thing in my life and I cherish them with great joy and pride.

As far as I can remember, after my first astral experience, I just fell in love with the astral projection. Today, after thousands of astral trips, this love has not weakened a bit and I cannot imagine my life without astral traveling. Many times in my early stages of psychic development, I have been training six to seven hours a day and have left my physical body more than seventy times on average. You can imagine the time I have spent on the astral plane and this does not include the astral trips that I have made at nights, which has usually lasted for more than five hours.

Despite all the amazing phenomena that I have seen throughout my years of astral traveling, I have also had many opportunities to encounter a UFO phenomenon and alien life forms. That has completely changed my point of view about life and reality on Earth. The knowledge we are not alone on this planet and that reality is not what it seems to be has pushed me to even harder and deeper exploration of the astral plane in a search of the truth about alien interaction with human species.

The things I have seen on the astral plane were one of the main reasons for me to write this book because it has become clear to me that behind the curtain there are many top secret projects that most people do not even dream about. Thus, from my own personal astral experience, I will try to present most of the data I have managed to collect about the subject of UFO and extraterrestrial life. Yet, these astral experiences are old dated because if I mention the astral travels that are up to date in this book, there is a real chance for them not to be understood, as they should.

Nevertheless, despite the subject about alien presence on the astral plane, I will give you a clear picture of how does it feel to be present on the astral plane and what does it feel like to move and act fully conscious. The fact is nobody lives forever. I believe that it should be selfish of me if the knowledge and the experience that I have managed to collect from the astral plane is not released in public and made available to everyone who wants to elaborate the astral science.

The knowledge about the astral science should circulate among all of us and remain vivid and vital. The more we share our knowledge, the more advanced it becomes. We all learn from each other and we all breathe the life breath given to us by the spirit of Earth. The energy of the spirit of the Earth is always around us and within us, connecting us in a special way. It is really a shame that we mostly forget the true values of the spirit in this Silicon Era of living. We all have to work very hard hopefully one day the balance between the technology and the spirituality will be regained.

During its physical existence, every astral being that awakes itself must go through many stages to become a fully awaken astral being. It takes time, but even Buddha "the awaken one" has once said: "At the end of time, every one will find his/her way to enlightenment."

Therefore, to help the process I will describe eighteen of mine carefully chosen out of the body experiences, which will clear up for you what can you encounter while you are on the astral plane, how to deal with it, where to go, etc. At the same time I will do my best to put a beam of light on the astral enigma in a way that I consider should be the most understandable of all for every one who encounters the astral projection phenomenon for the first time.

Subchapter 4.1
MY FIRST ASTRAL EXPERIENCE

Normally, you never forget your first astral experience. It happened to me in 1990, 21 April. The night was very calm and not very cold when I went to sleep as usual around 01:00 AM.

Sometime around the small hours, I became aware that I was in the middle of a strange dream. The dream was so vivid and I could think so freely. The theme of the dream was about the noble philosophy of the Tibetan lamas and their way of life. Finding myself in their wisdom, I wished with all my heart to become one of them. The wish was so real and intense that it had somehow changed the basic structure of the dream. With absolutely no warning in my head I started to hear a loud zooming sound like "zzzzz..." that had awaken me into a fully conscious state. Physically I was completely paralyzed and I couldn't move an inch. I felt a strong force running through my body that was giving me the impression of electrical nature. It was shaking me real good but I didn't panic. After a few seconds the force became much stronger and the sound much louder.

Deep inside, I knew it was the moment I had been waiting for. I strongly wished to leave my physical body. What a miracle! It started to happen. The feeling of the strong energy with the loud sound stopped and I felt elevating from my own body. After approximately twenty centimeters, I somehow managed to take control and stop elevating. I wanted to turn upside down to see my physical body and it happened in an instant. Down below I was lying on a bed with my head turned on the right side. The moment I saw myself down lying on a bed, I was overwhelmed with a great feeling of joy. People usually say that the first time you find yourself out of your body severe panic or fear follows it, but I felt so calm and wonderful. Moreover, how could you not feel wonderful when you had seen yourself lying on the bed while levitating above the bed and feeling completely alive and conscious? So, in my consciousness, those thoughts went like this:

"I'm thinking deeper and better than in my physical body. The fact that I'm levitating above my body means that the stories about the astral world are true. So, it must be also true that when we die we come here."

Then I managed to elevate higher and put myself in a vertical position. I could see everything in my room. It was strange for me because everything in the room was somehow illuminated but I was certain that when I went to sleep I put the blinds on the windows down and that the room had to be completely dark. Next, I wished to see my astral body and the silver cord that so many esoteric authors wrote about. When I looked at myself, I noticed I was a transparent double with the white line representing my human contour. It was the same size and shape as my physical body, like a perfect copy but totally transparent. About one centimeter all around the white line there was somewhat of small blue light flickering as if exposed to current air.

When I looked in the area of the solar plexus in my astral body and then in the same area in my physical body I didn't spot any connection between my two bodies. That put me completely out of control. It confused me a lot, because the belief of the silver cord was so famous that I was sure that connection had to be there but I could not see it.

On the other hand, I could perfectly see everything else and I even heard sounds of the cars that were coming from outside. In those moments of confusion, I felt I was losing my consciousness, but I managed to pull myself together and maintain the position of levitating in the center of my room. I loosened myself completely and after a second or two, I felt rafted by some strange and invisible current that was taking me backwards. I did not make an effort to fight it and I just adapted to that newborn situation because I was curious to see what would happen next.

The invisible current brought me close to the wall that represented the border between the rooms of my elder brother and my own. I walked through the wall amazingly easy. I remember that I got a very creepy feeling in the moment when I was slowly passing through the wall because I clearly saw the grey color of the concrete.

The next thing I remember was entering my brother's room, still flying slowly backward and still driven by that invisible force. The room was absolutely the same as it was in the physical world, and I saw my brother sleeping on his bed. The carpet, the pictures, the interior and everything else were completely the same as they were supposed to be. For a moment, I wanted to break out from the current that was moving me backwards, and in an instant, I felt like having gained full control over myself again. I turned my face towards the window and smoothly flew through it. The next moment, I found myself levitating at the fourth floor altitude. The feeling that I was on the altitude of the fourth floor levitating in thin air with no physical assistance was fascinating.

Even I did not believe that was really happening. I perfectly saw the front side of my building with all the windows and balconies on it and everything else that I knew so well, but this time from a new perspective. By the way, I lived in a building in a settlement in Skopje known as "Novo Lisiche". The building was not high and in fact, it had seven floors only in the two middle entrances and nine floors in the two side entrances. To be more precise, I lived on the fourth floor in one of the middle entrances.

When I managed to distant myself for about twenty meters away from the building, I could watch them all. In that precise moment, an interesting thought went through my consciousness: "That's why they called the astral plane a parallel world. Everything is completely the same as in the physical world".

After fifteen seconds of levitating twenty meters from my building, I came up with the idea to go around and land on the parking lot on the other side of the building to remember a registration plate on some car. It would serve me as evidence of my out of the body experience. Unfortunately, in that sensational moment I started to feel like loosing consciousness again. The next second, everything around me became completely dark. What was more interesting, I was still in a conscious state but I could not see anything. A few moments later, I felt I was back in my room again. My sight returned and I saw my astral body levitating in a horizontal position parallel to my physical body. In that same moment, I remember I felt strong force that pulled me down. I tried to resist it, but it was stronger than me and it pulled me down directly into my physical body.

The next moment I felt my physical body again and without absolutely any loss of the memory about what just happened I got up from my bed and said to myself: "Unbelievable. I did it."

I remember feeling overwhelmed with joy and happiness, almost as a child given the long desired toy. I had heard many things about astral projection but the experience of it was a completely different thing.

Subchapter 4.2
THE NEED OF HARD EVIDENCE

In the beginning of his/her astral voyages almost every astral walker has a natural desire to prove to him/herself that what he/she has seen and heard in the astral plane is not an illusion but reality. I was not an exception, so I strongly felt the need to prove to myself that everything I saw with my astral body was real. So, my first few astral projections were in fact a search for evidence.

This astral experience happened to me on May 28, 1990. The action took place around 07:00 in the morning. A very strong zooming sound like "zzzzz..." awoke me from the state of deep sleep again. It came without any warning like the first time, and it pushed me into a complete state of vigilance. I found myself lying on my left side but again fully paralyzed. The only difference from the first time was that it did not happen because of my influence on a dream but by itself. I could not even remember what I was dreaming about. Something unknown to me triggered the strange force in me and woke me up. It seemed to me that I was stuck somewhere between two dimensions. I could not move physically and I could not move astrally as well. I remember saying to myself: "OK Pane, just do not panic and remain calm!"
Luckily, I had already learnt from my uncle that the strange electrical force with the strong zooming sound like "zzzzz" was in fact a sudden rising of my Kundalini energy. Even then, I had been aware of the fact that everything that was going to follow up depended primarily on my reaction to the Kundalini energy.

It was clear to me that if my thoughts were calm and full of cosmic love, the Kundalini would bring the expansion of my consciousness, but if I panicked and showed fear, she would get wild and I did not want to know what it looked like in live experience. It was strange, but despite the fact that I could not open my eyes, I was seeing some strange blue light inside me while Kundalini was active. Anyway, after I focused on the cosmic love and everything else of positive nature that I could think of, the force increased its strength in a few waves. The zooming sound became unbearable and I thought I was going to explode by the pressure of the force. The Kundalini was streaming with all its strength and it was enlightening the bottom of my spine. The next moment the light started to go up in great speed. Somehow, I knew that the moment of separation with my physical body was coming closer. When the light reached my head I just wished to leave my physical body. The same second I wished for that, I felt the start of the separation from my physical body on the right side. When the head of my astral body had been separated, the zooming sound stopped and I did not feel any energy rising anymore. The first thing I noticed was that it was a morning. The room was lit with sunshine. I saw my body lying on the bed perfectly.

When I looked around my room, I saw a painting on the wall that was on my left side, the door, and the wallpaper with palm trees on the beautiful ocean shore that was on the opposite wall from my bed. I managed to separate half of my astral body when I heard footsteps on the parquet. I looked in the direction of the door again. I watched as the door-handle started to move very slowly and I saw my mother trying to be as quiet as she could, entering my room. She looked at my physical body, and when she noti-

117

ced I was sound asleep, she did not want to wake me up, so she continued to the other side of my room. She came close to the commode and opened the middle drawer. I found myself in a strange situation. I was fully awake; half separated from my physical body and watching the movements my mother made from a perspective that was impossible with my physical body because it was turned on the left side and with the back to the position where my mother was standing.

She pulled out one green t-shirt that belonged to me and after she closed the drawer, she went to the door very slowly intending to exit the room. In that moment, a good idea went through my consciousness. That was a good opportunity to test the reality of my experience. I joined with my physical body very fast and opened my physical eyes just in time to see my mother leaving the room with the green t-shirt in her right hand.

Two seconds later she closed the door and I was alone again. The sensation of triumph went through my mind. It became clear to me that I was not dreaming and it was real. Speaking from a physical point of view, it was impossible for me to see what she did because I was turned on the left side and with my back towards her all the time. I got up, and just for the test, I went to find my mother and ask her what she was doing in my room. I found her in the kitchen ironing my green t-shirt. Just for the jest, I started to complain that she was so loud and that she had woken me up. She looked at me with great compassion and said that she was so sorry, but she needed to iron my T-shirt because we would have to go to my nephew's house around nine to help him with the preparations for his wedding.

Again, just joking, I replied that I was looking for that green t-shirt all week and asked her where she had found it. She answered it was with the other t-shirts in the middle drawer of the commode all the time. My body started to shake with sensation. I replied to her again that I was just joking and I kissed her on the cheek and returned to my room.

I felt like having won the lottery, because it cleared up to me I was not hallucinating, and the event really took place. This was the second time that I proved to myself that I was capable of leaving my physical body and coming back, with absolutely no problems with the memory of what I had seen on the astral plane. The reality of this astral experience had given me a great amount of self-confidence and the sense that I was moving in the right direction. Yet, typically for humans, I needed much more to prove to myself that the stories about the astral world were true. I decided to train even harder than before. I was curious to find out what would happen the next time I decided to leave my physical body.

Subchapter 4.3
CLOSE ASTRAL EXCURSION

During my next few astral excursions, I continued collecting data, which would serve me as evidence that the things happening to me were real. This is one of them and it happened on September 3, 1990:

The action took place somewhere around 06:00AM, while I was sound asleep. I do not remember what I was dreaming about before I became conscious, but I do remember that I woke up because of some strange circumstance. The moment I became conscious, I realized that all I was able to see was a complete darkness but in the same time, I was strangely aware of my environment. Then about five seconds later, I started to feel like softly floating on some water surface. In the beginning, it felt nice and calming, but the situation changed in a few seconds when Kundalini became active.

It happened so fast. It caught me completely by surprise and I have to admit that it scared me a lot. It took me about five seconds to pull myself together and to realize what was happening. The bioelectric waves coming from the bottom of my spine were gaining on strength very fast and it seemed to me that if they became stronger I would probably have a difficult time dealing with it. The drama continued and the Kundalini started to produce even stronger sound but that did not disturb me as much as the sensation of the unbearable strong energy, which was going up my spine.

So, I remained calm with absolutely no effort to make any physical movement. At the same time, I knew I needed positive thoughts to be safe from the Kundalini's dark potential, so I concentrated the best I could on pure and positive things. When Kundalini reached the point in my head, (which I can define as a spot between my eyebrows) I knew that I had a clear chance to leave my body again. I did not want to miss that chance, so almost immediately I mentally gave a strong command: "I'm going out of my body."

I remember how amazingly easy that worked, so the next moment the separation started to happen. The best I can describe that separation, is like a feeling that between me, and my physical body there were thousands of tiny threads, which tore apart in a few moments accompanied by some strange sound I could not clearly define. The astral projection process finished and I found myself elevating up from my physical body. My astral body seemed to me the same as before, totally transparent and with the small flickering blue light around my human contours which were defined with white line.

Despite the fact that I felt the same joy for I was out again, I remained calm and focused. I elevated a bit more and when I reached the height of one meter above my bed I easily managed to change my position into vertical, which gave me a good perspective to closely observe my physical body. My eyes were closed, the breathing was normal and in fact, the whole expression of my face was giving me the impression of my other me sleeping as a baby.

After I examined my physical body and concluded that everything was OK, I focused on my room. Generally, my room looked normal to me, a little messy of some clothes I had put here and there during the day. Everything was in the right place as in the physical reality, so I looked upon the window with an intention to go closer. In an instant, I arrived there and I was a little surprised of how easy that was.

"OK, let's go and look around" – I thought. In a second, as if some unquestionable command was given I walked right through the window, made two steps on my balcony and jumped into the thin air. In the moment of falling, (which in fact was a product of me still thinking in the physical way) I lifted myself and managed to take a slow but smooth flight on the altitude of fifteen meters above the green park on the north side of my building. I was in ecstasy and felt great, as I never did before. Still, despite my effort to describe what I was feeling, the true sensation of flying in the astral body cannot be understandable for someone who has not experienced it at least once. The best I can come up with is like an ultimate freedom, which fulfills you in every way you can think of, and gives you a clear image of you as a part of the Universe, which is so much larger than you have ever imagined.

Anyway, after about thirty meters of flying I stopped in the air, turned around and started to stare into my building. Little by little, I started to get used to controlling the basic movements of my transparent double. All of what I looked at was so astonishing, because I found myself in a position to observe the balconies of my building from a perspective that I never had before. In my consciousness I remember saying to myself: "Wait until my friends hear about this".

I watched the building for about fifteen seconds, and then I turned around and spotted the small power plant that was about a hundred meters away from my building. Then I looked in the direction of ASNOM Boulevard that was so close to my building and spotted that it was starting to get crowded with people going to work. I remember that again I felt great sensation because it was an indescribable experience to be aware of the fact that my physical body was there in my apartment and I was here levitating in my astral body witnessing the awakening of my neighborhood.

I looked to the East and I saw the Sun rising from the horizon on a clear and cloudless morning sky. Generally, it was a pretty view to see. I let myself go again and without any fear of falling, I flew to the East. I flew above the boulevard and proceeded above the yellow wheat field just near by. I remember I was flying at the altitude of about 50 meters and the speed was about 30 km/h. I did not feel a need of speeding up because that speed seemed just fine to me; nevertheless, everything I did so far was experimenting with the way my astral body works, so I did not want to rush things on. I had just started to explore my new abilities and I didn't want to do anything stupid. I was just attached to the rule - nice and slow.

The sensation of flying was great. Soon I came to the end of the wheat field and now I was flying over a huge hole that construction workers had dug. They were coming here in big trucks to extract sand, which they were using at construction sites somewhere else. I did not hold myself long above the huge hole and soon, still flying to the East, I found myself over the biggest river in Macedonia. The name of the river was Vardar the stream of which was passing very close to my neighborhood, about two hundred meters from the ASNOM Boulevard. The riverbed of Vardar goes zigzag, and separates the city of Skopje in two almost equal parts. I never believed I would see the Vardar from this altitude and in this way. I looked straight ahead and I saw a few very high white poplar trees, which were so close to the riverbed of Vardar.

As I flew, I went very close to one of the trees, almost touching its white bark and continued in the direction of another area of Skopje called "Hipodrom".

Soon I arrived close to the buildings of Hipodrom. I decided to land directly on the parking lot of one building. It was interesting to me that I had landed amazingly softly, with absolutely no sense of weight while I was touching the ground. The parking lot was almost empty of cars, so I walked a few steps towards the nearby sidewalk and looked straight at the building. I started to observe the whole building especially the balconies and something on a balcony on the second floor caught my attention. It was a red bicycle, but the interesting thing was that one of the wheels was missing.

While I was looking at the bicycle, I felt that something was not right and that I was losing control over myself. After a few seconds, I started to see foggy, the building started to disappear from my sight and I felt that I was losing my strength rapidly. My concentration broke down completely and again I entered the state of complete darkness. It lasted for about two seconds and then I felt as if I was sinking directly into my physical body. When I felt that my control over my physical body was back, I remained still and did not move at all.

I was repeating all the data I brought from the astral plane in my mind, and when I convinced myself that nothing had vaporized from my memory, I slowly moved my arms and legs. As soon as I got up from the bed, I immediately took my diary and wrote down my astral experience.

Luckily, the place I visited in my astral excursion was a few miles from my area and it was possible for me to check the data I had collected. So, at noon I went to check the details from my astral trip. When I arrived to the Hipodrom area, I started to look for the building I saw in my astral excursion early that morning. Five minutes later I found it and went around the building to the parking lot. When I got there, I saw the same details on the building. Everything was the same and on the second floor on the same balcony, I saw exactly the same red bicycle with one wheel missing that I saw that morning while I was out of my physical body. The front side of the building, the park and the parking lot were exactly the same. After a while, greatly satisfied with a smile on my face, I left the place.

The truth is, in addition to this astral excursion I have made many others with a purpose to prove to myself that everything I do with my astral body is real. In time, I have stopped looking for evidence anymore and started to look at my astral excursions as equal as any other experience that I collect in the physical world.

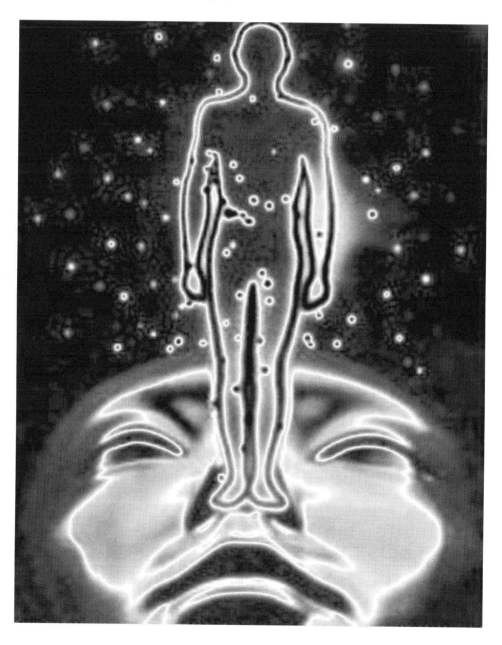

Subchapter 4.4
SHADOWS

On the night of December 6, 1991, I encountered a kind of an astral form, which sometimes can be found in lower and middle levels of the astral plane for the first time in my life. The truth is, in most cases you do not find this astral form because it finds you. However, first I will describe my astral experience and then I will comment it.

During the same night I had an opportunity to be present on the astral plane, twice. The first time I entered the astral plane was by using a dream control method, which in that time was the easiest way for me to leave my physical body. I remember dreaming that I was in Ohrid. The city of Ohrid is about two hundred kilometers from Skopje and is in fact on the shore of a wonderful lake; the biggest one of all three natural lakes that Macedonia possesses. To be more precise, I was dreaming that I was on the large summer terrace of the hotel "Mladost" located right on the shore of the Ohrid Lake, situated on the other side of the Ohrid hill, about 500m from the "St. John Kaneo" Church. I remember that the same evening my friends and I talked about Ohrid, so I find the dream about the lake not surprising.

However, there was an anomaly on the terrace in my dream and as soon as my perception picked it up, some trigger in my consciousness went on and the next second I became aware that I was dreaming. After becoming fully conscious that I was dreaming and in fact on the astral plane, I woke up on the same terrace of the hotel.

The anomaly was gone and everything had become normal to my perception. I saw my transparent astral body and a smile lit up my face because I knew that it was time for some astral stuff. I was out of my body again and that started happening very often lately, so it had given me a sign that I was improving the development of my astral consciousness. Straight ahead of me, reflecting the light from the city with all its beauty was the lake of Ohrid. The night was beautiful and starry. I jumped over the terrace about three meters high from the ground and walked close to the shore. The lights coming from the hotel gave the lake the effect of a wonderful dancing light on the surface of the water. I remember thinking to myself: "It's beautiful".

Loud disco music was coming from somewhere on the right. It proved Ohrid's nightlife fully active although it was winter. I was walking along the shore enjoying the beauty of the ambient. The beaches are mostly of small rocks but they are very beautiful. I looked at the lake enjoying the beautiful reflections on the surface of the water once again, especially the ones coming from the other side of the lake, and I remember thinking: "That is a wonderful site; it deserves to be seen". Then, I looked upon the stars on the blue velvet night sky. It fulfilled me with even greater feeling of joy and peace. Judging from the whole image, I assumed it was probably around 02:00 AM.

Then I made a mistake I was not supposed to. In a split of a second I thought of my physical body. The same moment I thought of my physical body I felt my consciousness changing somehow and taking some kind of liquid characteristics. The next second, I found myself in my room, part of me already in my physical body. The right part of my astral body was joined with my physical body but my left side was still out and I could still use it. After a second or two, pulled by some magnetic force the left side of my astral body also started sinking into my physical body.

I did not want to return to my physical body so soon and I decided to try to leave it again. The desire of leaving my physical body was so strong that I knew there was a good chance for a second astral projection. However, things started taking another course, different from the one I wanted to.

First, while I was still in my physical body I started to observe some dim light in the area of my forehead, or to be more precise in the point of my Ajna charka. After a few seconds, the smothered light took the shape of a black glowing triangle. I remember this thought went through my mind: "Well, this might be my third eye, very active tonight."

From the area of my third eye, I felt some force that started pulling me up. It felt as if I was becoming smaller and the black triangle becoming bigger and at the same time, I felt that I was being sucked into the triangle. Slowly and fearless I put some small effort to leave my physical body and the process began again. I felt my normal size again and inch-by-inch I managed to separate my astral body. At the point I had reached vertical levitation over my physical body, I saw something so disturbing that scared me a lot. Two strange shadow creatures were levitating in a horizontal position in the center of my room. The shadows had humanoid shape, but they were completely black and there was no aura around them. They seemed asleep, so I went closer to examine them better and to possibly find out what they were doing there.

In the moment when I got closer to them, the shadow creatures became alive and I remember them immediately taking vertical position. They had neither eyes, nor anything else but their blackness. Even today, when I remember the event I get the same creepy feeling. Anyway, I was seized by fear and with each second passing by they seemed as if they had come straight from hell to take me there. I was so scared that I did not know what to do. I remember a debate took place in my consciousness. I was aware that if I returned to my physical body, they would still be there in my room and if I remained on the astral plane and tried to fight them, I was not sure whether I would have a chance to win.

I decided the best option that I had in that moment was to take them out of my room. At that point, I realized they were reading my thoughts and one of them jumped at me. Before I had any time to react, the shadow had wrapped itself around my transparent astral body like a snake. Suddenly, I had exactly the same feeling as when a big and poisonous snake had wrapped all around you to tighten and crash your body to death. I knew I was in a difficult situation and I had to do something about it.

Two seconds later, I felt my astral body was losing energy. It seemed to me as if the shadow was somehow absorbing the life force from me, because I felt so much pain and a great loss of my strength. Driven by defensive instinct, I tried to shake it off, but that had absolutely no effect on the shadow. I started to panic and by inertia, I accelerated from the levitating mode into the flying mode. I was just above the green park in front of my building when the shadow tightened around me even harder and feeling so much pain (similar to the one when somebody stabs you with a knife), I started falling down.

Nevertheless, before I had hit the ground I managed to pull myself together and performed just one quick and sharp maneuver to the left. Then I directed myself to the West accelerating rapidly every second. The shadow was still wrapped all around me and when I looked back, I saw the second one catching up with me.

The panic reached its culmination and "my heart jumped into my throat". I had no idea where to go or what to do. I flew around and above many buildings on my way to the center of the city. No matter how fast I was flying, the second shadow was always a few meters behind me. I thought the moment of my death was close. The pain caused by the wrapped shadow was driving me insane.

Then, in those moments of despair I received a telepathic message: "Do not try to escape". I listened to that voice in my consciousness and realized that the voice was right and the escape was in fact the wrong solution. Although I was so weak, I stopped panicking and the fear was gone. I stopped for a second and in a blink of an eye, I felt the second shadow had touched my astral body.

The pain doubled that moment. I felt my whole astral body burning of pain, and I even experienced a feeling of overheating. Can you imagine yourself levitating between two buildings with two shadow creatures wrapped all around you like snakes? It was surely one of the most unpleasant experiences that I had ever experienced in my life. "If I return to my physical body I will bring the shadows with me, and they will suck me like parasites till I die. I must get rid of them here on the astral plane or I'm gone." – A monologue took place in my consciousness.

Somewhere deep in my consciousness I felt a mighty feeling of unconditional universal love. I opened myself to that pure feeling of cosmic love and allowed it to come out to the surface. In that particular moment, I remember my whole astral body started to shine. First, the beams of light illuminated the shadows like a negative and then the same beams threw them at least ten meters away from me. A moment later they disappeared in thin air.

I felt revived after they were gone. The light went back deep inside me and I knew that it went back straight to my soul. Still, I felt so weak and I started to fly slowly towards the area of Skopje where I physically lived. Two questions were forcing their way up to the surface in my consciousness:

"What if this ended the other way? What if I did not manage to get rid of those creatures, would that necessarily mean that it would end my physical existence or even my astral existence?"

As soon as I arrived above my area I saw my building and lowered my altitude. After a while I dropped to the altitude of the fourth floor and entered my room through the balcony. As soon as I approached closer to my physical body I noticed big beads of perspiration on my forehead. Still feeling terribly weak I succeeded to put myself into a parallel position with my physical body and started sinking into it.

The next moment the sense of my physical body was back. I opened my eyes and got up, but I sat again on my bed because the same moment I got up, a major wave of pain in my head hit me hard. I felt exhausted to the maximum. However, this experience did not end without any physical consequences. It took me about two weeks to get in shape again. Obviously, the shadows had sucked a huge amount of life force from me. To tell you the truth, I surely hoped I would not have to meet them again.

Comment: After long years of activity in the astral plane, concerning this astral experience I could say I did just fine considering my level of astral development in 1991. The term of this astral creature in the esoteric literature is known as "Shadow".

The Shadow is in fact a type of memory that comes from some consciousness, which has left the astral body the same way it has left the physical in the time of the physical death. In other words, the Shadow is a product of a natural process that transfers the consciousness from the astral plane into the mental plane. A part of the consciousness that contains some vibrations that cannot enter the mental plane because of their lower nature remains like a memory in the astral body that has been left behind to disintegrate in the astral plane.

As in the moments of the physical death the astral body leaves the old or not suitable physical body any longer, the higher principles of the soul leave the astral body when the time is right for it in exactly the same way. When that happens, the miniature part of the consciousness that contains a part of the memory of the being that has used that astral body is also being left behind. Because of the fact that this miniature part of the consciousness is still alive and it does not want to be destroyed, the only way to prevent its own natural disintegration into the astral substance is by stealing the energy from living life forms. This partly conscious creature becomes some kind of an astral parasite and as the amount of the stolen energy grows bigger, its disintegration into the astral substance takes much longer.

However, sometimes the Shadows can be found attached to the aura of living people on Earth. In these cases, the Shadows use every possible way to suck the energy from them until they draw them completely causing serious illness, even death. Another characteristic of the Shadows is that they cannot resist the calls directed toward other astral bodies from all areas of the physical world during the spiritualistic séances.

During these spiritualistic séances, the psychic him/herself usually does not have the ability to check out who is really present in the room and that gives the Shadow a perfect chance to manipulate him/her and the others. From the partly functional telepathy, it can easily read the thoughts of the psychic and the others, collecting a huge amount of energy with each question directed to him/her. With each question of the psychic and the others, the transfer of fluid or etheric energy is established and in the end, it results with growing of the energy level of the Shadow, but the energies of the psychic and the others become weaker. The longer the séances last, the bigger the amount of the absorbed energy is. If the séances become everyday practice and the psychic does not recognize he/she has been manipulated, it will surely end up with some serious consequences for him/her.

Despite of all that, it is also known that sometimes the Shadows can visit weak-minded people that often perform sexual masturbations. We all know that the energy cannot be destroyed but can only transform itself from one kind of energy into another. Through the orgasm, the released sexual energy goes into the etheric plane and stays there. In that case, all the Shadow has to do is to collect the amount of free energy. Just consider the fact that before the erection happens people feel so much stronger; they feel they can break the wall with a single punch, but after the orgasm, they feel so much weaker, almost like a flat balloon. The energy loss is obvious, wouldn't you agree?

I do not want to scare you that every time you make love, some dark creature waits in the corner to collect a part of your energy. I just want to say that this phenomenon is absolutely possible and real although rare.

In worst cases, the Shadow can become a part of all sorts of rituals of the black magic, with the purpose of harming someone or for realization of some selfish idea. However, the Shadows cannot fight the natural process of eternity, and eventually they fully disintegrate and fall into the darkness.

Subchapter 4.5
ANCIENT GREEK TEMPLE

I remember this astral experience as my starting point in my underwater research. After the astral excursion, which happened on February 2, 1992, my need for adventure had taken me many times into underwater explorations. I chose one of the many to present in this book.

Somewhere around two o'clock in the afternoon, I decided to go out of my physical body and to take an astral excursion. I put the window blinds down and I lied down into the position of Shavasana. In a while, I managed to bring my physical body into the state of total relaxation and started with the visualization of the seven figures of the technique I previously presented in this book. As soon as I finished the technique, I felt something pulling me up and the next moment I found myself elevating above my physical body.

It did not took me long to get full control over my astral body and in a few seconds I managed to land softly by my bed. From that position of standing beside my bed, I saw my physical body lying in Shavasana but I did not find any interest watching myself, so I started to run towards the windows intending to leave my room as soon as possible. After I went through the windows, I jumped over the balcony and strongly moved myself straight up towards the sky increasing the altitude fast.

When I reached the altitude from where I could easily observe the whole region of Macedonia, I decided to further move in the direction of Greece. The speed of my flight was solid, so pretty soon I arrived above Athens. The capital of Greece looked wonderful from above, so I slowed a little. Still, Athens was not my target, so I continued flying towards the Mediterranean Sea.

Despite the fact that it was winter, the sea looked wonderful from above. I diverted my direction to the angle of 45° and when I reached the altitude of about a few hundred meters, I continued to fly in the direction of a small group of islands, which were very close to the island known as Naxos. I flew around changing my altitude and enjoying all the beauties that this area of the Mediterranean Sea possesses at the same time.

Note: *It was a lot of fun, and it was one of the reasons I loved astral projection so much – while your body stays at home in the state of Trance, you are free to do whatever you like and go wherever you like. The only thing missing is you cannot bring a camera with you to take pictures and show others where you have been and what you have seen. Anyway, convincing people where I have been with my astral body has never been my objective, so for a very long time it has not made any difference to me. In that time I was feeling freed from the physical chains and that was all that mattered to me, until I started to see things that were very important to every one and deserved to be told.*

As soon as I had come at the altitude about ten meters above the water surface I decreased my speed. Although I was moving with the intention to reach Crete, I changed my course and started to circulate around the smaller islands of Naxos because the site was wonderful and I enjoyed it completely. It was all the more better that I had caught the period of the day, when everything around me was so calm and quiet, with exception of a few fishing boats. While flying above the water, I was looking down and sometimes I remember seeing a shoal of fish so beautiful in its shape and in changing its direction of moving. At one point, when I was following a shoal of fish, I noticed something shining at the bottom of the crystal clear water. Just of curiosity, I made a sharp side move and turned back towards the place where I had spotted the flickering thing. When I arrived closer to the surface of the water, I slowly started to go in. The feeling was so strange because I had never done it with my astral body before. It felt absolutely the same compared to the physical feeling of entering the water, except without feeling cold or warm. As soon as I had sunk up to my head, I started swimming on instinct. I remember the thought that went through my consciousness: "Don't be stupid, you are astrally here and you can not sink if you do not want that."

I stopped moving my arms and legs, and continued levitating in the water. I looked to my left saw a small island in the distance, but the reason I entered the water was on my right and very close to me. The water was so clear that I could clearly see what was lying on the bottom of the sea. I recall the sensation that overwhelmed me in the moment I realized that the thing that lay on the sand was the remains of some old Greek temple.

The columns were almost in great shape. Some of them were still standing, and some of them were partly visible because they were half covered with sand. The same moment I spotted the structure at the bottom, I dived towards it. As soon as I had slipped into the water, I found out that moving underwater was incomparably easier because you did not feel any resistance or pressure and normally, you did not have to breathe to stay alive. The floor was visible and I estimated it was probably about thirty meters deep. All around me, all sorts of smaller fish were swimming absolutely undisturbed, obviously not aware of my astral presence.

Note: *In those times, I thought fish could not sense my astral presence, but after a major underwater astral research, which took years, I realized I had been wrong and that sea life could sense an astral presence, especially dolphins and whales.*

However, it was a unique experience. The monument, which once had been an ancient Greek temple, was still in relatively good shape despite the factor of time. I had dove deeper and moved closer to some of the columns that were still standing. Although buried in the sand for one third of their size, they looked enormously huge to me. The part of the columns that was visible above the sand was intertwining with hundreds of small but dense seaweeds. The whole picture was giving me the impression that somewhere in the distant past this temple had looked similar to the Parthenon.

Suddenly I wanted to see up and overjoyed I saw the sunlight penetrating the surface of the water. It felt amazing because the sunlight was also penetrating my transparent astral body and that gave me a sensation beyond words. All those small things happening to me in the astral plane had made me love my astral trips even more. I thought to myself:

"Unbelievable. While my physical body sleeps in my apartment in Skopje, I'm here beneath the surface of the Mediterranean Sea, exploring a site of a historical monument."

After I had explored the monument in my own way, I decided to move on and see what else I could find underwater. I started diving south, always staying close to the floor. It was covered with sand and rocks, but there were areas, where the seaweeds were so dense that I felt like moving through some underwater forest. The sea life was so rich… I saw fish types that I had never dreamed about.

I had stayed for about twenty minutes more underwater, but I had not seen any other monument or some structure that belonged to the distant past. Still, I had enjoyed the astral exploration with all my heart and I remember feeling great regret when I felt a sudden weakness because I knew my presence there was over. The last thing I saw was my physical body lying in the Shavasana and the next moment I was physically awake. Normally, as a part of a standard returning procedure, I did not dare to physically move at all and after I had repeated the whole astral experience in my mind, I decided to open my eyes. I remember being angry with me for I had not been strong enough to remain longer in the astral plane and explore the underwater life, but soon I calmed down because I knew my underwater explorations had just begun. The interesting thing from a physiological point of view was that as soon as I returned to normal from the state of Trance, I felt so cold. In fact, I felt like I was freezing, so the moment I got up from the bed, I went to find some warm pullover to put on. After I put my pullover on, I took my diary and wrote about my out of the body experience on the next empty sheet. When I had finished writing, I lifted the window blinds up and went out on my balcony because I felt warmer with the pullover on. The sensation was still holding me tightly and when I looked into the sunny sky, I remember saying to myself: "What a wonderful astral trip!"

Subchapter 4.6
FIRST CONTACT

This out of the body experience represents the beginning of my contacts with alien species. The astral world is rich with all kinds of entities, many of them coming from the deep Space. Despite the fact that most of the people capable of astral traveling rarely encounter them on the astral plane, they are always there but they do not want to be seen. My first contact with such an entity happened on May 7, 1992. Basically, it was a very short contact but very important to me because they usually do not allow their presence to be known or even sensed, not on the astral plane and especially not on the physical plane.

I will describe the whole astral experience as it happened and the way I succeeded to awake myself on the astral plane. This experience is also a good example that there are numerous methods for entering the astral plane if you are familiar with the basic movements that consciousness makes during the state of dreaming. My dream was about a tall tree that my friend and I were climbing. It was daytime, but the sky was full of clouds and it started to rain a little in my dream. The place where we were was close to my neighborhood and it was just opposite the river Vardar.

Dreams are dreams; nevertheless the situation changed in seconds and it turned out that my friend was carrying a rope with him to hang himself. Before I was able to do something, my friend suddenly took the rope and was ready to do it. Thinking still physically, I remember saying to myself:" Good Lord, he is going to hang himself". The dream carried on and I started to climb faster, in order to prevent his intention, but the moment I had reached the height from where I had the possibility to save him, he jumped off the branch and hanged himself. Desperate as I was, I thought to myself: "Jesus, he is dead."

There was nothing I could do in that moment and still not realizing that I was dreaming I was awaiting for the separation of his astral and physical body. Nothing happened in the first ten seconds. Obviously, completely out of any awareness for my presence on the astral plane, I was stubbornly waiting for his astral body to come out.

Then it began and I remember saying to my friend:" Do not be afraid, you have just left your physical body for the last time."

The same moment I said that, a strong wind started to blow. The coldness of the wind woke me up, I realized that I was dreaming and a few seconds later I was standing on the same spot in my transparent astral body. Everything changed, day turned to night as it truly was, and the tree and the hanged body of my friend had disappeared, because they actually never existed and were only a part of an illusion that my sub-consciousness had created. The truth is, the astral plane allows our consciousness to create all sorts of visible illusions during the process of dreaming, and the nature of those deceptions always depends on our wishes or fears.

However, everything around me took normal appearance and I was watching my neighborhood from the other side of the river.

I remember saying to myself: "OK! Let's take an astral ride!" I felt great need to lift myself from the ground as much as I could. The instant I wished for it, it started to happen. I felt great inner strength awakening somewhere inside me, and two seconds later, I was somewhere on the altitude of two kilometers already. I remember the clear starry sky. I made a huge somersault that gave even greater élan to carry on flying. It does not matter how often you go on astral trips; every new one is a different story.

After completing the somersault, I carried on flying to the West, towards the center of the city. Skopje looked so much nicer from above, attired in thousands of lights shining in the night. I dropped my altitude on one kilometer and continued to fly over the city for a long time at low speed. I was thinking about the purpose of my life. This was strange, because almost always, when I was out of my physical body I was completely occupied with something I was doing or seeing on the astral plane. In contrast to the usual, on this astral excursion I was deeply thinking about the purpose of existence and of life itself in the Universe.

It was completely irrelevant where I was going, what I was going to see or hear. With no special intention, I changed my direction of flying to the North, or to be more precise, towards the Skopska Crna Gora Mountain, one of the mountains that surround the valley of Skopje. In a while, with no particular reason again, I was preparing myself to leave the area of Skopje, when all of a sudden I felt something was different in my environment. In my consciousness, it felt just like the feeling when you sense you are being watched, but you cannot see anyone.

I tracked the feeling, and when I determined that the strongest signal was coming from somewhere behind me, I turned my head back to see if I was going to spot something suspicious. The instant I turned around, I saw a transparent astral creature that was following me, keeping distance of about thirty meters. I did not manage to analyze the creature, but the moment I saw it, judging by its contours, it cleared up to me that the creature was not human. Although it was humanoid in form, it was much smaller in its astral size than the average human, and its transparent head was much different, similar to the being from the science fiction movies - big head with large black eyes.

To tell you the truth, it did not seem a bit friendly and with no intention to communicate with me, so I decided not to irritate him. The whole of its appearance was strange, so I stopped on the spot to examine the creature. When I stopped and focused on it, I felt something like a strike of a strong tornado. It felt as if someone had blown away all my strength and left me completely helpless.

I was sure the creature had something to do with it. I remember well the feeling of a sitting duck. The next moment a strange and strong voice appeared in my consciousness:

"The humans do not have the clearance to be here fully conscious. Do not come again".

Without any warning a bright light flashed for a second and suddenly I found myself levitating above my physical body. Unwillingly, I slowly started to sink into it and awoke physically. I recall getting up from my bed. I had a glass of water and wrote down the astral experience in my diary. Many questions appeared in my mind, which concerned the strange creature I had met.

Comment: It was the strangest being I had encountered in the astral plane ever. It acted as if it were the host in the astral plane and that I had somehow trespassed in its private property. I remember its transmission put in a form of command not to enter the astral zone on my own will again. Until then, I had not backed off from anything or anyone in my life, so I did not intend to start doing it just because some strange creature said so. Later, when I started contacting them (almost on a daily basis), I learned that most of them come from the constellation of Zeta Reticuli and that they did not want to be mentioned by their real name. They preferred the term that people aware of their presence had made up for them - "Grays."

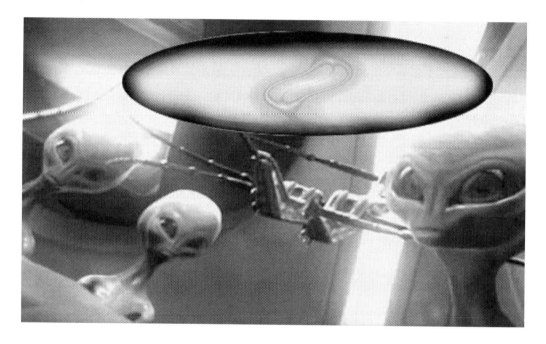

Speaking from experience, their presence always radiated a great hidden mental force and in 90% of my contacts with them, they were aggressive and evil. However, they had not shown any emotions at all, and that led me to a conclusion either they did not have any emotions or they could control them in an unbelievable and effective way. Anyway, the greatest interest they had shown in the beginning of my astral traveling had been about my strength and clearness of my consciousness and my capability to move across the astral plane. To tell you the truth, I was beginning to feel as a part of some major experiment with each day left behind, which started to bother me a lot and it surely made me persistent beyond words to find out what was really going on in every possible way.

Nevertheless, they had not shown any concern until they realized my efforts to find out more about them, but as I said before, they were focused only on my spiritual improvement, and they had been monitoring me, each time I had become conscious on the astral plane.

Subchapter 4.7
TUNNEL

This astral trip happened on November 30, 1992. After I had left my physical body, I reached the altitude of about five kilometers above Skopje and started to fly with great speed to the East. Words could not express the joy that the movement at that speed gave me. Constantly changing the altitude, I flew over mountains, forests, lakes, and from time to time above the Indian Ocean. After a half an hour of astral traveling, I reached the air space of Vietnam. I started to drop my altitude and went into the free fall towards the huge Vietnam jungle that extended as far as my eyes could see.

A few moments later, something strange appeared in the sky. I noticed huge distortion in space, which appeared from nowhere in the sky and I remember asking myself was it visible only from the astral plane or could it be seen from the physical plane as well.

I became so curious, that I stopped my free fall above the jungle and flew straight towards the space distortion. A doubt seized my consciousness whether I should or should not enter the sky distortion. Well, the explorer in me was dominant. I considered it a good chance to explore another phenomenon, which I had never seen before on the astral plane, so I decided to enter the space anomaly. So I did and the same moment I had gone through the space distortion I felt very unpleasant because my whole astral body was beginning to become extensible. The next second, I found myself in a strange tunnel. I remember questioning myself: "Where am I?" I was expecting transportation to some other place in space and time or something else but not a perfectly circled tunnel. Fully surpassed, I started to examine the tunnel.

The tunnel was illuminated with some kind of phosphorus light but I didn't manage to determine the source where the light was coming from.

"It must be ten meters in diameter" – I thought to myself. I looked behind me and then again up front and concluded that the end was not visible from either side. Guided by curiosity, I slowly flew in the direction in front of me and noticed the tunnel was going zigzag with

142

long turns. I was flying to the left then to the right, then to the left again and so on and on.

After a while I increased my speed because the end was still not visible to me. I decided it would be better if I came closer to the wall of the tunnel to examine the material it was made of. It seemed the walls of the tunnel were made of some strange phosphorus astral matter and not of classic astral substance. I remember that the phosphorus light was coming directly from the inside of the tunnel's walls and had given a wonderful effect to my transparent astral body. I carried on for miles and miles and yet I had not reached any exit point. My curiosity vanished and some unpleasant feeling started taking me over. Then the situation changed, but I was not sure whether it was for better or worse.

I spotted some strange yellow-white light about thirty meters ahead. It was very similar to the appearance of the Sun in the middle of the day. I cannot explain this completely, but somewhere from the deep of my consciousness, some flashes and visions from my distant past started to appear. In some special way, they were somehow related to this tunnel or at least to the light I was seeing. My consciousness became agitated when all of the sudden I remembered my friend Velibor's words:

"Pane, sometimes you can encounter tunnels that are infinitely long in the astral plane and there is no return, no way out from some of them".

I realized this was not a game anymore and I should start looking for an escape. The first thing that crossed my consciousness was to try to get out through the tunnel's walls. The moment I thought about that, by default my astral body lifted itself and I passed the bounder of the tunnel. I found myself in a complete darkness and the light that was visible inside the tunnel was not visible from this side. As soon as I separated the legs of my astral body from the wall, I experienced a strange feeling, like the time had stopped. Everything around me seemed frozen.

Then, that feeling was gone and I felt like moving in slow motion through the infinite dark space. I couldn't see a thing and there was absolutely no sound at all. The feeling was similar to the one when you are walking through a deep cave - you cannot see anything; it is completely dark and you feel the unpleasant moisture in the air.

A feeling of bitterness overtook me and the absolute silence was making the situation even worse. It did not take long before I sank down again into the tunnel. The strange light was still there. It was at the same distance from me and it did not move. As soon as I moved toward the light, it also moved away from me at the same speed and distance.

I increased my flying speed and started chasing the light. I was flying very fast always changing the direction of my flight, constantly adapting to the turnovers in the tunnel. Every single moment seemed to be as long as eternity. Although I was constantly increasing my speed, the light was always getting away keeping the same distance. I thought to myself: "How can I catch this light when it is constantly getting away"?

The tunnel seemed to have no end. I panicked and I kept asking myself if there was an exit from this tunnel. I started to move even faster and the more I sped up, the more it was clearing up that I should not had entered the distortion in the sky in the first place. How could I be so stupid and made this foolish mistake?

It was obvious that I had been trapped there and that there was a real possibility I would remain there for a very long time. The question was how long my physical body would be able to remain in the state of Trance before it became weaker and finally died.

The turns were changing all the time. I was in the tunnel for more than an hour and I still could not catch the sight of the exit. The light was still about thirty meters ahead, always getting away. I got rid of the panic that was present in my consciousness and started to search for any solution of the problem, because if I stayed there for more than a day, there had been a big possibility for my physical body to die.

I was focusing on returning to my physical body for the last twenty minutes but with absolutely no result. It was as if the connection with my physical body had been completely cut off. I tried to astrally teleport on some other place for more than ten times but that did not work either.

I started emitting telepathic messages to my astral guide; still that did not improve the situation at all. I tried to reach my friend Velibor on the astral plane, but that also ended up a failure. I even tried to communicate with the light, hoping it would explain to me where I was or why was this happening to me? I felt the light could sense my thoughts, but there was no response from it. It seemed it did not want to communicate with me.

The time was passing by, and I had shot all the solutions I could think of, except for one. The only solution left was to reach the light and see what would happen. I decided to push my speed to the limits and let something happen. Anyway, I did not have anything to lose, so I accelerated. I felt something similar to turbo bust, strong increasing of the speed in a few jumps. I had passed the long turns in only a split of the second and I felt my whole astral body driven by its own force that was out of my conscious control.

I felt a new jump that greatly increased the speed of my flight and another one in a short while. The distance between the light and me started to shorten. I lost completely the control of the speed and let myself to the "light speed" that seemed to have had its own bust. The last thing I saw was the light about two meters away. Then I found myself in pure light and had the same experience of everything frozen and the time stopped. The next moment I felt a strong and painful dive into my physical body.

You cannot possibly imagine the relief I felt when I opened my eyes and slowly moved my physical body. Joyous and happy for I had come back alive, I wiped the sweat on my forehead and said to myself: "Good Lord, this was close".

Comment: This type of tunnel can be found on many locations on the astral plane. My best advice to every astral traveler, especially to those who are not so advanced is to avoid it or be very careful when they encounter any strange lights, space distortions, whirlpools, black or red holes, geometric shapes that levitate in thin air and similar on the astral plane.

To enter such a phenomenon is often an easy case, but to exit it is a completely different story. Despite the fact that they are usually located in space, such phenomena can also be seen here, on Earth although occasionally. Some of them are gates that will transport your astral form to distant places or take you into different time, and sometimes both. Some of them will give you the entrance to the Acasha – a hidden dimension, which is a part of the astral plane but has a completely different frequency from its seven basic levels.

However, I have to repeat that for the beginners or for the practitioners who do not have at least five hundred successfully pulled astral trips, a strong advice would be to avoid this kind of astral adventurism. In addition, I must say that when I had encountered the above-mentioned phenomenon, I did not have that much of experience. I think I had been very reckless and it is a miracle I had stayed physically alive and able to retell it. If I knew then what I know now, I would never enter such a thing with the astral skills I possessed at the time. The light that I had encountered on this astral trip is a natural astral elemental that can often be found in tunnels similar to the one I had mentioned. Usually it has a role of a gatekeeper for the dimensions that are not touchable for the human kind but also, they can be a part of a very perfidious trap set up by not so positive entities.

A similar tunnel to the one I had entered in the above-mentioned experience can be found at the distance of eighteen light years from Earth. It has a phosphorus illumination, too and it is visible only from the astral plane. It is long about a light year and has strong magnetic forces around it. It can be entered only from the endpoints and if you find it and try to enter through its walls, you will find that there is a strong energy field all around it. My advice to every advanced astral traveler who is capable of making this far is not to enter it. There is no way out from that tunnel and that is all I can tell you about it.

Nevertheless, there are many tunnels that can be found on the astral plane but the most popular and known to people is the one that one usually experiences throughout the short time of clinical death. It is a black tunnel with bright light at the end, which in fact is a passage through this world to the next one. This tunnel leads to the highest levels of the astral plane and only those who have been honest and have not done anything seriously wrong during their physical existence will pass through it. It is popularly known as *the land of the eternal summer*.

In contrast to the honest people, those who have spread only pain, sorrow and negativity all around them during their physical existence here on Earth, take a different tunnel and go to places where there is no color but black and white, no love, compassion, peace and joy. That place is divided into a few sublevels that can be classified as the most materialistic and the most brutal, sublevels not so materialistic and not so brutal and sublevels with a chance for repaying the Karmic debts. The legend, which is spread in many cultures and traditions for judging our deeds in our afterlife, is not a pure fiction.

Reality there is just as real as you are reading this book, even more real. So, always keep your heart pure, give your best to always do good things for others and avoid doing things that you would not like done to you.

The third kind of people that are the most rare ones, belong to the spiritual group of people and through a certain light they will gain the chance to go much higher than the astral plane with no need to incarnate again. Usually, when this kind of noble spirit is leaving his/her physical body for the last time, many light beams are present above him or her. Those lights are only the portals that will lead the individual to other realms of existence. The best representation of this process is put in the "Tibetan book of death". Special gifted and trained lamas who managed to map the whole Universe from the levels with the most density to the subtlest ones using their more subtle bodies wrote this very old Tibetan book, translated from Sanskrit. From my point of view, that book is the best manual for life after life guidance with all the manifestations that human soul depending on its purity, will have to go through after its final separation from the physical body. Generally speaking, there are many tunnels on the astral plane that carry potential danger.

Advanced astral travelers should also be aware of the strange phenomenon that exists in the empty space fifteen light years distant from Earth, in the direction of the Orion constellation. It is a very dangerous trap and I do not advise anyone capable of making that kind of long distance astral trip with his/her astral body to enter it; on the contrary do not enter it at any cost.

The tunnel itself is not visible, except for the entrance and only from one side. Hopefully, you can get in the tunnel from nowhere else but from the entrance. From its visible side, the astral sight captures it as a green square. The left upper corner is a starting point for a double line that connects it to the right lower corner like a diagonal. There are three symmetrical black circles on the lines. From the other side, the entrance is completely invisible to the astral eye. If some astral traveler exploring the Cosmos and seeing only empty space full of stars ahead hits the exact point of the entrance (which is ten meters large in diameter), he will enter the tunnel he will never be able to come out from.

Concluding from all the data I possess, the tunnel has been designed by a very old and advanced civilization. Not a single case of anybody that has entered it and returned to tell about it exists as evidence. Once you enter it, no one knows how long you will travel to an exit. In my opinion, it leads to the parallel Universe from which there is no return because the entrance functions like the diode does in the electronics - it allows the life form to pass only in one direction.

Subchapter 4.8
ACASHA HOLOGRAMS

During the last few months of 1992, I encountered many astral phenomena, which were unknown to me and the one that will follow is one of them. This fascinating astral trip happened on December 11, 1992. I used the method of "Dream control", and I woke up in my astral body levitating twenty meters above some sea surface. After I got fully conscious I was out of my physical body, I felt joy because I was above some sea, and I loved seas and oceans.

Judging by the light on the sky, I realized it was an early morning; the sun had not risen yet. I dropped to the altitude of five meters above the sea from where I was in a position to easily see the fish swimming. When I looked around me, I concluded I was deeply off shore. I could not see any land anywhere around. That did not bother me a bit, so I decided it would not be so bad if I took the chance of high speed flying above the surface of the sea. The next moment, I was already flying above the surface without touching the water and soon I reached the speed of about two hundred kilometers per hour. I did not know which sea I was flying over, but it did not make any difference to me. I knew I could easily check it out if it did by increasing my altitude to the point from where I could view the whole region or even the whole continent if I needed to. What was really important to me was to fly at high speed close to the surface of the water. I enjoyed it so many times before and I had never got over it.

The feeling of flying free as a bird was wonderful. I made some efforts to increase the speed in my consciousness. The speed started to increase rapidly and in a few seconds, I reached the speed of about 700km/hour. At that speed and so close to the water you could hardly notice many things that were going below you, so I reached higher altitude for about 100 meters.

I reached the land, flew over for a couple of seconds and then I reached high sea again. During the flight, I made a turn and started to follow the line that separated the land from the sea as best as I could. Everything was moving so fast that I could not see what was going on below, but the feeling of great power dominated over slowing the speed.

Then I continued straight ahead, and the ambient was changing so fast. For a second I was flying only above the sea, then above the shore, then above the land and then again above the shore, then above the sea and so on and on. My consciousness wanted more and I increased the speed of my flying. The speed was fantastic and no words can describe the feeling of power I felt while flying that fast. If some of you had experienced the speed of 300Km/h driving the Kawasaki or Honda bikes – imagine speed three times faster than that. Still, it was not enough because I felt that I could go even faster. In that moment, I felt as if something exploded deep inside me, as if something did let go in my astral body that caused the unbelievable increasing of the speed. I also had a strange feeling like some liquid flowing in all directions on the surface of my transparent astral body. Soon, I had no knowledge of the speed. It lasted for about half a minute and somewhere in the distance, I noticed blackness. As I was moving towards the blackness, it grew larger. A few moments after I entered the blackness, I spotted some horizontal straight blue line, which separated the blackness into two equal parts. When I got closer, I noticed that the blue line was in fact the passage and I flew right through it. The moment I passed through the passage, I entered the space of complete whiteness.

I did not know if I was flying or falling through the space, because I could not orient myself and I was not able to see anything but whiteness. Then the situation suddenly changed. Some strange phenomena started to appear. At first, I started to see some strange

150

transparent geometrical shapes and forms, which were shining with all sorts of colored auras around them.

Those geometrical shapes were in many sizes and some of them were much bigger than I was. They moved in all directions and after a while, they started to take different colors and their shinning glow changed into even more intensive.

"Impressive" – I thought to myself. I remember my consciousness was strongly focused to find out the meanings of the hologram projections that were flying all around me in complete whiteness. After a while, the whiteness changed and the ambient became black and blue. Some strange lights started to appear and the moment I saw them I felt some strong pain, which made me think that I was going to lose my consciousness.

The sudden instability of my consciousness caused my expelling from that strange astral place. I found myself in a different geographic location from where I was before I entered the blackness. Because of the fact that it was morning before I went into the blackness and now it was a starry night, I determined I was on a completely different side of the planet.

However, at that point I was flying with the speed of about 200Km/hour and I was not above the sea anymore but close to some big city. Again, I increased the speed and flew towards the big city. After a while, I reached the city and started to fly above the buildings.

The city was very nicely illuminated. I got closer to the buildings and started to fly between them. Down, below me, I could hear loud noise and when I looked down I saw the streets were suffering a heavy traffic-jam. At one point, when I was flying between the buildings and my attention was diverted down, below me, a high building got in my way.

There was still time to go around, but I went right into the building. I managed to pull some interesting maneuvers while I was inside. Still not slowing down, I went through the glass, which was on the front side of the building, and encountered one wall in front of me but in a split of a second I made a strong maneuver to the right and found myself in a floor passage. The passage had many doors and one of them was open. The moment I passed through the door, I saw a man cleaning the carpet. Again, I made a strong maneuver and before I went through the cleaner I turned left and went outside through the windows. I pulled all that in less than a second as if I had already known each corner of the building.

Note: *It was interesting because in the beginning of my astral excursions I did not possess this ability, but in time it developed to a superb level. As far as I could learn from my experiences, I would say that this ability was all about the constant connection of one's consciousness with the environment. Imagine that you are flying in your astral body at great speed through a deep forest which you have never visited before. Despite the fact that you are there for the first time, you feel as if you have known every tree, brook, the plants, even every stone for many decades.*

Basically, this quality of the astral body varies from the level of the awareness of the astral consciousness, as there are different levels of symbiosis starting with the weak symbiosis with the environment to a perfect symbiosis. The secret is in the sharing of the astral substance. The astral substance exists in every living or non- living form connecting all things in a special way. Everything that should be done while we are out of our physical bodies is to become aware of its presence. I see this ability as a very important one in the process of astral development.

However, people usually think that as soon as they separate from their physical body, all of the capabilities of the astral body will be under their control and ready for use. Unfortunately, that is not how things work here. Usually, it takes some time before basic things are learned, but for those more advanced abilities of the astral body certainly years have to pass by. So everything depends on our natural gift for accommodation of our consciousness to function out of the physical body.

After I left the building, I carried on flying over the city. When I was above some huge football stadium, I felt sudden weakness. I sensed that my time in the astral plane is up and that I would join with my physical body in a few seconds. I was correct and it happened almost instantly. I felt the reunion with my physical body and as soon as I regained the physical control, I opened my eyes and noticed that it was late morning in Skopje.

I thought: "What a great ride!" I went to the bathroom and after a while, my mother made me a cup of coffee. I took the coffee and while I was drinking it, I wrote down my astral trip.

Comment: I had encountered the phenomenon from this astral experience many times during the years that followed. In time, I learned that the place that contained those hologram projections was in fact a part of the astral plane where Acasha records were kept.

To the best of my knowledge, these Acasha records contain the whole history, present and the future of all life forms that were, are or will be present in this galaxy and further. In fact, The Acasha is a library and although it can be accessed from the astral plane, it can be visited from a special place in the physical plane as well. That special place is the city of Shambala, which in fact is the capital of the underground kingdom known as Agharta. In Shambala, there is an entrance to the Acasha library and the citizens of Shambala can enter through it and acquire the true knowledge, no matter the subject.

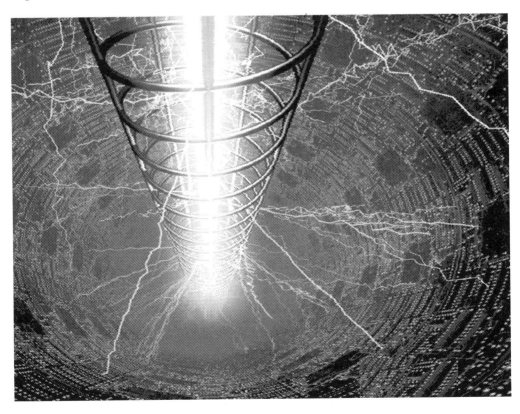

Just for the record, the city of Shambala is situated deep in the center of Earth, and technologically and spiritually, it is far more advanced from the human civilization that lives on the surface of the Earth. Before I go further about Agharta, I will distant myself from the subject for short. According to the scientists, Earth is divided into four main layers: the crust, mantle, outer core and inner core.

The crust is much thinner (0-30Km) than any of the other layers, and is composed of the least dense calcium (Ca) and sodium (Na) aluminum-silicate minerals. Most of the Earth's mass is in the mantle (30-2900Km), which is composed of iron (Fe), magnesium (Mg), aluminum (Al), silicon (Si), and oxygen (O) silicate compounds. In basic, the mantle is solid at over 1000 degrees C but can deform slowly in a plastic manner. The outer core (2900-5200Km) is composed mostly of iron (Fe) and about 10% of sulfur (S) and again, according to the scientists, it is so hot there that this layer is molten. The inner core (5200-6350Km) is under such extreme pressure that it remains solid (Fe).

Nevertheless, most of the scientists agree with this simple fact: "We know more about the surface of the Sun than the depth of the Earth!"

To the best of my knowledge, the Earth's outer and the inner core do not exist at all because our planet is hollow. The space that belongs to the interior of the Earth and corresponds to the outer and inner core of our planet is not what scientists make us believe. The truth is that one of the most advanced civilizations ever present on this planet lies there. If you do not believe me, go research the subject and you will find out that there are many anomalies, which concern scientific facts about the Earth's core. I know this from my own experience, because I have been there astrally many times and I have communicated with many of those who belong to their civilization.

Generally speaking, the civilization of Agharta is so far more advanced than ours seen from all directions of evolution. I had a chance to admire the wonders of this underground civilization many times through my astral trips.

Still, the library that contains Acasha records has been constructed on the foundations of a much older civilization than Agharta once present in our solar system. That happened millions of years ago and they recorded the Acasha records in the form of holograms. One can find recorded data about the long forgotten history of Earth in this library, and among them data about the rising and fall of the Lemuria, Atlantis and Mu are just a tiny part of the whole. The most fascinating thing of all is that there is a record of the whole history of this part of the Cosmos, with rising and falls of many civilizations that once existed. There are also many records about all life forms that existed, their present incarnation and their future incarnation if there is any.

I had never seen anything similar to that and to me it looked like a pulsating knowledge that was so alive and vital because it contained more data than any physical computer could ever handle. It might sound contradictory, there are more data about civilizations that have once existed on Mars, Venus and the only planet between Mars and Jupiter that has been destroyed while orbiting the Sun, than about all other civilizations that have risen and fallen here on Earth.

Unfortunately, not everybody can reach the library with the Acashic records from the astral plane. In contrast to the people that live on the surface of Earth, the citizens of Agharta have constant access to the library. Many times during my astral excursions into the library, I had had a chance to encounter many astral beings that belonged to Agharta but they had always been busy watching the holograms and in the beginning, they did not pay any attention to my presence there.

Anyway, despite the fact that scientists represent their standpoint that our planet's interior is full of lava, from my point of view, that is true only to a certain point. In fact, the origin of the lava flows is so much closer to the surface of the planet than to the center of our planet. A very advanced civilization, which is the  keeper of the true knowledge existed and still exists in the center of our planet. From all the data I brought from the Acasha records I learned that in ancient times there had been a massive destructive war between the alliance of Atlantis and the negative alien civilizations that had come from deep space on one side, and the alliance of Lemuria, Mu and the other positive alien civilizations on the other.

After the war that caused a great mass destruction to our planet and a global flood, the survivors of the Lemurian race retreated safely, deep underground and built an electromagnetic shield for protection. Today that protective electromagnetic shield is on the border of the outer and the inner core and it is the main reason for those readings to the scientists' equipment.

Anyway, apart from the seismologic science, my point is this: Despite the fact that many thousands of years have passed since then, the electromagnetic shields around Agharta still stand because the negative alien forces (among which the Reptoids and the Grays are majority), had never left our solar system truly. They still present danger for people who live on the surface of the Earth unaware of their presence and for the underground people of Agharta as well.

If you read in some report that some witnesses had seen the battle between two or more UFOs, be sure that at least one of the UFOs belongs to Agharta. When a human attends the astral plane regularly, he/she gets a picture that many things are not as they seem, or at least not the way they are presented to him or her scientifically. In time, a human capable of astral excursions understands that somewhere in his/her past incarnations he/she possessed much greater psychic powers and knowledge about the forces of the nature and starts to work hard to regain what naturally belongs to him or her.

Unfortunately, alien influence on people reduces the chances of changing things for the better. The Grays have the technology to easily trace and control most of the human population. The worst part is that they possess the knowledge to do that on the astral plane, too.

To achieve fulfilling of their purposes, the Grays abduct humans and implant the micro devices into our physical bodies with their advanced technology. With those implants, which are usually put through the nose into the head, the Grays can easily trace the humans any time, change their actions or abduct them for conducting genetic researches, which are part of their global genetic program. Well, almost the same we do with animals, but the Grays do it in a more sophisticated way. I know it sounds like science fiction, but believe me it is happening all the time. Moreover, the worst part is that government divisions throughout the whole world have been more or less aware of the fact for more than fifty years and with terms similar to "Top Secret" have been hiding the truth from the public.

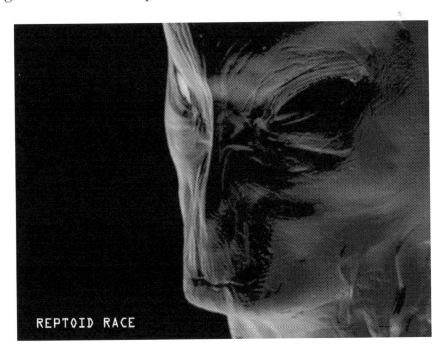

REPTOID RACE

157

Subchapter 4.9
SECOND CONTACT

My second contact with a creature that belongs to the alien race known as Grays, happened to me on January 24, 1993. It was early in the morning when I managed to project my astral body and after I left my apartment, I went flying in the direction of the natural border of Skopje - the Vodno Mountain.

The Vodno Mountain (with its highest peak Krstovar 1,066m) is one of the mountains that surround the Skopje valley. It was sunrise and very beautiful. I felt great sensation because more than two weeks had passed from my previous astral excursion. I was flying at solid speed already, and a few moments later I left the Vodno Mountain far behind me.

I was flying at the altitude of about 800 meters and passing over a huge field area. I saw rare village houses here and there. Although it was winter, there was not any snow there, but the area was wonderful anyway. I flew on the left side of my astral body with my hands clenched into fists. I was not moving fast enough in my opinion, so I rapidly increased and reached the speed I estimate was about 600Km/hour.

I fully enjoyed the huge panoramas I was passing over and felt as if I possessed a rocket engine. At that speed, it was difficult for me to follow all the activity below, and the ambient was changing rapidly because Macedonia is so rich with mountains and valleys. I flew over the mountains, rivers, and valleys, on and on. During the flight, I pulled some acrobatic maneuvers, which pushed me up all the more. From a physical perspective of speaking – my adrenaline went up.

After a while, I lowered my altitude to about 100 meters above the ground. I was above some rocky area when I noticed some hills straight ahead covered with snow. The next second, I flew over them and encountered a wonderful huge valley. It was covered with snow and I remember it as one of the most beautiful valleys I had seen on my astral trips. Ten seconds later I flew over it and again encountered a new area of snowy mountains.

I continued flying not knowing anymore if I had been over Macedonia, Bulgaria or Turkey. I also did not know what distance I had traveled because I had changed the direction of my flight many times, but judging from the Islamic structures below, I assumed I was somewhere above the Turkish territory. After I spotted the Islamic structures on the ground, I wished to return to Skopje. I made a semicircle maneuver to the left and I flew to the direction I had arrived from. I felt very strong and I increased my speed to the point where you get the impression that everything around you is moving in indescribable speed beside you and you are the one that stands still. The truth is, I did not really know the exact path back home, but I relied on my inner compass to guide me.

However, after five seconds or less, moving with that speed I felt I was nearing Skopje. I decreased my speed instantly, and the moment I did that I flew over the Skopska Crna Gora Mountain. I arrived from the north side and at the speed of 200Km/hour; I entered the air space of Skopje. In my consciousness, I started to analyze:

"When I left Skopje, I did that from south, and now I came from the north side, which means that my flight was in semicircle way. Anyway, that is not so important to me compared to the fact that I arrived from Turkish territory in just a few seconds, which is solid time for that distance. However, I still have not tested the real limits of my astral body."

As I flew over the Vardar River, I intentionally started to decrease the altitude and soon I landed in "Karposh 4" (one of Skopje's settlements), close to the primary school. I used to study in this school. The name of the school was "Ivan Goran Kovachich", and I knew each corner of it by heart. I came closer to one of the walls, which was on the front side of the school and slowly passed through it. I elevated again and slowly started to fly through the halls and classrooms. The school was empty because it was still early for classes.

After two minutes of flying in and out of the classrooms, I went to the gym where I remember playing basketball with my classmates. Then I lifted my astral body to the ceiling and went outside. From that altitude (which was about 30 meters from the ground), I saw the sun rising from the East and when I turned my look to see what was going on around the school, I saw some people probably hurrying to work. Everything seemed perfectly normal to me, so I chose to make a somersault and softly landed in the schoolyard. The schoolyard was large and nicely arranged and decorated for a change in contrast to the days I was a student there.

Then all of a sudden, I noticed something that did not fit into the ambient. Some creature was standing at about 15 meters from me, with its back towards me. It was almost totally transparent. It looked as exactly the same alien creature I had encountered on my astral excursion on May 7, 1992.

Although I recalled all the things that happened on our last meeting, I did not fear the creature. I started to walk in its direction slowly, intending to come closer to it and start a possible communication with it. I succeeded to near it and it was obvious that it happened to be the same creature I had met the first time or at least it belonged to the same species. Despite the fact that it was humanoid, it did not look human at all. The head of the alien was very big compared to the proportions of its body, and its eyes (although focused on something else on the other side) were completely dark and gave bad impression. I found it so strange that the whole astral body of the alien was transparent except for its eyes, so I wondered how that could be possible. Anyway, when I reached the distance of about one-meter from the Gray, I stretched my transparent arm with the intention to touch it on its shoulder.

It turned out to be a bad mistake. Its astral body felt as cold, almost as touching ice. The Gray turned around and looked at me with its big eyes. Instantly, I felt something was not right. The black eyes of the Gray started to flash with white light and I felt as if hurricane was striking me when I sensed its extraordinary mental power coming from its eyes. The last thing that I recall in my memory was sharp and strong pain and I woke up in my physical body in an instant.

Comment: From one point of view I felt great joy because of the success of the fast flight I had pulled off, but from another I felt embittered in my soul because of the second contact with the alien. It became clear to me that despite all the extraordinary abilities I possessed, I was no match for that creature. It expelled me from the astral plane so easily, just like the first time, if I assumed the fact that it was the same alien. Compared to the first time, I found out that at least I managed to see it from a very close range. The thought that it was not going to end like this annoyed me a lot. If it was the same creature, it was certainly following me for some reason. Usually, when I was present on the astral plane, my telepathy scanning was so well developed, or at least I thought that it was, but this time I did not even manage to touch the consciousness of the alien as if it simply had not been there. I remember I felt somebody watching me during the first contact, so I felt something, but this time I felt absolutely nothing. In addition, the "Haragei" – the feeling of potential danger in my environment, was alarming me in many situations when I encountered all kinds of astral entities, but not this time.

Note: *"Haragei"* is a term that has its root in ancient Japan, and it denotes a special ability, which once fully developed, starts appearing in the mind of the samurai or ninja, like a strong alarming sensation when potential danger is somewhere very close to him.

However, the conclusions came to me by themselves. It was as if the alien did not possess any emotions at all. If he had bad or good intentions, I believe I would have felt something, but I sensed nothing and that upset me a lot. Obviously something was going on and I felt like a part of an experiment I did not want to participate in at all. Anyway, one thing was certain. If the alien wanted to hurt me, it probably would have. Yet, he just expelled me from the astral plane. In my mind, all kinds of questions started to appear. What was really going on there? The astral plane started to look to me more vital and alive than ever. It was obvious that I was on the beginning of my astral science studies and I had so much more to learn.

Subchapter 4.10
THE MYSTERY GOES ON

This was a sensational astral trip. For the first time, a higher rank Gray communicated with me almost as with an equal. Until this astral trip, I was always under the impression that the Grays were considering me a lower creature with no potential to harm them. But, I was wrong. This time I discovered that they were considering me potential danger for them, and they revealed to me much more than they wanted to. It happened on February 8, 1993, and here is what the whole astral experience was like:

That afternoon I decided to make the astral trip to one small city in Croatia known as Lepoglava. The city of Lepoglava is about 700Km away from Skopje, and it belongs to the region of Croatia called Zagorje. The area is one of the most beautiful places in Croatia. My mother was born there and I had many relatives that I had not seen for a very long time. That is why I wanted to make the short astral excursion and visit them.

I went to sleep somewhere around 00:05 AM. I finished the whole technique and entered the well-known Trance from which I was able to easily achieve astral projection. After I successfully projected my consciousness into my astral body, I left my apartment. I passed through the windows and after I jumped over the balcony and took off, I decided to go straight up. As soon as I thought about that, I found myself about hundred meters above my building. I took a short look to my neighborhood and thought to myself: "Novo Lisiche is always beautiful at night". From the still position, I greatly accelerated my speed and flew northwest. In my consciousness, I knew where I was going because I had only one destination – Lepoglava.

I was moving so fast that in about five minutes I reached Zagreb, keeping the same altitude as before. I did not decrease my speed a bit and flew over Zagreb joyously, watching the city from the superman's perspective. After I left the capital of Croatia, I increased the speed even more and soon I encountered a deep forest region. It was very dark. The only light was the moonlight, so I would say I was blind flying. Still, I did not pay any attention to the direction I was flying, because I relied on my inner compass completely and just followed its guiding impulses. I simply knew that I was going to arrive where I wanted to.

Soon, I arrived above the area that was recognizable to me. I slowed a lot because I felt I was close to my final destination. I arrived above Lepoglava from southeast and immediately dropped altitude to about ten meters above the ground. Although it was February and this area is usually covered with deep snow at this time of the year, there was not any. The night sky was very beautiful and crystal clear.

I spotted the highway passing through Lepoglava and flew parallel to and above it. I followed the road until I reached the point where I should turn, so I turned and continued further. The road leading to the house of my relatives was not asphalted; it was a kind of macadam road but with miniature rocks and in very good shape. There was a high hill on the right with vineyard and a small brook on the left. I flew two meters above the brook because I knew that it led to the house of my relatives. The excitement for visiting my relatives was surprisingly big. Straight ahead, I recognized the house I was searching for and a smile lit my astral face.

The house was very big and had a huge cellar, ground floor and two other floors. My relatives had a big courtyard on the front side of the house with a beautiful flower garden and a large vineyard in the back, which extended to the top of the hill. I was devoted to that place. As a little boy, my Mom used to bring me here in summer time to play with my female cousins, and the memories flooded me and gave me a warm feeling.

After I flew above the large iron fence, I noticed that the garage was not finished yet. It was just the same as it was when I last saw it during my last visit to the place physically. I had not visited my relatives for more than 10 years, and many things (except for the garage) had changed. The house was finished, and the court was even more beautiful.

I approached the balconies of the house and went straight up to the second floor. I entered the living room through the wall. The room was in semidarkness, but I clearly recognized the counters of the commode, the sofa, the luster, etc. Many years after, they were still in the same place. The moment I entered the living room I noticed somebody was sleeping on the sofa. The man was covered with a blanket and his head was turned towards the wall, so I could not recognize who it was. The next moment I slowly walked closer to the sofa and bent to see who it was. It was Pero, the husband of my once removed cousin Seka. I went through the wall into the passage between the rooms. The door of the room on my left was half-opened and I noticed a pleasant smothered green light of a table lamp coming from there.

I thought: "Fascinating! While everybody else is asleep, I am wandering around in my astral body and paying visit to my distant relatives."

Very excited, I elevated myself 20 centimeters above the passage carpet and moved closer to the half-opened door. I encountered an interesting site.

The physical bodies of my twice-removed cousins Sanja and Sneshka were in their beds, sleeping. I felt warm at heart because they were the daughters of Pero and Seka, and they were the ones I had played with as a little boy. The air coming from their exhaling proved it was very cold in the room. It did not surprise me, because as far as I could remember they always liked to sleep in a cold room.

It was an extraordinary thing to see their astral bodies three meters from their beds, sitting on the carpet preoccupied in funny conversation. Both of them were very exited but unaware that they were out of their physical bodies and shared the same dream.

Simplifying:

I will have to simplify this as possible as I can. Every one while dreaming leaves his/her physical body, usually unaware of the astral plane. Because of one's unawareness, his or her astral body can often be streamed by all kinds of natural astral currents. In this case, the astral body floats around swept away by these astral currents, constantly changing the level of the awareness from totally unaware to partly aware and rarely one is completely aware of the presence on the astral plane. However, his/her astral body mostly stays more or less close to the physical body but sometimes it can float away very far. During this process, the astral body is fully capable of receiving all kinds of expressions from a positive or a negative character, who in fact are the basic creators of the phenomenon that we call dream.

165

The situation changes when under certain circumstances, one becomes aware that he/she is dreaming. If the consciousness is even half-calmed and not caught by panic, one has a good chance to remain in the astral body during the process of awakening. If we assume that one has succeeded to pull that off and become aware of the astral plane, the clearness of his or her astral vision will vary from totally foggy to total clear which will be determined by his/her mental strength.

The duration will be determined by one's wish to stay active in the event and by the stability of one's thoughts. However, the memory of all the things one has managed to hear and see there, will vary from the level of total and clear recall to the level of total amnesia of his/her out of the body experience. So, it is not a miracle when some astral traveler encounters a transparent astral body close to his/her physical one, floating totally unaware or doing some half-aware activity thinking that he or she is still in the physical dimension. Even if some advanced astral traveler comes up with the idea to try to awake a different astral body unaware of the astral plane during the dreaming process, he/she will rarely achieve his/her goal. Even if the advanced astral person manages to awake the sleeping astral body, the chances for remembering the event after returning to the physical body are usually very small, because of the low level of psychic development.

Since my astral body vibrated with much higher astral vibrations than the two unaware astral bodies of my cousins, I was invisible to their dream appearance. More levitating than flying, I came closer to their transparent bodies. I landed on the carpet and I thought: "I am standing in front of them, yet still they can not see me."

Their astral bodies were identical to mine but the aura around them was smaller. I turned around and walked to the window to see what was going on outside. The moment I approached the window, I bent and the higher part of my astral body went through the glass of the window while my lower part remained in the room. It was an amazing experience. I was partly in the room and partly outside enjoying the view of the vineyard and the blue velvet sky. On the right, I saw the forest that is near Lepoglava and on my left there were other houses situated at the top of the hill. Words cannot describe the amazing feeling of experiencing such a thing.

In slow motion, I returned into the room. I turned toward my cousins again because I wanted to gently touch them instead of saying goodbye before I left. I stretched my arm and touched Sneshka tenderly on her shoulder. When my hand touched her astral body I felt very cold and the very same moment Sneshka astrally awoke. She looked at me, and the expression on her transparent face gave me the impression she was very confused. Two seconds later she disappeared and a moment later, she woke up physically. Sanja was still in her dream sitting on the carpet, obviously seeing something in her consciousness. Sneshka got up from her bed and when she saw that everything was OK in the room and that she was dreaming, she went back to sleep. I did not want to cause any more trouble and decided to leave their room. As soon as I passed through the wall, I found myself in the kitchen. The moonlight coming from the window helped me notice the kitchen

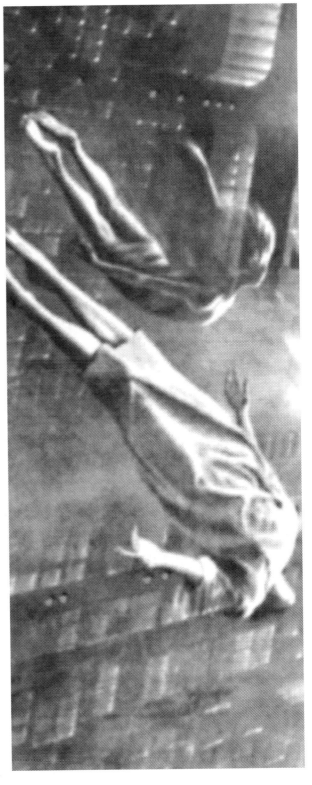

was so nicely fixed and everything was in perfect order. I saw a newspaper and a pair of glasses (probably belonging to Pero) on the table. I walked towards the wall that separated the kitchen from the hallway and went through it.

Then, something strange happened. With absolutely no idea that it would happen to me here, in my relatives' house, I saw a little Gray standing in the hallway. I saw his black eyes focusing directly on me. That lasted for about three seconds. Then, its whole appearance changed. It took undetermined form that grew, and in a second it took the form of my good friend Dejan.

Many thoughts crossed my consciousness in an instant: "Calm down Pane! Do not panic and act wisely! How can this be possible? It must have used telepathy to read my thoughts and chosen to take the human form of Dejan. Why him? What is this Gray trying to pull of me? Is it going to expel me from the astral plane like before or what? I do not feel comfortable in this hallway, so I will go outside and then, depending on the situation, I will see what I will do next."

I felt something was cooking up against me, so I moved my astral body to leave the house immediately. I jumped from the hallway through the bathroom that was on the right to the floor entrance door and went outside. I did not intend to run away, so I stayed close to the roof of the house, hovering in thin air. I was curious to see what would happen next.

After a second or two, the alien that took human astral form of my friend appeared from the house. He flew around me, sat on the boundary of the roof and started to look at me again as if scanning me. I telepathically asked it: "Can you see me?"

First, it made an expression on its face as if I had asked a stupid question and then it replied that it was true and it could see me. Although it had that expression on its face, I knew well it was probably nothing more than good acting because the Grays either rarely had feelings or they did not possess any.

No matter how perfect the astral body of Dejan looked to me, I was always aware that an alien entity was in front of me, and obviously it wanted something from me or was just testing me, because if the Gray wanted a fight it would have started it already. At that point, I noticed a very strong bright light somewhere behind me. It was coming from above and it was so strong that even shadowed my astral body. I noticed that the light was moving by the moving shadow that was on the tiles of the roof and the two for me visible sides of the house. I wanted to find out what the source of the strange light was, but I did not dare turn my back on the alien that was still producing the hypnotic illusion of my friend Dejan. I thought to myself:

"It's probably an object that is moving up in the sky and judging by my inner sense it is at least 50 meters above us."

I knew my time was running out, so I focused on the alien and tried to find out something more. That turned out to be a failure. I could not touch its consciousness because the alien was blocking me all the time. I concluded that it used mental methods not familiar to humans because I noticed that its thoughts were streaming on a completely different frequency from ours.

However, it looked as if it had a very high opinion of itself and it was obvious to me that it was not just an ordinary Gray, it was one with a higher rank. Also, it did not show any interest in my scanning and without sensing it was coming, it asked me a question: "Where do you intend to go?"

I did not want to answer its question because I was aware the Gray already knew the answer. I was just levitating two meters away from it, watching it disdainfully. Still not answering its question, I transmitted a thought that I was perfectly aware that it was not who it appeared to be, so why the masquerade?

The seconds were passing by and the light was coming closer. Now, the whole court and the house were illuminated. I was on stand by to move out of there as fast as I could, when I sensed a telepathic communication between the alien and the object in the sky. Suddenly, as if the show was over, the alien gave a sign with its head and in an instant a light turned off and then on again. In my consciousness, a voice was screaming: "Get the hell out of here, you stupid fool!"

Still, I was not ready to leave the place yet, risking the possibility of my astral abduction. There were many questions about hidden activities on our planet, so I promised myself to find out as much as I could. The next moment I sensed that approval for ending of my astral duration had been given. Then, for the first time I felt that the physical body of the alien was on that flying object. The next moment the Gray took its original form back. The look of its big black eyes gave me an inexplicable creepy feeling. The last thing I saw on its face before it disappeared from the roof was something close to despair and that gave me a feeling that things did not work out the way the alien wanted.

A second after its disappearance, I felt that my consciousness had been cut off by some strong force and I started to sink into total blackness. For a few long moments I did not know whether I was falling, flying or teleporting. I felt that they were doing something to me, but the next moment I was relieved to see my physical body in my bed. The next moment I returned to my physical body and that felt so good. I remained motionless, because I was repeating the whole astral event in my mind. That used to be the standard procedure I had gone through each time when I had experienced something very important on the astral plane. When I became sure that nothing had been deleted from my memory during the connecting process with my physical body, I opened my eyes.

I got up from the bed and noticed that the light in the kitchen was still on. When I opened the door I saw my Mom still reading a book. I looked on the display of the stereo to see what time was it. It was 1:07 AM. She asked me why I woke up, but I just waved an empty gesture with my hand and thought to myself: "You would not understand even if I told you." I returned to my room and closed the door. What was I supposed to say to her? "Mom, I had just returned from Lepoglava, I saw our relatives, encountered an alien in their house and I was so close to a shining UFO that was above me while I was levitating over the roof!" – She would think I was nuts.

The next day, while I was out of home, Sneshka called and talked to my mother. She told her that last night she had seen me in her dream and that she wanted to know if we were fine. Sneshka also told my Mom that last night everybody in the house had been forced to wake up by some strange light, which had illuminated the whole area around the house like daylight.

She revealed that everybody was so scared because the electrical equipment in the house stopped and the moment her father encouraged himself to go out on the balcony to see what was going on, the bright light was suddenly gone. Luckily, as soon as the strange light disappeared, the electricity was back to normal. At first, my mother thought she was just joking, but when she realized that Sneshka was dead serious, she began wondering what that light could be. In the end, Sneshka concluded that her father believed a UFO passed over their house the previous night.

Comment: The question that the Gray asked -"*Where do you intend to go?*" had connected many segments into one big picture. Perhaps the aliens discovered to me more than they had planned to, or they considered my intelligence low. I was not sure, if that was their mistake or just an extraordinary deception created with the purpose to deceive me.

Five days before this astral trip happened, another out of the body experience happened to me that had changed my plans for the future. Astral entities from Shambala came to visit me while I was out of my physical body. They explained to me what should I do and where to go if I wanted to fulfill the purpose of my physical incarnation.

I felt honored because they actually invited me to come to Shambala from the secret entrance that still exists in the region of Gobi Desert in Mongolia. They told me there were other gates leading to their territory but the one in the Gobi Desert was the safest one and closest to Shambala. When I asked how I would know where the entrance to their kingdom was, they answered that as soon as I reached my destination in the north region of Gobi it would be visible to me and to nobody else. They also promised they would protect me on my way there because the Grays would surely try to stop me.

I told them that I was curious to find out why the Grays were so interested in me and they replied that it would be something that was in my DNA, which was connected to the rare ability to change the reality of dimensions. When I asked what that exactly meant, they said that once I had reached Shambala it would be explained to me. Normally, I did not miss the opportunity to ask what the Grays were doing here, to which they answered that their race was just an emissary of another race known as Reptoids. They said that the race of Reptoids was what the surface people would call "the incarnation of Evil".

171

So, the Grays were aware of my contact with Shambala, my potential physical trip there and they wanted to prevent it. Still, my spirit was determined to complete the training and change so many things that were happening on the surface of the Earth. Nevertheless, I was perfectly aware that the only way I could make a difference was by using an extraordinary force that I would have to develop over there, on Shambala. This astral experience helped me understand many things that were not clear to me. However, the mystery ball was rolling on and all I had to do was to wait and see what future events would bring.

Subchapter 4.11
ELECTRONIC PERCEPTION

After having consulted some astral travelers throughout the world (whom I respect as experts in the astral projection field), I have concluded that the astral ability I am about to mention next is so rare that even some of them have never heard of. Thus, this out of the body experience has been put in this book primarily for understanding the rare ability of the astral body to scan an electric circuit to the level of observing the stream of electrons in it.

It happened on February 23, 1993. After leaving my physical body, I moved myself about hundred meters away from my building in thin air for about 15 meters above the ground and watched my neighborhood. From the levitating position, I was clearly able to see the small power plant straight ahead, the buildings of Novo Lisiche on my left and the Skopska Crna Gora Mountain on my right.

While enjoying the view, I remained completely still for about one minute with a purpose to collect as much inner astral force as I could – something like a battery charge. When I sensed that I had enough amount of the astral force in me, I strongly addressed myself with a strong mental command - Now!

I had not even finished my thought yet, when I found myself flying with the speed of more than 700 Km/h. The feeling was similar to a suddenly turned on rocket drive in my astral body. In less than three seconds, I passed above the region of Skopje known as Petrovec and started to increase altitude. The next second I was around 200 meters above the ground and after I left the valley of Skopje I made one big semi-circled maneuver to the right and moved again towards the city. I prefer not to bother you with explaining the pleasure and excitement the movement at that speed gives, so I will only say that it is something you have to experience yourself. As soon as I arrived above the Vodno Mountain I made one big semi-somersault, gained a little on altitude and pushed my self in flying to southeast.

I wanted to have fun with high-speed maneuvers and I was doing just that. When I came above the area where the river Vardar leaves the city, I made a sharp turnover to northwest. Just for the record, the river

Vardar enters the Skopje region at the Derven canyon from northwest and leaves it at the Taor canyon southeast from the city.

Flying at that speed, in about 5 seconds I was very close to leaving the region of Skopje. I wanted to fly above the Treska Lake, an artificial lake used only as a bathing beach for citizens. For the record, the lake itself is about 9 km away from the city center and it is 700m long, 300m wide and 2,5m deep. Anyway, the next moment I greatly decreased my altitude and speed. Almost instantly I saw the lake in front of me and I nearly touched the surface of the water as I flew. Then, with the smile on my face, I returned to the same altitude but increasing my speed rapidly just in time to fly over the mountain that was on my way.

After about 30 seconds of non-stop flying, I reached the city Tetovo and continued to the West even faster. Soon, I left the air space of Macedonia and entered the Albanian air space. I rapidly decreased speed and in a while I was flying at the speed of about 200 Km/h., I saw some settlement in the distance. When I got closer to that inhabited place, the structure of some building still in its construction phase, grabbed my attention.

It was at the end of the settlement and to the left of the construction site there was a yellow crane. I arrived at the top of the building and sat there to take a view. There was a wonderful valley in the distance. I thought to myself: "Although it is February, the nature here is so beautiful".

There was a nice river in the middle of the valley, which made the valley even more beautiful. "Nice place" – a thought crossed my consciousness. I wanted to see the river from a close distance and as I was sitting on the top of the building, I suddenly jumped into free fall. About 5 meters before I touched the ground I gave myself a little boost and flew towards the river. It was very beautiful, so I landed by the river intending to enjoy the pretty site. After I sat on the bank, I looked at the sky, so clear and full of stars. The sounds coming from the water were so calming and gave a mystical note to the whole experience.

I thought: "The astral body offers me infinite chances to go and visit so many beautiful places that I have never dreamed about." Strangely, but I remained there for more than 15 minutes enjoying the peaceful nature and I rarely stayed long somewhere while on the astral trip. A thousand words would not be enough to describe the sensation I felt. I would just say I had not felt so fulfilled for a very long time. Before I left, I stood up and gave one last look to the river. The next moment I said to myself – "Up" and I felt some strong force lifting me up, almost like catapulting. When I reached the altitude of almost 300 meters above the valley, I changed the direction of my flight and flew parallel to the ground.

Soon, I increased the speed to about 600 or 700 Km/h and redirected myself south. Down, below me, sites were changing fast. To be more precise, they were changing every second because I pushed the speed of my astral body even harder. I had changed the directions of my course a few times, and I did not really know which territory I was above. However, the flight took me above some forest region when something bigger than me passed me by. It was some air force plane.

The visual contact with the plane was so short because it was flying to the west and in that particular moment I was flying to the southeast. Still, in that split of the second I noticed that the military plane was carrying big missiles under its wings. Almost instantly, an idea to turn around and chase the airplane seized my consciousness, but on the other hand, I realized there was not much sense in doing that. I decided not to chase it and remained the same course.

Twenty seconds later, the need of even higher speed took me over. I felt my consciousness so powerful and vital and knew it could take much higher speed. In fact, it wanted more. While thinking about that, I felt a strong boost and the speed rapidly increased. Then, a few other boosts came out of me and I clearly saw my astral body becoming different. It seemed as if some strange liquid was flowing on its surface. The ambient bellow me had disappeared from my sight and the constant changing of the ground appearance took place. I cannot explain clearly, but it felt so amazing since everything in front of me was now moving towards me.

The experience was so vivid that I thought to myself: "I'm moving too fast and I can not clearly see what I am flying above. Should I lower my speed or should I go up toward the stars?"

I was not in the mood for space exploring because I enjoyed the things I actually was experiencing, so I slowed instantly. The ambient bellow became clear and I noticed that I was above some steppe region. I flew over the steppe for a while and I noticed some big mountains straight-ahead in the distance. Before I got closer to the mountains, I slowed even more. I had enough from high speed, so now I was flying at about 30 Km/h. I spotted some road with telephonic poles near by. I approached closer to the road and flew in straight line above the poles, which carried telephone cable.

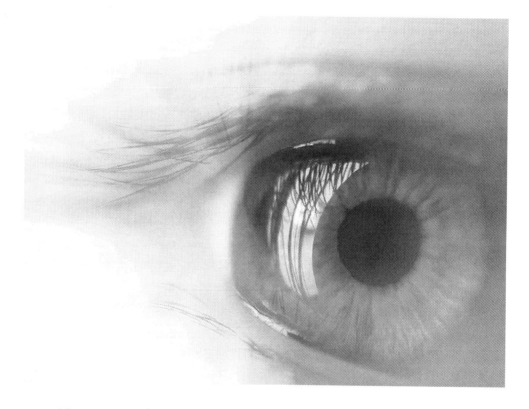

Here comes the new element. While I was watching the cable with no special intention to do anything in particular, my astral vision suddenly changed. I felt something new in my consciousness; something I never knew existed in me. (The best I can describe it is as if the normal astral vision has been upgraded with a new quality, which provides you with a new dimension of electronic perception). I was completely surprised by that, so I thought:

"Wow! I can see electronically, too. This is interesting."

It hit me as a very strange thing. Until then, I knew how to change my astral perception (which also lies hidden from the normal astral vision) to see the deeper levels of the aura that surrounded life forms, objects and places, but I did not know that something like that was possible.

During the first few seconds I was staring at the cable still not believing how that could be. I was able to see so much more clearly as the tiny electrical impulses were moving along the cable. Another amazing stuff hit me when I realized that when I was looking at the sky and the stars I could see normally, but when I was looking at the cable, I could see the electrons flow. I could see completely normally; in addition, I had the ability to see electronically. I tried to sharpen my astral vision to prove to myself that this was not some kind of anomaly in the astral perception, but nothing changed. I experimented with the new ability for about five minutes and I discovered that I could switch it off and on again if I wanted to. That was a final proof that this kind of visibility is not an anomaly of the astral vision but a real part of it. When I turned around, I saw that the road, which I was above, was going beside the mountains. I traced the cable, which was actually disappearing in the horizon. It was amazing to see the tiny lights moving along the cable. However, it turned out that this kind of concentration sucks a great amount of astral energy and at one point I felt my strength was becoming weaker.

I allowed loosening myself. The next moment I fell into complete darkness and I knew my astral journey was over. I did not want to resist the force that was pulling me back to my physical body, because I really had enough. A few moments later, I opened my physical eyes and a smile lit up my face. I was completely satisfied because not only I had a great astral flight, but I also had discovered a new ability of the astral body.

Subchapter 4.12
BLUE CRYSTAL

This one is among the most unusual astral experiences I have ever experienced. It happened on March 13, 1993. That night I went to a party and had good time with my friends. It was around 01:00AM when I came home and after I took my clothes off and put my pajamas on, I went to bed. The night was still young for me because it was my astral life's turn. I took my zener cards that stood beside my bed and started to concentrate on them intending to increase my ESP level.

I sat on the bed, closed my eyes and started my training. The first deck went bad. It was somewhere around the middle of the sixth deck when a drastic improvement came forth. The only unpleasant feeling was a small pain in my head; it was just a common effect as a product of my focusing on the zener cards. To be more specific, my pineal gland became irritated because I had made a mental effort to send amplified psychic waves through my third eye with intention to sense or see the symbols, which were on the zener cards, and I didn't pay much attention to that.

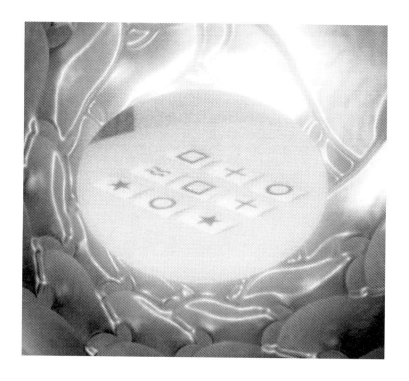

Psychically, I started to feel stronger and soon my astral vision became very sharp and clear. I passed to the next level of training in which I was forcing myself to sense or see two cards at the same time. After a while, I was done with that, too, so I started to put three cards at a time and nine cards beside me very soon. When I passed those tests, too, with my eyes still closed I started gaining the astral vision of my whole room.

As soon as my whole room became visible in my astral vision I just pushed myself out and found myself standing in my astral body. The moment I saw myself sitting on the bed with the nine cards beside me, I smiled. It was time for another astral excursion, and that felt good. I moved closer to the wall, which separated my apartment from the apartment of my neighbor Diana. I passed through the wall and as soon as I went to the other side, I looked around. The whole room was a mess and I saw Diana sleeping on her bed. Anyway, I didn't have any attention to stay there long so ten seconds later I moved towards the wall that separated Diana's apartment from the next one. I stepped forward and after I went through the wall I found myself inside the next apartment in which a very old lady had passed away about 20 days ago. An unpleasant feeling got over me because I did not have any intention to disturb her spirit if it was still around. However, I was already there, so before I left that apartment too and went to the next one, I took a close look. The blinds on the windows were put down. The apartment was in complete darkness, which made me feel even more unpleasant. All of a sudden, my Haragei – a sense of potential danger in my environment rang a bell. In the next few moments, the inner impulses became stronger and it was clear something was not right. Suddenly, a blue dot appeared in the center of the living room. I thought, "What is this"?

The bright dot very fast became a wonderful blue line, which in a few moments became a beautiful blue light. I was surprised to notice that from the center of the light a blue crystal was coming forward and growing rapidly. It grew up to about one meter and there were hundreds of small crystals of about a few millimeters in size all around it. The moment it stopped growing and took the final shape and size I felt as if hit by some energetic shock that resulted with the biolocation of my consciousness. I became fully aware that I was sitting on my bed and at the same time, I was fully aware that I was standing in my astral body in front of a strange blue crystal. The next moment, without my conscious will, my whole consciousness transferred itself directly into my astral body and I had lost my awareness of my physical body. In an instant, I felt some strong magnetic force pulling me towards the crystal.

I could not resist the power of the blue crystal and a few moments later it pulled me directly to it. Nothing happened when I touched the surface of the blue crystal, and I could freely move my hands over it. While I was still occupied with the observation of my transparent hands as they smoothly glided on the crystal surface, something changed again. A strange humming sound appeared and I felt a strong source of energy coming forward from the crystal. Deep in my consciousness my Haragei was alarming of great danger; still, before I could do anything I felt that the force was taking control over me completely. Then, a flash appeared and I sensed that all across my astral body something very powerful went through. I tried to remove my hands from the surface of the crystal but I encountered an unpleasant surprise – I could not pull my hands back because a strange powerful force would not let me. Although until then I was thinking of myself as of a man with solid experience in the field and that rarely something could scare me on the astral plane, I was obviously wrong. Honestly, I started to panic completely taken over with fear. Instinctively I immediately transferred my consciousness directly to my physical body intending to switch dimensions, which looked to me as a possible escape from this unpleasant situation. As soon as I regained awareness of my physical body, I opened my eyes and clearly saw my room but in my inner astral vision, I was still standing in front of the blue crystal with my hands attached to its surface.

I realized that it did not work, so I closed my eyes again. The moment I did that, I found myself again standing fully conscious in my astral body in front of the crystal. Again, I put the maximum effort to release my hands from it but unsuccessfully. The moment I was pulling, another strong flash came out with no warning from the crystal. It struck me like electric shocks do, and my astral body started to shake badly. The Haragei was screaming in my consciousness, but again, I could not do anything. The situation became similar to a horror film.

The worst part was, that whenever I opened my physical eyes I found myself sitting on the bed, but whenever I closed my eyes I found myself standing before the crystal still stuck to it. Nevertheless, a minute after having switched the location of my consciousness, I managed to put the panic aside, regroup myself and telepathically asked, "Who are you"?

Instead of getting an answer, I found myself in a strange crystal cave that was 30 meters large and at about the same height. The walls of the cave were carved with thousands of tiny crystals, which were reflecting a beautiful rainbow light. Along the middle of the cave's floor, there was something like a path that led straight to a smaller exit that was the only visible way out. I headed towards the exit constantly on guard asking myself if something would appear from nowhere and still I had no clue where I was. Luckily, nothing tried to stop me and I reached the exit, a very small one, about a half of a meter. It was made of very long and tiny crystals, too, which also reflected wonderful light that influenced me in some indescribable way.

While I was passing through the exit this was the thought that went in my consciousness, "This might be a trap and it could cost me a lot, yet there is nothing else to do". Therefore, slowly and very cautious, I went through the exit and found myself out on a snowy mountain.

The snow was all around me but in my astral body, I did not feel cold at all. I noticed I was somewhere very high and about 400 meters close to some mountain peak, which was only one of the many peaks visible from the spot where I was standing. Deep down, I knew that I was on the Himalayas. Still not paying too much attention to where I was, a monologue took place in my consciousness: "Did the blue crystal release me or did it not? I will soon find out. I want to return to my physical body!"

I had not even finished my wish yet when I found myself in my physical body sitting on my bed with the zener cards beside me. I opened my eyes physically and encountered a disappointment. I was still seeing things through two dimensions. I was looking at my room and at the same time I was standing in front of the crystal with my hands stuck on it.

I closed my physical eyes again but instead of finding myself in front of the blue crystal, I found myself in the same crystal cave and on exactly the same starting point as before. I did not waste any time and I went towards the exit again but this time I was running. As soon as I had passed the exit and found myself outside, I noticed that everything was the same as it had been the first time. Deep in my consciousness, I was worried a lot, because I did not know what was truly going on there. However, the snow glittered so beautifully that the whole mountain looked unforgettably beautiful, too. It was so beautiful and peaceful that I thought I should never leave that place. Although aware of the situation I found myself in, still, it was as if a part of me was fascinated and somehow charmed by that natural beauty.

I headed towards the top of the mountain to see what would happen next. I noticed a big rock on my right and a small footpath nearby. So I followed the footpath and continued my way up. I was aware that I could take off and reach the mountain peak in an instant but some inner sense was telling me that it was for the better to continue walking. As soon as I passed beside the big rock, I discovered that the footpath led towards the top just over the edge of one side of the mountain. When I looked down, I saw an abyss with no end. Anyway, though it looked dangerous, I was completely aware of my astral presence there and I knew I could not fall if I did not want to.

I continued following the footprint wondering where would it take me. After about two minutes of walking, I saw something so strange that made me feel a strong doubt whether I was dreaming all this or was it happening for real. Not so far away from me, I saw four big stones levitating in thin air like a magical bridge between two mountains. I looked down again and the abyss looked even more dangerous. Still not believing what I was seeing, I looked forward again and noticed that the stones were in a precise position and at a distance a human could cross over. I assumed that if someone wanted to make it to the other side he was able to achieve that in five long jumps. Despite the fact that I was fully aware I was on an astral dimension, the whole environment looked to me somehow unreal. I thought to myself, "Dear God! Am I hallucinating or is this really happening?"

On the other hand, I was able to see much clearly, and what is more interesting I was seeing things through my transparent astral body. Just for the test, I wanted to lift myself a few meters and see what would happen. As soon as I thought of lifting myself up, I found myself three meters above the snowy footpath. From that perspective the abyss looked terrifying and I did not feel like exploring it, not even astrally. Nevertheless, I remained relatively calm and focused myself on the stones. The stones were just levitating there in thin air as if they had been there since the beginning of time. In those few seconds, so many thoughts crossed my consciousness: "So, it's real. I'm here and those stones are here. Perhaps, they are leading straight to the entrance of Shambala. Should I go to the other side or should I stay on this footpath and see what awaits me at the end."

I assumed I would probably find the answer at the end of the footpath and thought it would be great to explore those stones if there was time. Therefore, I hit the footpath again and continued to walk. The magical stones stayed way behind me. Close to the footpath, I encountered a strange gate made of rocks. Nevertheless, the footpath was leading straight up and I wanted to check out the gate first. There was some kind of inscription on the gate in strange symbols. I thought: "Since I'm on the Himalayas it should be some kind of Sanskrit but these marks do not resemble Sanskrit at all."

In the depth of my consciousness, I sensed that some inner program similar to computer software was searching for the information about that inscription, but I blocked it intentionally and went through the gate. When I reached the other side, I found myself in complete darkness. Even the radiance that surrounded my astral body did not illuminate the complete darkness somehow. Suddenly, as I was getting ready to leave and return to the footpath, a familiar blue light started to appear from the darkness.

In a few seconds the blue light illuminated the surroundings and I clearly spotted I was at the entrance of a huge tunnel which led deep down in the mountain and I knew the blue crystal had returned. I found myself in the same position as before again.

Attached to the crystal surface my hands were with absolutely no chance to free them. Panic mixed with great fear started to rule over me. It was completely strange but somehow I could feel that the crystal was feeding on my fear. Still, that awareness did not change a thing and the situation became worse when I sensed something very powerful had touched my consciousness. I heard an echo: "You will remain attached to me forever!"

Indescribable panic went through me. Once again, I tried to release my hands with all the strength I had, but nothing happened. The panic became despair. I telepathically called for Orska to help me and I started calling my friend Velibor if he was present on the astral plane.

Note: *The green crystal, which I have mentioned before is a divine life form, which possesses almost unlimited power. Physically, it exists on one planet known to me as Orska, which is about 33 light years distant from our planet in the direction of the Orion constellation. The civilization, which inhabits this planet is among the oldest ones in this part of the Cosmos and*

certainly among the most advanced ones. To the best of my knowledge the life form that lives inside this green crystal controls all of the Orska civilization. However, I learned about Orska by my friend Velibor Rabljenovich who in fact had introduced me to the Orska beings.

Despite all of my telepathic efforts in the following five minutes, neither there was anybody to help me, nor the situation changed. I was starting to accept the fact that my physical body would die and that I would be attached to the blue crystal who knows for how long. The moment I truly gave up and thought it was over the green crystal appeared beside me.

As soon as I had recognized it, I thought that there was hope for me. The green crystal flashed with a strong green light, which shadowed the blue light coming from the blue crystal. I saw as the green light passed through my astral body and that same moment I felt the magnetic force of the blue crystal was becoming weaker. Then it flashed again and I managed to pull back my hands. I was relieved and I thought to myself: "Thanks God, I'm free."

The green crystal was present for about 10 seconds more and then the same way it suddenly appeared it was gone. I did not even have time to thank it. I turned around towards the blue crystal and noticed that its appearance was starting to fade. In the next few moments it became completely transparent until it disappeared and only a weak blue light remained. In the end, the light became only a pale blue dot, which stretched itself in a tiny line and in a split of a second it disappeared from my sight.

The blue crystal was gone and I remained to stand in complete darkness. I did not feel any presence around me and my inner sense of danger had shut off. At last I was feeling free. I thought of my physical body and the next moment I found myself returning to it. I opened my eyes and saw the zener cards beside me.

The inner vision was gone and I did not observe multidimensional any more. I was constantly opening and closing my physical eyes to make sure that things were back to normal. In my astral vision the blue crystal was gone and I felt a great relief because this time the situation was really critical. I even did not want to think about what would have happened if the green crystal had not helped me.

I got up from my bed and went to take a shower. The next day I told the whole astral event to my friend Velibor. He told me not to worry. In fact, he said he should congratulate me, because from now on the green crystal would protect me. Yet, in the end he also mentioned: "Do not talk about that to anybody!"

Nevertheless, the truth is that the night before I could have ended up badly. If somebody ever asks me if there is any danger on the astral plane, I will surely tell him/her "yes" and I will mention that experience of mine to prove it.

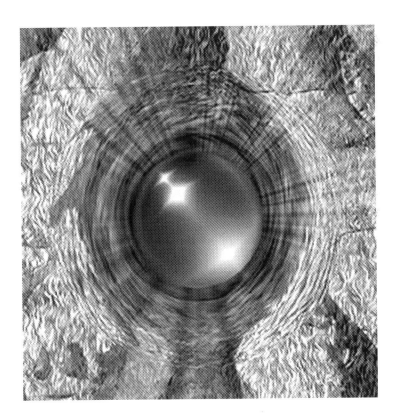

Subchapter 4.13
ASTRAL FIGHT

I remember this astral excursion of mine as a very unpleasant one. Again, as many times before, if my friends from Orska did not help me I surely would not be here to tell about it. Some of you might say, "This man is strongly oriented on convincing us not to experiment with the astral projection phenomenon". I can assure you that it simply is not true, but I have to point out that the astral world can bring many unpleasant experiences some of which can be very dangerous, some even fatal.

However, a true astral seeker willing to go deep into the exploration of the astral plane has to clearly understand that there are risks just like there is potential risk of crossing the street on the physical plane. It simply comes with the territory. The astral plane is an even larger area than the physical one, so it is logical to assume that it possesses even greater varieties of life forms.

That is why one should know that he/she is going to encounter all kinds of astral entities some of which are not positively oriented toward humans. The bottom line is, once some of those life forms get in touch with a human astral traveler, they become very aggressive almost instantly. So the threat is real and the astral traveler should always be on the alert. It is as if you have packed your things and went to some foreign country you have never been before. You can encounter different kinds of people and anything can happen to you.

Anyway, a naïve astral traveler who thinks very high of him/herself as of a perfect and the strongest creature in the astral plane very often ends up as a victim of his/her own deception. Despite all other dangers one can encounter, strong negative energy radiates from some places. I am not speaking about places on the lower astral plane but places that are in the middle belt of the astral plane. A well-trained and experienced astral traveler can easily detect them by their dark aura but it is a totally different story for an inexperienced one.

This astral excursion happened on May 19, 1993. I went to sleep with no intention whatsoever to walk across the astral plane, but practice is practice, and very soon after I fell asleep my consciousness had

188

become aware of dreaming. To be more precise, I used the method of dream control by becoming aware of some anomalies that I had seen in my sleep. Anyway, in my dream I found myself walking in some deep and dark forest. I awoke myself in front of a tall tree strangely shaped. The first thing that I did was to inspect my body and see if it was transparent or not. As soon as I realized I was completely transparent and that I was in the astral plane, I said to my self: "So, here we go again."

I was walking through the deep forest for about a minute with no intention to lift myself up and fly away because I wanted to investigate the inner signal of potential danger that was constantly alarming me that there was something wrong in this forest. At one point the Haragei became much stronger when walking among the trees I spotted a little stone cabin about forty meters away from me. The cabin's aura was very dark and foggy and it did not match the global aura of the forest at all. Anyhow, I went closer to the stone cabin and noticed there were not any windows on it. There was only a wooden door and generally in a very bad shape. In fact, the door and the roof were the only wood visible from outside the cabin and everything else was made of stone. It became very suspicious to me, but curiosity had done the job and I walked through the wall.

It turned out to be a big mistake. As soon as I found myself inside the cabin, I realized it was almost in a complete darkness. There were only two small rooms in the interior. The whole space was divided by only one wall supposedly with a door. However, the space where the door was supposed to be was empty. Only a tiny light was coming from there. It was in fact coming from the damaged entrance of the cabin. In almost complete darkness, I managed to register that the wall that separated the two rooms was also made of stone. Suddenly, deep down I felt the Haragei was going stronger. I started to feel some strange and disturbing presence close to the spot where I was standing.

The Haragei started alarming stronger and stronger each second. The moment it reached its culmination, some small humanoid transparent creature appeared through the wall and jumped over me. In a split of a second, I recognized that it was some small alien from the Gray species. Exactly the same moment, I defended myself on reflex by rejecting the Gray with mental power. I just looked at it and using the mental strength I pushed it back through the wall it came from. My defense came somehow natural and on instinct and the strength of the PSI-wave surprised even me.

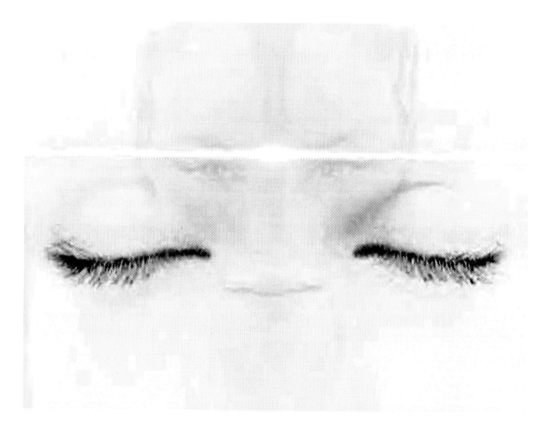

In that moment, I felt capable of producing a strong PSI-wave that could wipe everything on its way. However, this was far from over, so while I was accumulating mental energy, the Haragei alarmed me again just in time when two little astral creatures came out of the wall. Everything happened so fast, maybe in a second but before I produced the second defensive PSI-wave and pushed the two Gray astral beings through the wall, I thought: "What do they want now?"

They disappeared from my sight and I was alone again. I felt embittered because they would not let me go in peace. Their presence promised nothing good and it cleared up to me that they were again in the aggressive mood no matter of my reaction to them. For a few seconds everything was silent. I reached deep down within to feel the inner danger sense. The Haragei was silent, so I concluded that the danger was gone, at least for the time being. I stretched my transparent astral arm and pushed straight through the wall.

My transparent arm disappeared in the wall and the next moment I pulled my arm back. Then, I passed through the wall and found myself on the other side. I looked at the old wooden door, which was in a very bad condition and noticed it did not perfectly fit into the door space because tiny light-beams were coming from the small holes between the door and the wall.

I was just getting ready to leave this creepy cabin through the door when the signals for great danger returned even stronger. It was twice stronger than the last two times and I was fully aware that this time the danger was much more serious. It was high time to get out of there, so I commanded myself to lift up and fly away, but I encountered an unpleasant feeling it was too late for that. Some strange and very powerful force pulled me back on the ground and did not let me leave. The next moment four transparent appearances started materializing around me. In the beginning, all of them were the size of the average Gray, but a few moments later the appearances started to grow and took exactly the same size of my astral body. Although they took human form, I knew they were Grays.

Note: *I really did not understand their reason to change the size and appearance of their astral bodies, when that never worked for me. Although sometimes their masquerade was fun for me, I never allowed myself to forget how advanced they were and I was certain there had been some secret reason for their behavior. Maybe it was just their way to cover up their presence here on Earth from humans. It made sense because that way they would not leave any traces of their activities in the memory of human subjects. Nevertheless, throughout the years, I learned one thing straight: "Never underestimate a Gray!"*

Strange, but since the first moment they materialized, I felt that one of the astrals was in charge. I did not pay much attention to their appearances but I constantly looked for the solution to free myself from the strong energy that was pulling me down to the ground and would not let me go. After a few long moments, they attacked. They were all levitating in the same distance from me watching me highly concentrated. I started to feel a severe loss of my strength and I knew I was not in position to defend myself. Their joint mental force had tied me so strongly; even my thoughts started to move slowly across my consciousness.

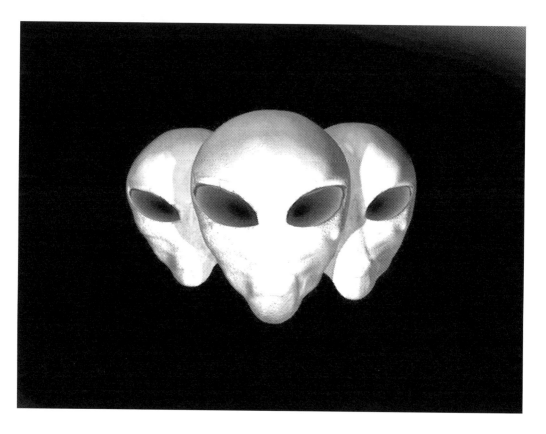

The panic found its way itself. In my consciousness I was screaming: "I want to immediately return to my physical body!" - But that did not work. I was still not able to move on my own will because they were constantly blocking me. Something in my consciousness started to hurt so much that I felt my own thoughts burning me. I could not think and I could not concentrate any more. The next moment a white light appeared around my astral body and I felt indescribable pain. The white light lifted me from the ground and started rotating me very fast. They were burning my consciousness in a way I had never felt before. Somehow, I managed to construct a simple thought in my consciousness: "This is definitely the end!"

I was not able to stand the pain anymore and I started losing my head. One of the Grays transmitted a simple message to me: "If you do not cooperate with us, we will eliminate you!"

When I had completely lost my hope and when I thought that I was history, the door opened as if been hit by a tornado. I saw the light coming from the outside and the dark room became illuminated. The next moment I heard a strong voice in my consciousness: "Let him go. He is with us."

At that point, the white light around me disappeared and the force that was spinning me around became so much weaker. Three of the four astral entities that were around me, retreated for about a meter distance from me. They were looking at the one with a higher rank who did not back off from me. They seemed as if they were asking approval to fight or not. I barely succeeded to move my head and noticed that the leader of the Grays was looking straight at me with so much hatred, which was not average behavior of a Gray. "Be sure that next time it will not end like this!"- His message whipped my consciousness. Finally, the leader backed off me, and in an instant, I felt incredibly weak.

The moment the Gray in charge released me I fell down on the ground. I felt a small amount of my energy returning to me, but I still could not think without feeling any pain. "Orska"- I thought to myself. Two astrals from Orska came closer to me and lifted me up from the ground. They were levitating close above the ground never touching it. A strong white aura was visible around their transparent astral bodies. "I'm saved. Is it possible?"-I did not believe I was saved. I tried to stand on my own but I realized that the legs of my astral body could not hold me. I was feeling so bad, almost like the Grays had drained my life force. The friendly astrals looked at me with so much compassion and took me out of the cabin.

It was so much more pleasant to be outside and quite the opposite from the inside of the cabin. They continued dragging me for another 30 meters from the stone cabin. There were more than 20 astrals from Orska waiting for us. They were all looking at me compassionately and I felt as if I was a juvenile not able to take care of myself. Anyway, I swallowed my pride and turned my head around for one last look at the cabin. The leader of the Grays was still standing on the doorstep and looking straight at me. As soon as the alien noticed that I was looking in its direction, it made a strong move with its head, and almost instantly the door closed so loud that it echoed for a while throughout the whole forest. I turned toward my astral friends again and I succeeded to give them my gratitude. I felt a spinning in my consciousness again, but I managed to pull myself together a little and asked: "Where are we?"

They all replied like one consciousness: "We are at Dulce, New Mexico. Though you had not noticed, the small cabin is above one of the largest underground bases on the planet. Here a genetic program is being conducted on many subjects, mostly humans. Do not come here again because they have technology to detect presence of a life force that emanates from the astral body of an intruder. They can easily trap your astral body inside the electromagnetic force field and your water vessel will die."

"I did not come here on purpose. Maybe they have something to do with it? However, I was not looking for trouble, so why did they attack me? – I asked.

The voice inside my consciousness did not give a straight answer to my questions but perhaps it was enough:

"You resist them, but they are determined to extract a part of your genes from you. So, be very careful of where you move in your astral body because we can not protect you everywhere."

The spinning in my consciousness became faster and I lost control over my astral body completely. The last thing I received in my consciousness was: "It is time for us to take you back to your water vessel because your life force is leaking very fast."

The next moment, I sank into complete darkness, traveling back to my physical body. I managed to open my physical eyes but I could hardly move myself. I felt strongly embittered and the pain was striking my whole body. Emotionally I felt broken into a thousand pieces, completely drained, and exhausted to infinity. I was aware that if my friends from Orska had not helped me I surely would have not survived to speak about it. In my mind, the same sentence was repeating itself: "What if they had not come in time and what if all this ended differently?" All this was becoming very risky and it started to disturb me a lot. I started asking myself whether I possessed a gift or was I just cursed.

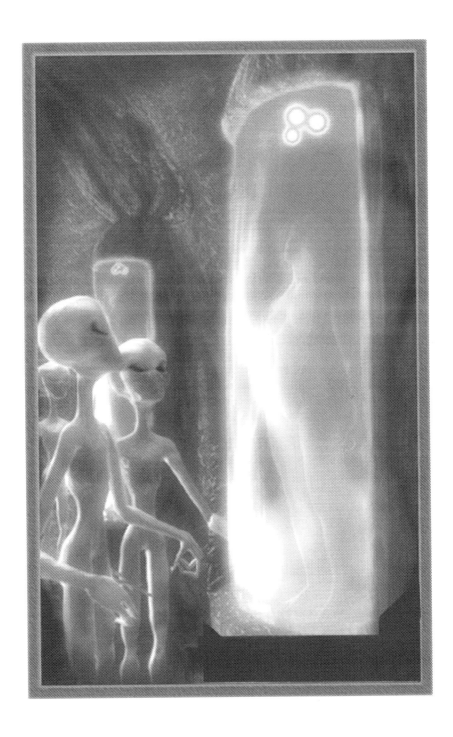

Subchapter 4.14
STRANGE ENCOUNTER

My contacts with the Grays continued and very soon, I was a witness of an event in which 3 flying objects performed an amazing show in the crystal-clear night sky. The UFO encounter happened suddenly in the time when my contacts with them had become more frequent and I did not think they would let me see a part of their technology in action so soon. For the record, this astral excursion happened on May 24, 1993 at 02:00AM. After I had finished my astral projection technique, I slowly elevated above my physical body. There was no need for me to stay in my room, so I left my apartment at great speed and flew to the west.

The high-speed flight took very long and rarely I needed to go higher (only if I had to fly over like a mountain) than approximately 200 meters. I passed over many mountains, rivers, lakes, forests and valleys. The sky was clear and starry, which gave me a wonderful and mighty feeling at the same time. I was thrilled to be out there flying completely free, able to experience what most of the people could not. I do not want to give you the expression of my showing off, but really, I was feeling like I was special.

I assumed I was somewhere in Spain when I arrived above some large forest region. The area of at least 20 kilometers was uninhabited so it was very quiet.

The whole ambient was unforgettably beautiful and I slowed my speed to about 100 Km/h. "Wonderful", – I thought to myself and lowered altitude to about 20 meters above the ground completely enjoying the pretty site. The forest was very large and I still could not see its edge. A few kilometers away I spotted some road disappearing in the horizon. Just for fun, I made a flying maneuver and started to fly exactly above the road because I was curious to find where it led. Then, suddenly and completely unexpected, something in the sky started flashing and grabbed my attention. Just a half of a kilometer higher on my left I saw something shining in the shape of a disk moving across the sky at very low speed and with absolutely no sound. It was obvious to me the object was not one of ours. Anyway, the Haragei was calm and it was not alarming me, so I assumed there was no potential danger for me.

Still surprised, I simply continued following the UFO on its path. Suddenly, some information emerged on the surface of my consciousness: the flying object belonged to the Grays and had been constructed somewhere in the Zeta Reticuli constellation. I did not know from where all that data was coming from. Sometimes, during my presence on the astral plane I felt like a huge amount of data existed in the depth of my consciousness. In other words, it was a feeling as if you possessed an archive that contained an infinite zip files ready to unzip. Yet, I did not have any access to it and the data came spontaneously and without my own will. So far, somehow, not even once that hidden inner knowledge had shown wrong or false and there was no reason for me to doubt the information.

"So this is how their flying ships look like" - I said to myself. The disk shaped object continued to shine in short flashes. The rhythm of the flashes was not changing so far but the light of the flashes was changing from light yellow to dark red. No difference whether the flash was yellow or dark red, it was leaving a small light trail in the sky, which was disappearing very fast.

A debate within me began. I was wondering should I get closer to the flying object and take a good look of it or should I stay at a relatively close distance where it was probably safer. I decided not to look for trouble so I kept that distance from which I was in position to easily monitor everything happening. The object continued to fly parallel to the ground for about a kilometer further when I spotted another two flying objects on my left moving in parallel formation towards the first one. They were the same size and shape as the one I was watching at so far.

Again, some information appeared in my consciousness from nowhere all by itself: "They are returning from their daily abduction activity. They are done for now and they will now leave Earth and go to their base which is located on the other side of the Moon."

I shortly looked down at the forest and saw the tall trees swinging in the wind. I looked up again and saw the three objects flying across the sky making no sound at all. The distance between the objects became closer, and when they reached the intercepting point they all stopped. I was wondering what was going to happen next. The UFOs levitated in the sky for about 5 seconds and during that short time, nothing happened. Then, they started to change the intensity of their lights in longer or shorter flashes as if they were communicating with each other. 15 seconds later all three objects flashed with a very strong light forming one big yellow-red circle line all across the night sky. The sight was fascinating. The next moment all three objects moved with a great speed flying in parallel. They were gaining on altitude fast and soon they disappeared from my sight.

It was strange, but somehow I knew what maneuver they were going to pull. I felt telepathically connected to them. It seemed they were aware of my presence the whole time and that in fact, they allowed me to see this as a preparation process for our further contacts. However, I remained to levitate above the forest for a while. I was looking at the stars trying to see if the Grays were coming back though I was aware they were done for that night. Then blackness swallowed me and I started to feel that I was returning to my physical body. I recall opening my eyes and with an expression of triumph on my face, I got up from my bed. I took my diary where I was archiving all of my astral experiences and started to write.

Comment: Many years have passed by ever since, and I have had so many opportunities to admire alien technology. Although technology here on Earth is undergoing a very fast development, comparing it to all other technologies I have seen on my astral trips that belong to other civilizations, sometimes I still cannot avoid the feeling that we still live in the Stone Age.

We can have 300 billion visible stars in our own Galaxy...That's around 30 billion planetary systems... Conclusion: We can have One million civilizations in our own Galaxy...

Subchapter 4.15
CONTACTS GO ON

This astral voyage happened on September 12, 1993. Unusual for me, I went to sleep about 11:20PM. Still, I did not have any intention to sleep, but to induce an out of the body experience. Therefore, after ten minutes spent in the position of Shavasana I successfully accomplished the astral projection. Very fast and very smooth I left my apartment and found myself at the altitude of about 50 meters above the center of Skopje.

During the flight I sensed some unusual feeling concerning my physical body. To be more precise, I felt my physical body protesting because of an uncomfortable position. The astral excursion ended in a second and I opened my physical eyes. As soon as I gained control over my physical body again, I turned from the position of Shavasana to the left side. It was a very rare case for me to feel uncomfortable in the position of Shavasana, but it has happened a few times before, so I did not pay too much attention to it.

After I found a suitable side position, I induced an out of the body experience again. The moment I lifted myself in my astral body above my physical body, a strange flash appeared in my consciousness. It was very strong and I felt my consciousness becoming liquid somehow.

The next moment another flash appeared and I was teleported to space instantly. The sudden change of my location had confused me at first and I was asking myself where I was. It happened so fast, and it caught me by surprise, because I did not give any conscious command to leave the planet. A few moments later I put myself together and started to look around.

The space around me was so foggy that I thought I was somewhere in space. There were many high-density dust particles. My astral vision became clear and I saw that in fact I was in the middle of an asteroid field. There were so many asteroids around me and some of them were quite big. The view was amazing from that perspective. I noticed Jupiter on my right in its full glory. I thought: "God, it is huge!"

Although it was so far away from me, the planet was obviously a giant one in size. Suddenly, I felt a contact in my consciousness. It took me by surprise because my Haragei did not alarm me of any presence and I was thinking I was completely alone up there. The telepathic message was quite unusual and its contents said: "Look around you. This asteroid field is all that remained from the planet that had been orbiting this Sun once, too."

The same way the contact appeared in my consciousness, so suddenly and abruptly it disappeared. With a bit of caution and fear, I looked around myself and about a hundred meters or more away, I spotted a large UFO by a bigger asteroid. This asteroid moved slower than the rest of the asteroids. "Unbelievable" – I thought and instantly looked at my transparent astral body to make sure I was truly there and that the UFO that I was looking at was real. Everything was in order and I accepted the newborn situation. "OK. I'm truly here. Let's see what this all is about."-I thought. The UFO was not disk-shaped but more like in the shape of some modern vehicle.

The space around the UFO was strongly illuminated with some strange blue radiance. It seemed that the radiance served as a protective shield from the asteroids but I could not tell for sure. By its appearance, the UFO looked made of some kind of black metal with a very smooth and shining surface. The whole experience was more than amazing because deep down I felt a stream of a strange fluid between that flying craft and me. Somehow, I knew it was there because of me. "What do they want now?" – A logical question ran through my consciousness.

The same moment another flash appeared in my consciousness and I felt an incredibly fast movement through space. I was transported somewhere unwillingly and that started to disturb me because they were playing with me like with a child's toy. Anyway, I could not do anything about it, so I just adapted to their game. The moving stopped and I found myself in a very familiar environment. The first thing that caught my attention was some very strong radiance of blue light on my left. When I turned left, I noticed I was close to Earth. The blue radiance was coming from the Earth's atmosphere, which was giving the planet an indescribable wonderful appearance. I looked at the billions of stars visible in deep space. The Moon was hiding behind Earth, but slowly becoming visible. I turned around again towards the deep space to admire the beauty of our Sun for a few seconds. Visible in the distance, it was shining gloriously. I was overwhelmed with the beauty. No words could describe the true beauty of the experience because watching space on TV or in a movie is one thing, but watching in live feels completely different. Believe me one does not have any clue how beautiful the space looks until getting there physically or astrally.

From my diary

When I felt like going deeper in our solar system, the same UFO appeared again. In contrast to the first time, the strong radiance around the craft was not visible any more. Seen from the distance I was levitating at, I assumed the UFO was about 200 meters long, 50 meters wide in its slimmer part and 100 meters in the larger one. I did not notice any windows or anything similar, which in fact did not surprise me at all. Suddenly, more than 10 white light spheres equally sized, materialized from nowhere. The light balls took some kind of formation and started to move in my direction. Before I had the time to react one way or another, the spheres passed me by in a second and entered the Earth's atmosphere. Two of them passed very close to me and I realized they were probably 10 - 12 meters in diameter. It seemed so strange that all of them went into the direction of Earth and not even one towards the Moon.

"What's happening?" - A creepy question appeared in my consciousness. As many times before, I wondered why they would allow me to see this. Without any hesitation I took action. I was chasing after the light balls fantastically fast. The acceleration felt powerful, but it did not last long because they suddenly sped when I managed to catch up with them, and disappeared out of my sight. The interesting part was that before they disappeared from my sight I saw them splitting up and moved in different directions diving fast into the Earth's air space.

I was sure I was quite capable of catching them, but obviously in those short moments I did not react fast enough, because either I was not skilled enough or I just respected them too much knowing what they were capable of doing to me if I pissed them off. Despite the delay of my action, I intended to fix the mistake, so I continued diving at high speed. A few moments later, (judging from the contours of the continent I was flying above), I was landing somewhere in Russia. I made a smooth maneuver to the left and continued flying at drastically lower speed of about 500 Km/h. I adjusted my altitude to about 300 meters above the ground and continued to move north. All the time I bewared of the possibility that some of the light balls could appear from somewhere. Where the white spheres went and what their mission was had been the only constantly active question in my consciousness.

Anyway, none of them showed up so far. I noticed a large forest area below, but I did not pay much attention to it, because I was looking everywhere to see if some light ball would appear in the clear night sky. After about 20 minutes of flying, I arrived above some mountain region. I stopped for a while above one of the mountain peaks, looking again in all directions in the sky. I spotted some clouds above me that made the night sky look more beautiful. The clouds were illuminated by the moonlight and remembering that I recently arrived from space gave me a strong feeling of self-respect. I cannot describe the sensation I felt. All I can say is that I felt presence of something Cosmic in myself.

Then, suddenly the ambient disappeared and a few seconds later a new one appeared. There was no particular reason why it happened, but it was certainly not because I had something to do with it. I found myself in some kind of astral dimension where the ambient was very dark. Anyway, I felt I had hit some invisible wall directly. It did not hurt, although sometimes it does if you are still thinking partly in a physical way. It was strange at first, but I adapted to the situation very fast. I wanted to pass through the invisible wall and I was aware that I could not succeed with the standard procedure (just passing through it), because I would not hit my astral body in the first place. It was clear to me that I was facing something like an invisible energy barrier. Therefore, one of the possible solutions to reach the other side for me was to make a change into the structure of my astral body. To be more accurate, I thought of changing the astral substance of my astral body.

It worked. I intentionally changed the density of my astral body into some liquid substance and joined myself with the substance of the invisible wall. I did that even to the atomic level and the next moment I just moved my substance deep into its substance and exited on the other side. When I found myself gliding on the inner surface of the energy barrier, my astral body gained on density again and I took my normal human astral form. I smiled when I regained my normal shape again.

The view in front of me was indescribable. About 30 meters away from me, a square was rotating levitating in thin air. Its sides were about

20 meters long and totally black. At first sight, the whole image seemed very suspicious to me. I thought: "Could it be one of those traps I encounter on an astral plane occasionally?" Since I felt tired of looking for solutions to get out of many dangerous traps, I decided to get out of there before the things became worse. Thus, I did that concentrating on my return home to Skopje. The square vanished and I found myself above Skopje at the altitude of about 200 meters. I did not even think whether I had left the square too soon or not. I did not even care if the Grays had something to do with it, and I simply accepted my decision as final and went on. I put my astral body in free fall and just a few seconds before I touched the ground I gave myself a little boost and continued flying between the buildings downtown.

After a few minutes of fun, I reached Avtokomanda (another settlement in Skopje). While I was performing a maneuver that would redirect me to Novo Lisiche settlement, which was my physical home, everything around me vanished again with no particular reason. The next moment I started sinking into total blackness again with a clear feeling I was falling down. The interesting part of it was that before I had been pushed into the total blackness, I was flying at the altitude of 50 meters above the ground, yet I was feeling that I was falling rapidly for more than two hundred meters at least.

I was expecting a quick return to my physical body, but 5 seconds later a new reality opened in front of my eyes. Again, I was in some other dimension trying to figure out where I was. I was probably somewhere in the deep Astral. A strange levitating path was visible for me in that space. It consisted of many thin dark green rectangle-shaped slabs.

I had no explanation until then, but the feelings that this was not the first time I had been there was very intensive. However, everything wouldn't have looked so complicated to me, if I had not seen a little Gray sitting on one slab about 30 meters away from me. I was already tired of them and I went straight to it to finally clear the whole thing and find why they kept following me for so long. I really had enough of them, and I wanted to tell them to leave me alone because I did not want anything to do with them. The truth was I was tired of backing off from them, and in that particular moment I had lost myself in my anger, even hatred and I was ready to fight strong for my freedom.

As if the alien was reading my thoughts, as I am sure it was, as soon as I arrived to the slab it was sitting at, it just disappeared. Still, before it vanished from my sight I received a telepathic message that it was the one responsible for everything I had seen in space. It did not explain the most important thing to me – Why? Anyway, the transmission ended very fast and I felt that now my astral trip was going to be cut off. I was right because the next moment everything around me started to distort and again, I sank into total blackness.

I saw my room and my physical body lying in the bed still turned on its left side. I slowly came closer to my physical body and started to rejoin with it. As soon as I felt I could control my physical body again, I only opened my eyes and did not move at all for at least a minute. Meanwhile, in my mind I recorded every single detail about my astral trip. Then, I got up from the bed and took my diary to archive the events of my astral activity. Anyhow, this astral trip had raised many new questions in my mind. I was wondering what was really going on here on Earth. What did they want from us? What did they want from me? Why me?

Still I had no solid answer to any of my questions and I was not sure about anything anymore. Nevertheless, I hoped to find out more in every new contact. The worst part was that at that time I stopped speaking about my astral experiences even with my best friends because I was not sure of their reaction if I told them what I was experiencing. For the first time in my life, I felt alone - alone with my abilities and alone with the troubles that those abilities bring.

Comment: Today, after so many years, I have found some of the answers. The planet that was also a part of our solar system once was in fact property of the Reptoid race. Two species of the race known as Grays also had their base on this planet but they were in an inferior position to the Reptoids. The Reptoids were in charge of everything and the Grays were always obeying their orders. To the best of my knowledge, even today, nothing has changed – the Reptoids are still the ones who run the show and some of the Gray species are still doing the genetics and all other dirty stuff for them. However, thousands of years ago a massive destructive war had been going on in this part of the Galaxy. A highly advanced civilization that once existed on the planet Mars put tremendous offensive fight and succeeded to completely wipe out the whole planet of the Reptoid-Gray collective.

So the asteroid field that I had mentioned in the astral experience from 1993 is in fact all that has been left from the planet once orbiting our Sun between Mars and Jupiter. Unfortunately, at the end of the war the whole planet Mars has been destroyed on the surface and become unsuitable for life any more. Most of the survivors of their civilization went to deep space to look for a new home. However, a small part of them came to Earth to join the forces of Lemuria against the aggressive alliance that consisted mostly of Reptoids, Grays and Atlantians. Many of them had died in the massive destructions, some of them had left our solar system for good and some of them had retreated deep underground in the Earth's interior with the rest of the survivors of

Lemuria. Today, some of them still live in the capital of the underground kingdom – Shambala.

What I can say with certainty about this astral trip is that at that time the Grays were showing me a lot of their technology with a purpose to convince me to cooperate with them. They needed me because there was a gene known as "Meta gene" in my DNA. They wanted to extract the gene from me, using their advanced technology. However, the Meta gene cannot become active by force; it needs special environment to activate itself naturally; time to develop and even longer time to become fully active inside the DNA. That is why they were letting me do what I wanted to in the astral plane and even helping me discover and develop my astral skills even faster. I came up with that conclusion because they were always in position to abduct me and to extract the Meta gene from me with their advanced technology.

As far as I know, they wanted to duplicate the Meta gene from me, as well as from other people like me, in their own DNA by making hybrids that are partly human and partly alien. I know this might sound like pure science fiction, but believe me some of those activities are still going on, even now. The Grays are still monitoring some people, who are naturally gifted by this gene.

What is so special about this gene? – The Meta gene is some kind of natural accumulator of everything that could be put in the area of paranormal. Its basic purpose is to accumulate the natural energy that flows freely in the Cosmos. If the subject possesses a small amount of Meta gene in his or her DNA he/she is surely capable of telepathy, psychokinesis, astral projection, super hearing, ability to heal with bioenergy and much more. Those are only the smallest effects of what Meta gene does, and the stronger effects are passing high above the barrier of modern science of parapsychology. I am not speaking just about physical levitation, materialization in a sense that Sai Baba successfully demonstrates, or manipulation with magnetic fields etc. I am speaking about physical teleportation, physical flying, opening a multidimensional hole in space and time, teleporting the whole space ship or larger objects to the distant quadrants of space and much more. I am talking about real psychic power that is passing beyond the limits of average human understanding. By using the Meta gene, one (well educated in special science of PSI-energy) can change the reality of the physical and astral Universe. Today on Earth, this is a privilege for only few ones who live in Shambala. One of them is the King of the World also known as Sanat Kumara.

The Reptoids and the Grays cannot reach the territory of Agharta without destroying the whole planet. That is the reason they are trying to get the same effect with the people that live on the surface of Earth, speaking of which, I must mention that the Grays have had ongoing genetic programs for a very long time. Can you imagine how secretly and precisely they have performed this genetic program for thousands of years? I know it is scary but it has been happening and it is still happening. Go and make a small research in the public records, in government records or on the Internet and you will find plenty of evidence of this. Nowadays, it has become a kind of a public secret, everybody knows about this more or less, but still nobody or at least only a few are trying to do something to bring the truth out to the surface. Finally, if we do not care about ourselves, shouldn't we care about our children? I do not want to sound impolite, but wake up people! What are you waiting for?

The shadow government is a top-secret world organization that knows and runs the exchanging alien technology program in return for the major cover up of alien presence here on Earth and their interaction with humans. The US government officials claimed for so long that the Area 51 or Dulce did not exist, but the satellite images and so many other proofs show something different. What do you think they keep there – cats and dogs?

The worst part is that Area 51 and Dulce are only two of so many underground bases throughout the world in which there is current alien activity. Thus, despite the fact that aliens have a huge base on the other side of the Moon and that the radars and other electronic equipment picks them up almost on daily basis, some of the leading governments in the world are still keeping this evidence from the public a secret. It is so obvious that some of ours know what is going on, but they still cover it up very well by putting strong efforts to discredit all the reports, which concern UFOs or alien activity on Earth.

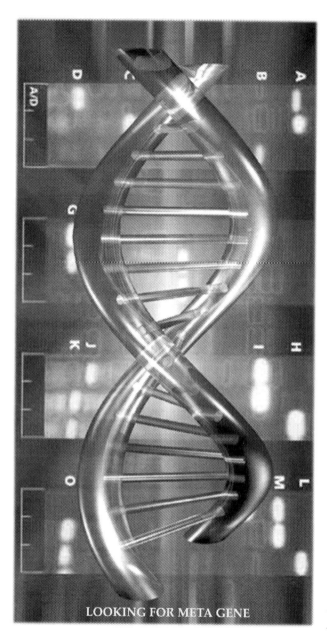

LOOKING FOR META GENE

However, the main purpose of the genetic program that aliens conduct with humans who live on the surface of this planet is to duplicate the effect or to come even close to fully functional Meta gene. If that hasn't been the case they would've surely wiped us from the face of the Earth long time ago. Thus, this which I call both-side problem, has roots in the simple truth that there are not many species in Cosmos that are capable of generating unlimited psychic power in a natural way or in other words with simple use of the single focused thought. Fortunately or unfortunately, humans are one of the rare species in Cosmos that are potentially gifted with Meta gene. Perhaps this will strike you as a shock, but the Grays also possess Meta gene with one basic difference: theirs is in the state of atrophy, which causes them many anomalies through their utilization of mental powers.

This anomaly in their gene responsible for their mental powers comes as a result of all kinds of genetic programs they conducted on themselves trying to save their own race from the frequent exposure to radiation during the numerous cosmic wars they have participated in.

However, they are trying to fix that by crossbreeding with human females and creating a hybrid race with the basic characteristics of Grays. The crossbreeding is the main reason for the physical abductions of human females usually at the age of 14 - 35.

The human genetic material in that particular case can serve as a complement to a part of the Gray's DNA, which is in the state of disintegration. As far as I know, they have already succeeded to create many of these hybrids, but the effect is not as they wanted it to be. The human DNA and the DNA of the Grays are little compatible and the Meta gene is producing only 10% of the real power.

When they abduct a human female for purposes of crossbreeding, they induce pregnancy by extracting alien genetic material and inseminating. Then they remove all conscious recalls of the event from her memory and she will soon realize that she is pregnant not having a clue of how could that happen. After a period of two months or so, the aliens abduct the human female subject again and remove the embryo from her body. Then, aliens put the embryo in vats with special liquid and monitor the further growth of the hybrid.

When the female wakes up the next morning, she will realize that she has had a miscarriage and that her pregnancy is over. Normally, like the first time, the Grays will not leave any conscious memory of their contact. What they do to human race is a real tragedy, and what is even worse is they have been doing it for very long time. As far as the Meta gene is concerned, all we know is that the Grays have a different program for it. First, which is the most important for humans is that the Meta gene can be found in one of 50 thousand people. However, it must be clear to everyone that in every one of these individuals the Meta gene is in a different phase of development and its maximum power is variable.

Anyway, they know about all the humans that possess the Meta gene because they have been monitoring the humanity since the time of the global flood. In most cases, their genetic program for one human subject goes on for thousands of years and they trace him/her from incarnation to incarnation not allowing him/her to leave this solar system. Still, they first allow the subject to reach top level of development and afterwards they abduct the human and extract the Meta gene from his/her DNA. To the best of my knowledge, they have no use of the Meta gene when it is in a latent state but only when it is developed to a certain stage. Finally, they absorb the Meta gene through their skin while they swim in major vats filled with human plasma.

The fact that they are present here on Earth for a very long time leads to the logical question–which stage of development their genetic program is now in. The answer is unknown to me. In my opinion, even the M12 who are the head of the top secret shadow government concerning UFOs and alien top-secret projects do not know the latest achievements of the alien genetic program. However, they have made a mistake signing the alliance with the aliens, which results with great suffering of the human race now.

It may sound the other way around, but if we analyze the problem of UFO appearances above our sky, we can conclude that they do not act very secretly. The secret programs for cover up do the job for them. The top-secret organizations that are led by M12 are so powerful that an average human cannot even detect their existence at all. For 85% of the human population, the UFO phenomenon is only a myth and I do not blame them for that.

The top-secret covered up projects are fully operational and brought to perfection in covering up the data or distorting the truth from the public about the UFO and aliens. Did the M12 made disastrous mistakes that cannot be fixed? – In my opinion, Yes and No.

When they realized the technology the aliens had given them was mostly to be used in telecommunications systems or in flying crafts technology (which they have been testing mostly in the Area 51 for quite some time), it cleared up to them that things are not going well for humans. Now it is probably too late and only an outer intervention could stop the aliens and push them away from this solar system.

Nevertheless, I believe perhaps it is not too late for the humanity and perhaps there is still hope if "The great gathering" really happens as the prophecy of Shambala says. The prophecy says that in 2012 the gathering between the forces of Sirius, Orska, Shambala and some other positive forces from space will happen and the final fight will take place in this galaxy. If that happens, the negative alliance of Reptoids and Grays will be pushed away from this part of the Cosmos for a very long time.

Unfortunately, the Reptoids and the Grays are aware of this possibility and they will surely do whatever it takes to prevent such joining of the positive forces. They will also increase their strength with alien renegades from deep space, which will help them to overcome the attack of the positive alliance. Anyway, everything has its own beginning and end, so the tyranny of negative alien forces will end some day. Therefore, there is nothing else to do but to hope and wait for whatever happens in 2012.

Subchapter 4.16
ASTRAL TRIP TO THE HOME PLANET OF ORSKA

This is one of the best astral trips in my early years of astral traveling. This unforgettable cosmic astral trip happened on July 15, 1995, while I was on vacation in Kushadasi - Turkey. My friends and I arranged with one travel agency in Skopje to find us a nice place close to Kushadasi. It turned up to be a nice hotel about 8 kilometers away from Kushadasi called "Sunny Bay". The days passed wonderfully, the weather served us well and we had really good time.

That night, most of my friends and me decided we should have some rest from our nightlife going out every evening to the famous Pub Street. Most of the pubs and discotheques made the place a pleasant summer environment for the young population coming to Kushadasi from all parts of the world.

However, the night did not go by without any party and we had good time with the people that remained in the hotel. It was about 00:15AM, when the party was over, so I decided that some night swimming in the hotel's swimming pool wouldn't do me any harm before I returned to my room. As soon as I arrived there, I found about 10 people also enjoying the night swimming. The water was nicely warm and while I was swimming on my back I looked upon the stars. They were so beautiful and I knew that this night nothing was going to stop me from going up there.

After about 20 minutes of enjoyable swimming, I left the swimming pool and went to my room. The hotel was not a big one and since there were 14 of us, all friends from Macedonia, we had to take 3 bedrooms on the same floor. When I opened the door, I noticed that the light was off. My friend Sasho was sleeping in his bed, while my other friend Slavcho was absent and probably having fun in the Pub Street.

I lied down on my bed and started a complex pranayama rhythm. Well-trained breathing process and soon I was in the state of Trance. The metabolism of my physical body was on minimum; my heartbeat was so slow, but on the other hand, my mind was fully vital. I was wondering which method to use to leave my physical body and I chose the

Kundalini rising as a quick launch of my astral body. I held back my breath and concentrated on the Muladhara chakra. The same moment my lowest energy center started to pulsate. I was still not breathing, although more than four minutes passed.

The pulsating became stronger and I knew that the Kundalini would rise soon. I was right, and after a few moments a loud zooming sound like "zzzzzz…" appeared. I knew from my previous experience that if my thoughts were calm and filled with cosmic love, the Kundalini would bring the expansion of my consciousness, but if I panicked and showed fear it would get wild and I did not want to remember what that looked like.

Anyway, after I had focused on the cosmic love and everything else I could think of that had positive nature in me, the Kundalini increased its strength in a few waves. The zooming sound became almost unbearable and I thought that I was going to explode by the pressure of the force. I was able to see the dark blue illumination in the bottom of my spine with my inner eye as always before.

The next moment the light started to go up very fast. I remained calm because I knew the moment of the separation with my physical body was coming close. As soon as the light reached my head I just wished to leave my physical body and the same second I felt the start of the separation. The moment I mana- ged to lift up the head of my astral body the zooming sound stopped and I did not feel energy rising anymore.

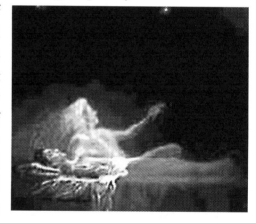

A few moments later, I elevated myself up and found myself floating one meter above my physical body. From the position of flat levitation, I turned around towards my physical body intending to see the way it breathes. I faced myself and noticed that the breathing was very slow but normal. It was interesting that I was in that face-to-face position, more than 20 seconds and started to feel some magnetic force pulling me back into my physical body.

When I backed off a little, the invisible force became weaker. I turned to the right and saw Sasho asleep. It was a potential risk if he awoke, so I decided to project 1% of my consciousness back to my physical body to watch over it. It felt like a tiny part of me had separated and entered my physical body, but despite the separation, there was still a connection. The best way I can describe it, is like you possess thousands of eyes and you put one eye apart, but you sense and see what that single eye is watching, and the opposite.

Note: The reason I did that was because there was a possibility my friend would get up and come up with an idea to wake me up for a chess or card game that we all used to play until dawn. So, if he tried to shake me even once, he probably would cause a real harm to my physical body. In that case my astral body would return to the physical so fast and hit it with full strength. That is something that every advanced astral traveler avoids, because it can easily overload some chakra and cause a serious energy shock which can sometimes produce negative effects that can last for days or even weeks. That is why I left a miniature part of myself to watch on the environment around my physical body. To all my colleagues (astral travelers), I friendly suggest to use this method while they wander in their astral bodies meanwhile their physical bodies are in a room with other people. The astral trip does not lose on quality and the astral body can be alarmed on time if something unexpected appears in the environment of the physical body. However, despite the above-mentioned reason, I was doing it whenever I intended to move very distant from my physical body or use the maximum potentials of my astral body.

As soon as I flew above my friend I went through the wall and found myself in thin air. I flew smoothly, made a little turn to the left and directed myself toward the sea. After a few seconds, I reached the coast and slowly started to gain on altitude. I stopped about 100 meters above the sea surface to see what it looked like from that perspective. The sea was so beautifully illuminated with lots of lights coming from the coast. Obviously the summer night was still young because there were voices and loud music coming from everywhere.

I felt my capacity was growing stronger, so I did not move, and started to prepare myself for the trip towards the stars. In about 15 seconds later, I felt at full power and I gave myself a strong command - "Now, straight to Orska"!

I felt something mighty turned on inside me. The acceleration of my astral body was indescribable and I found myself moving at fantastic speed towards the stars. I passed our Sun in a second. You cannot imagine how beautiful the space is until you have seen it with the eyes of your astral body. I increased the speed more so that everything around me looked exactly like the visual effect of "warp speed" in the science fiction series "Star Track". I was flying in the space tunnel full of stars that appeared as tiny lines because of the high speed. A million words cannot describe the experience. Another amazing thing was that with the help of the small part of my consciousness I had left in my physical body I felt my physical body shaking as if experiencing the same speed too.

There was a high risk that my friend could be awaken by the movement of my physical body and would probably think there was something wrong with me. If that happened it would seriously complicate things for me, but luckily, that did not happen. The astral body of my friend was somewhere in the deep astral, dreaming and completely unaware of the physical environment.

The interesting thing was that whenever I increased the speed, the contact with that tiny part of me weakened or disappeared, and when I slowed-down I felt the connection again. Believe it or not, I flew across star systems, around many clouds with huge proportions and I saw many strange things visible only on the astral plane. Many star constellations appeared and disappeared from my sight in just seconds, so I was looking for the ones that were known to me.

I could only say that it was an astral ride I would remember all my life. After about 40 minutes of unforgettable traveling through the space I came closer to the border of the territory in Orska's control, so I rapidly decreased speed. I was satisfied with myself for arriving up there and remembered my friend Velibor Rabljenovich – also an extraordinary man - sketching a star map to me a long time ago, with all the directions that led to Orska. As several times before, I was just looking for the constellations that I remembered were on the map. Looking from the Earth's surface on the night sky Orska is a planet in the area close to the third planet in a straight line from the constellation of Orion.

It was my fourth time that I astrally traveled to Orska and I knew from experience that they would sense me coming. A few minutes later I spotted their planet about 2 million kilometers straight ahead. Almost the same moment I felt the presence of millions of consciousnesses in the astral plane that were aware of my arrival. From experience, too, I did not want to start a communication without their approval so I just carried on. I noticed an incredible sight in the distance. I saw high frequency of flying crafts with all kinds of shapes and sizes coming and leaving the planet.

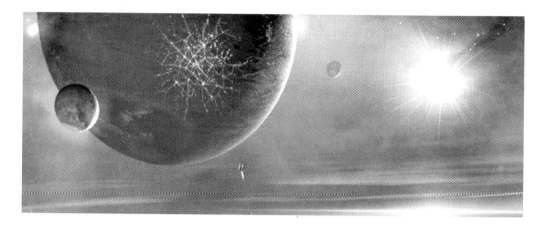

Figuratively speaking – it was breathtaking. The speed they were moving at was amazing. Simply, it felt like being in the middle of a traffic jam with vehicles moving incredibly fast in all directions. When I moved closer to the planet's orbit, I saw a "parking lot" for thousands of flying vehicles. Some had the size of only a few meters and some of them were so big that I assumed they were about 15 kilometers long and about 7 kilometers wide.

The view was unbelievable for me because I knew all I was seeing in front of me was a part of one of the most advanced and oldest civilizations in this part of the galaxy. There were billions of little lights coming from the surface of the planet and it was obvious even this far that there were big cities on the surface of the planet. It represented a clear image of highly developed technology that overcame the wildest science fiction movies. Suddenly, while I was watching at the planet, one spacecraft passed close by me at the distance of about 50 meters. I turned around by reflex just in time to see the craft accelerated and disappeared into subspace. That moment I felt a contact with Orska.

The best way to describe the telepathic contact would be if you could imagine a million of consciousnesses gathered in one and they communicate with you through that one. Deep in my consciousness I started to see visions that contained many transparent balls, pyramids, cubes and other combined geometrical shapes. The geometrical shapes were altered by complicated mathematical schemes, which at the end, were also replaced by the complex code systems.

While I was receiving the geometrical shapes and mathematical schemes I felt OK, but when the code streams started to appear I felt something like pressure in my consciousness. They started with simple codes and as my consciousness was adapting, they continued with codes that were more complex. It appeared strange to me, but somehow my consciousness perfectly knew them all, by some natural way as some hidden software installed deep inside me, but out of my reach. The communication started to go smoothly and the pressure was gone. I understood everything they transmitted to me so clearly as if I knew that code language better than the ones I speak on Earth. The total communication lasted about thirty minutes or more and most of it would be:

--**Orska**- Welcome! You should know by now that your life force is very strong considering the fact that you possess a "water vessel" which is not fully developed. We congratulate you for that.

-**Me**- Thank you, but I'm aware that I still have so much to learn.

--Correct.

-Can you explain to me, please why do you use the term water vessel for my physical body?

--Biologically, the life forms that live inside the water vessels on the surface of your planet are offspring of the water creatures who were brought to Earth 5 millions years ago. The origin of those creatures was a planet that belongs to the Vega star system.

My first logical conclusion was that they were calling the human physical body a water vessel because two thirds of it is water, but I was wrong.

-Why did you mention the water vessel on the surface of Earth?

-- Another civilization inside your planet possesses a water vessel, too.

-Is there any difference between them?

--Yes. In the interior of Earth, the water vessel is in the original form while on the surface it is genetically modified.

-What do you mean by genetically modified?

--The Gray collective had made a genetic modification on the DNA molecule on most of the water vessels that survived the global flood. The main purpose for doing that was to limit the capacity of the water vessel's brain and after the genetic modification the water vessels were no longer capable of using large spectrum of their original mental abilities. The only exceptions were the survivors from the Atlantis.

-When did the global flood happen?

--6000 years ago.

-Is the present state of our DNA permanently damaged and will we ever again be capable of using our full mental capacity?

--No. But to regain back your potentials a new global genetic modification should be conducted.

- Did you mean Agharta when you mentioned the inner civilization?

--Yes. A very high cosmic life force by the name of Sanat Kumara is present there in the main center you already know as Shambala. The great "Green crystal", which is the leader of our civilization, communicates with Sanat Kumara whenever there is a need or a purpose for it.

-Does Sanat Kumara possess a water vessel?

--He takes every form that he considers appropriate. The most important thing for you is to know that his life force arrived from the planet Venus when Shambala was still on the surface.

-What location was Shambala situated in then?

--Today you call that place the dessert Gobi. In those times, the dessert was a big sea. The surface part of Shambala was located on an island close to the northern coast.

-Is the Shambala only a city?

--Much more than that.

-Why did Sanat Kumara arrive on Earth?

--In those times, the aggressive forces of the Reptoids and Grays wanted to destroy the solar system, so the help of the Sanat Kumara and his numerous followers was needed to prevent the destruction.

-Was there a chance for a peaceful solution of the crisis?

--No. The civilization of the Reptoids is spread all over this and other galaxies and wherever they go, they approach with violence and without negotiations. They are considering the whole Cosmos their property and they are determined to achieve that goal. The civilization of the Grays is in inferior position to the Reptoids in the relationship and they usually just follow their orders.

-Why do the Grays have to obey the Reptoids?

--There are many species of the Grays and only three of them are slaves to the Reptoids. Those three species obedient to Reptoids are genetically reprogrammed to do so. If the Grays do not obey them, they will be destroyed.

-Do the Reptoids conduct genetic engineering on the water vessels that live on the surface of Earth?

--Rarely. The Grays are doing most of the genetics on the surface water vessels for them.

-Does that mean that they cannot abduct the water vessel from Agharta?

--Yes. There are electromagnetic shields around the Agharta, which prevent the teleportation of the water vessel from Agharta directly to their ships.

-So, are you telling me that we are constantly exposed to abductions from the Grays?

--No. On periodical basis when they consider there is a need for it.

-How do they realize that?

--The Grays implant a small electronic device in every subject they consider necessary for the genetic program, which allows them to locate and monitor the subject all the time. When there is a need for abduction they just teleport the subject directly to their ship.

-You mean implants?

--Yes.

-How come we cannot detect them?

--During the abduction process, tiny objects are implanted on different places into the water vessel but most commonly into the head of the subject by direct penetration through the nose. They are visible only if for some other reasons the subject takes what you call x-ray image close to the spot where the implant is put.

-How come there is no infection and the tissue does not rot, because the implant is a foreign object in the organism after all?

--In most cases, there is a tiny gray shell around the implant designed to make a compatibility of the device with the environmental tissue and produces nerve stimulation as well.

-Do they use implants only to monitor and teleport the water vessels?

--Depends on the device. Most of the implants are constructed to serve many purposes, but besides the monitoring and locating activity they are designed to control the behavior of the subject, cause blackouts in his or her consciousness or even eliminate him/her completely if they consider it necessary.

-Does my water vessel contain an implant?

--Not yet. Otherwise, you would not be here now in your astral form communicating with us. Yet, that does not mean that the Grays do not possess other technological and mental methods to track you down if they want to.

-I understand. I am curious: does the whole underground world on Earth belong to the Agharta?

--No. In the major parts of the continents that you call North and South America today, there are many underground bases, which mostly belong to the species of the Reptoids and Grays.

-Do you mean there are other alien races present and active on Earth?

--Yes, besides the Reptoids and the Grays, there are four that have lived underground for a very long time and two alien races that land on your planet periodically.

-Besides the two alien races known to me, are other aliens friendly oriented to the subjects that live on the surface of Earth?

--Only two races are compassioned to the water vessels but they avoid contacts with them because of the Reptoids.

-What is the relationship of Agharta with all of the rest alien species?

--They are constantly in conflict with most of them. The Reptoids are determined to finish the extinction of the survivors of the Lemurian race.

-The subjects that live in Agharta are the offspring of Lemuria?

--Yes. After the massive destructive war, the survivors of the Lemurian race retreated to deep underground inside the planet.

-Who was the enemy of the Lemuria in the global war?

--Atlantis, Reptoids who were mostly situated on the planet still orbiting the Sun between Mars and Jupiter at the time, Grays who had their colonies on Earth and many other smaller groups whose goal was terror in this part of the galaxy.

-Had Lemuria an alliance too?

--Yes. Lemuria's allies were Mu, Sirius, Orska, Venus, Mars, and other smaller civilizations whose goal was peace in this part of the galaxy.

-So, the negative alliance won?

--Depends on the point of view. Eventually, Earth was left flooded. The Atlantis and Mu were destroyed. Most of the Lemurian race managed to retreat underground and escaped the destruction. The planet orbiting the Sun between Mars and Jupiter with the 80% of the Reptoids was completely wiped out. Mars was almost completely destroyed on the surface. Venus became a death planet, Sirius suffered great damage; we lost 40% of ours and the Grays suffered a severe loss. You can come up with only one conclusion – nobody won, but everybody lost.

-Did Reptoids and Grays leave our solar system after the war?

--Only for short. Soon after the war was over, they returned even in greater number but there was not much to conquer any more. Only 10% of them stayed ever since.

-Is there any possibility to push these negative forces out of this part of the galaxy?

--Yes. That should happen in the year 2012.

-Do you mean by military operation or by something else?

--Both.

-Is the Green crystal a God?

In that moment, I felt something powerful in my consciousness I was feeling all the time since the communications had begun, but in the background like a silent observer.

Green crystal---I am what I am.

I was surprised of the strength of its thoughts. They were echoing themselves like they were coming from everywhere and not just from one source.

-I apologize if I have offended you.

I did not get any approval or disapproval, but it continued to communicate, as if it had not received my apology.

---I am only a transmitter of the will on the Ultimate force of creation that your race calls a God.

-How old are you?

---If you mean physically, almost 8 billions of years.

-How come this planet is not visible with the telescopes we have on Earth?

---Advanced technology.

-Do entities of Orska possess sexes like male and female?

---No. They get their physical carrier from me.

-You mean they are reproducing through you?

---No. They are all individual cosmic life forms. I only materialize the physical carrier for them.

-How long does that physical carrier last?

---2000 years.

-Do they have a need for food like the water vessel?

---Not in the way your race is consuming it. They do not have a mouth like your species because they feed themselves on the natural energy that floats freely throughout the whole space.

-Do they possess a brain?

---Yes. It is smaller than the brain of the water vessel but 100% functional and fully under control.

That moment I received a complete hologram vision of what their physical carrier looks like. It was like computer 3D simulation with lots of statistics in it. Although I have had close contacts with them many times before, the data the Green Crystal was revealing was unknown to me. I will try to describe the being from Orska for you:

It is humanoid by shape. The skin is completely white. The form of the head of the entity of Orska is similar to the one of the Gray but the color of the eyes is different. The entity from Orska possesses green metallic colored eyes. Its arms are longer than the ones of the Gray and with two fingers on each hand. The legs are very thin and the entity has only three toes on its foot. Generally speaking the entity of Orska is likable and does not leave aggressive or even scary impression like a Gray does.

-Are all the citizens of Orska active in the astral dimension?

---Yes. They spend most of their lives in the dimensions much higher than the one you are in now. As you already know, our civilization is one of the oldest in this part of the galaxy and since the beginning of our presence here, we have had full access to all the dimensions that exist in this Universe.

-Can you help me complete my training?

---Only to a certain point. You have to dislocate your water vessel into Shambala, to achieve the goals that I see from your consciousness you want to achieve.

-How should I find the entrance to Shambala?

---It is known to me that the water vessels from Shambala made several contacts with you and explained to you very clearly what you should do. So, why are you asking me about the same subject?

-Forgive me, but I want to be sure.

---If you are pure of heart and if your mind is clear, you will see the things that a shadowed mind cannot.

-I understand.

---Be prepared to encounter some resistance during your dislocation there. The Grays are aware of your potential and they will do everything they consider necessary to stop you from reaching Shambala.

-Can you or Shambala protect me against them on my trip up there?

---Only to a certain level. During your dislocation to Shambala you must control your mind as never before because the Grays will hit it hard. If you manage to keep the control of your mind and block the Grays' influence you will succeed. Otherwise, you will fail.

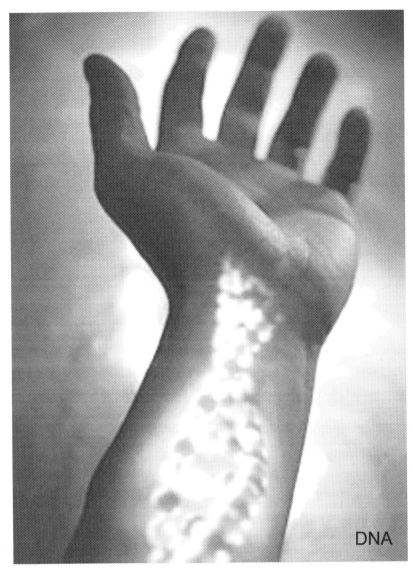

DNA

-Why do they find me so important?

---Two aspects. The first is because your DNA contains a gene that an average surface water vessel does not possess. The other one is because your consciousness contains major data concerning the knowledge that even some older civilizations than ours have left in you.

-So, that is why I feel filled with something very heavy but I cannot reach that area even if I want to. It seems to me that there is a blockade of some kind like a code missing or something similar. Well, that explains the effect that very often, with no particular reason, data are coming from the depth of my consciousness and I am sure I have never acquired that knowledge during this incarnation. What does that knowledge consist of?

   ---For now, the knowledge that you possess is sufficient. You will be told the rest of it when you reach Shambala.

   -Is there anything else I should know?

   ---When you will be searching for the entrance to Shambala, do not forget to believe with all your heart that you will find it. Only if your heart is pure and filled with unconditional love and compassion you will succeed. Do not think of your family because if your heart is not determined and split in, you will fail. The Grays will hit there the most.

   -Thank you.

   ---You should go now.

Suddenly I felt the collective of the consciousnesses had retreated from my consciousness. It was time for my return and I said to myself: "I'm going home"! Meanwhile, I was accumulating astral energy. I started to wonder how long it would take me to reach Earth without using teleportation. It was a good chance for me to see how fast I could go. Thus, the moment I felt in full capacity, I turned around to the direction I arrived from and moved myself at top speed. Then, the real speed flight began. I felt familiar liquid feeling along the surface of my astral body because of the fast acceleration. I think that the best association of the speed I was moving at would be the one in the movie "Star Gate" when Daniel and the rest of the military personnel had entered the portal.

So many star constellations had changed in front of my eyes in a split of a second. I had never felt so powerful in my life before. The things I had seen moving through space at that speed, I believe are something that every astral traveler wishes to see and experience. I had passed across many asteroid fields, light fogs, planets and all kinds of space appearances. That was something I would never forget. I was overwhelmed with joy the moment I recognized our solar system while I was passing close to our Sun. I could not believe myself I had traveled 33 light years for less than 15 seconds. I had beaten my personal speed record and that meant so much to me because it had given me a sense I was improving myself.

   While I was thinking about the time that took me to return from Orska and beating my speed record, a smile lit up my astral face when I started diving into the Earth atmosphere. I sensed the tiny part I had left in my physical body again and I locked on at that signal. The next moment I found myself at about 500 meters above the area where the hotel "Sunny Bay" was.

   The sea looked so beautiful from that perspective. I pushed myself into free fall and in a few seconds, I stopped 5 meters from the balcony where my physical body was. I passed through the balcony quickly and entered the hotel room. I flew above my friend and by pulling a somersault I jumped directly into my physical body. I felt a strong strike and my whole physical body shook. The return of the physical feeling was so good that I opened my eyes in five seconds. I remained completely still not moving a millimeter, recalling even the tiniest detail of my astral trip. When I made sure that I remembered everything, I got up from my bed. My friend Sasho was still asleep and the bed of my other friend was still empty. My other roommate, Slavcho had probably been stuck with some girl in Kushadasi and would probably come back the next day around noon. I went on the balcony and looked at the blue velvet, clear summer sky. I felt like crying from all the happiness. I felt like I was special and a part of some higher cosmic plan. The power of the speed was still holding me tight and that felt so good. I looked at the stars again and said to myself: "So, it is obvious now that all my roads lead to Shambala."

GOBI DESERT

Subchapter 4.17
SPACE EXPLORATION

It was on the night of March 28, 1996 when my friends and I went to the "Hard Rock" discotheque, which at the time was the most famous one in Skopje. The bad part was I was not feeling well because during the night I had a strong stomachache.

Anyhow, the nightlife ended for me somewhere around 03:00AM when I arrived back home. The moment I entered my apartment I felt even worse and I was forced to throw up, so I hurried up towards my bathroom. That was a relief and I started to feel much better. My brother and my mother had probably fallen asleep long ago, so I walked tiptoed on the parquet trying hard not to wake them up. As soon as I closed the door of my room behind my back, I went to the balcony to get some fresh air because the throwing up had left bad taste in my throat and my mouth. The stars in the sky were so beautiful for observing but it was so cold that I had to return to my room after just 10 seconds standing there. I felt much better and said to myself: "I had not been anywhere in the astral world for the past two days, so it should not be so bad for me to go and take some astral excursion."

I lied on the bed and started to make the necessary preparations for a quick launch of my astral body. I blocked all my thoughts and in a few seconds, my mind became completely empty. Soon, many astral pictures that can be used for the remote viewing or as portals for a direct astral projection started appearing on my mental screen. It was a well-trained method for me. Shortly after, I managed to project my consciousness through one of the first astral pictures that appeared on my mental screen using strong mental efforts to pull the astral picture towards my third eye and pushing my consciousness towards the picture forcefully at the same time.

The astral trip I made did not last long, two hours maybe at the most. I cannot describe fully all the details I have seen and experienced during my astral flight because it will take more than 30 pages, so I will stick to the most important ones.

The first thing that happened as soon as I had blocked all my thoughts and my mind had become completely empty was the appearance of a picture on my mental screen, which in fact was an astral reflection of a blue tunnel. That tunnel exists on the border of the astral and mental plane and after having recognized it I projected myself directly into it. The next moment I found myself in the middle of the tunnel that was rotating in the clockwise direction. Its structure is so amazing because it consists of both the astral and the mental substance. It looked like millions of jellyfish, joint together in one great, beautiful blue-colored unity.

The tunnel vibrated so high vibrations while rotating that my astral body started to spin in the same direction. The speed of the rotation of the tunnel and my own was synchronized to perfection. It led straight up and I was climbing increasingly when I spotted the white light. I knew the light would not let me pass if I remained in my astral body so I had to replace it with my mental body (which possesses subtler vibrations). While I was moving up, I started to concentrate on my heart. A source of the white light started to appear from the chest of my astral body when I released the cosmic love that was so deep inside me. A few moments later, I became a white light with human contours. I was in my mental body now and I was moving towards the light at the end of the tunnel. The distance was decreasing and when I came about 50 meters from the white light, I made a stupid mistake. A memory image of a similar white light I have seen so close to Earth's atmosphere appeared in my consciousness. In a split of a second, the ambient of the blue tunnel and the white light at its end disappeared and I found myself in space above our planet.

I wondered how I could have been so stupid to make such a mistake. I had missed a clear opportunity to explore the mental world. It was not all the same to me because every time I had entered the world above the astral world I felt overjoyed that sometimes I wondered should I come back to my physical body. The presence of so much consciousness in one place filled with so much love had made the mental world so beautiful that I would not exaggerate to call it "A place where Heaven begins."

However, it was no use crying over spilled milk anymore. I loved space exploration almost the same as the mental plane. The space was offering me an infinite number of places to explore and with no hesitation I flew towards the Moon at great speed. A few seconds later, I approached the surface of the Moon and continued to fly over it at solid speed completely enjoying myself. The flight over the Moon's surface was offering me many interesting sites but the craters took the most of my interest. This time I did not encounter any UFOs, although I was seeing them almost every time I was coming even close to the Moon. I continued flying in Zigzag over the rocky surface for about 10 minutes more and then I increased my altitude and went up again.

I did not want to go to the other side of the Moon because I knew there was the main base of the Grays where from they were observing the activities on Earth. Judging by my previous experience, the contact with them had never brought any good, so I tried to avoid them as much as possible. The silence, rarely disturbed by the sounds of tiny meteors passing close from time to time gave Earth indescribable beauty that made me just look at it for a while. The Sun was shining brightly and in the moment when I almost decided to move towards our star, I remembered promising myself to visit Mars. I was in no hurry, so I was not in the mood to teleport myself directly there. I wanted to travel at lower speed and not to miss all the indescribable sites that our solar system offered on the way there. So, I moved my astral body towards the red planet. The flight there took a while and I really enjoyed myself moving through space. I thought: "Wow, if only I could bring a camera with me and show these sites to my friends… all of them would remain speechless."

I was constantly changing maneuvers during my flight for more pleasure. (The astral traveler, who has not yet experienced this, does not have a slightest idea how wonderful all this is. You are a free soul flying through space and your physical body is somewhere distant on your home planet). In about one hour, I arrived at Mars, which seemed to me two times smaller than Earth. The planet was almost all red covered as a result of the red dust on the surface and it did not look very hostile to me.

However, it happened that my course took me in the direction of the major scar of Mars visible from far away. Seen from above, the red planet had many scars on its surface. You do not have to be a genius to

determine that the planet has suffered a massive destruction because of some terrible war that happened a very long time ago. Although it was an interesting spot to explore, I had not come for the scar. I had come to visit the region of Cydonia. While those thoughts were rushing through my consciousness, I made some strong effort to teleport myself above that area.

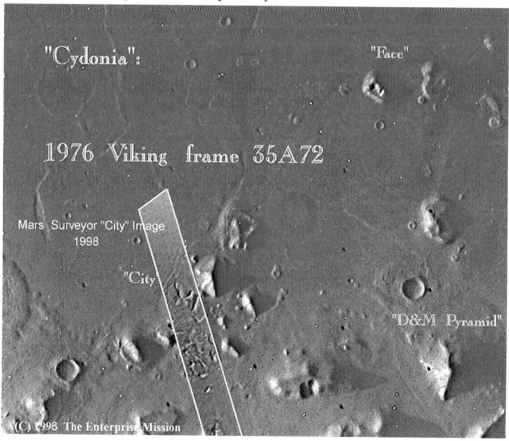

Not having finished my wish, I was already there. Sensation beyond words passed through me, when I recognized the most mysterious spot visible on the surface of Mars. Down below me I saw the huge pentagon pyramid and when I looked more up I saw the great monumental structure - The Face of Cydonia.

For the record, I had passed here for more than 10 times before during my previous astral trips and each time I had come here I was wondering if something had changed on the structures. I looked a little to the left and I saw a complex of 12 pyramids that looked as if they were part of a major city that once had existed there. In the complex, five pyramids looked bigger than the rest of them and it was quite obvious that some advanced civilization had built those monumental structures.

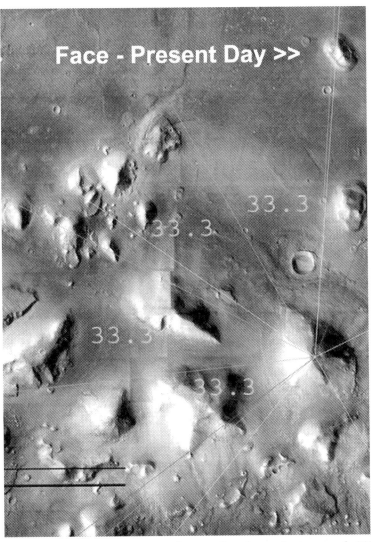

Face - Present Day >>

From the complex of the 12 pyramids to the East another monument was visible to me. High above the desert plane there was an amazing mound of the soil of the planet. To observe all that while my physical body was on Earth was an incredible feeling. I focused again on the sphinx face and moved myself very fast straight to it. A strong sensation went through my astral body while I was dropping my altitude towards the face. When I reached about 500 meters above the face, I stopped. While I was levitating above the majestic monument, a monologue started in my consciousness:

"No matter what efforts the powerful secret government puts to cover up their artificial origin, the pyramids and this human face can not hide the simple truth, which is so obvious. The artificial origin of those monumental structures is so obvious that every 10-year-old child would notice the difference instantly. It is also obvious that the face is not in the same condition it was in 1976, when the Viking 1 took a photograph of it from space. It is about 1.5 kilometers wide and about 1.3 kilometers long, but despite the fact that it still looks like a human face, it does not possess the sharp lines any more. Looking at it from this perspective it seems that somebody has ruined the monument on purpose. Pyramids on the other hand resemble those on Earth in the region of Giza. Anyway, it is a solid proof that life existed on some of the other planets of our solar system."

"The City": Surveyor Confirms the Existence of "Giza scale" Pyramids on Mars ...

GIZA   CYDONIA

(C) 1998 The Enterprise Mission

I hovered above the face for about 5 minutes, and then I decided to go on and moved myself to the western horizon at very high speed. It took me 15 minutes of flying at very high speed before I encountered

240

huge channels on the surface of Mars. I slowed rapidly wondering whether I should go towards the stars or straight down to explore the channels. I decided to explore what is down there and cautiously headed in that direction. It was interesting that the channels were straight angled. Most of the channels differed in depths, but the one I went in was about 2 kilometers wide, 3 kilometers deep and about 30 kilometers long. I found it very interesting that it had no ending point. It continued in straight angle to the right connecting to the next channel. It was amazing how smooth the walls of the channel were and it was obvious they were not made by the hand of nature but by some very advanced technology. I arrived to the end of the channel very soon and made a quick straight angle maneuver to the right, then continued to fly into the next channel.

The next one was connected with another channel and I realized that it was not just a few channels but a whole net of channels in front of me. Suddenly, when I was flying in one of the channels I noticed that the surface of the channel started glowing with some strange dark blue light. Haragei – my inner sense of potential danger started to alarm me and by reflex I went straight up away from the channel. In less than a second I reached a safe distance of about 200 meters above the channel, just in time to see as the dark blue light was materializing into a laser beam at the same point I felt the danger. The blue beam reached the ending point of the channel in a split of a second, but it did not hit the wall. It was amazing to see the laser beam turning in a straight angle towards the next channel as if redirected from some invisible mirror. The same happened with the next channel and the laser beam had passed through all the channels visible to me from that perspective.

In a second, it was all over. The laser beam disappeared somewhere in the distance and the dark blue radiance was no longer visible. I was wondering what would have happened to me if I had stayed in the channel. I assumed that somehow the channel that was built by some advanced technology with so subtle sensors had sensed my life force like an intruder and the defense mechanism had activated by default. I decided that further exploration of the channels was not a good idea. After I gave one last look to the surface of the planet (which was hiding many mysteries), I strongly moved at cosmic speed and left

Mars. The next moment the red planet behind me remained just a small red dot. I felt so powerful moving at that speed impossible to be described to someone that has not experienced it yet. From the physical perspective, I would say it was way beyond the adrenalin rush.

After a few seconds, Earth appeared and I slowed my movement drastically. Still, the speed was high and I went in a search for the Adriatic Sea as a guiding point to easily find the territory of Macedonia. The moment I came very close to Earth where from I could easily observe the relief below, I realized that if I continued flying down on this course, I would land somewhere in Japan, so I strongly moved west. I increased my speed again and in a second or two, I spotted the Adriatic Sea bellow me. The next moment I pulled a fast dive towards the Macedonian territory. Two seconds later I spotted the lights of Skopje and thought: "I'm home!" Then, I continued to move towards the settlement of Novo Lisiche and very fast arrived above my building, made a sharp maneuver and stopped at two meters distance from my balcony. Very smoothly, I continued straight, and in a few seconds I passed through the window of my room and landed directly into my physical body. I opened my eyes instantly and with a smile on my face I took my diary and wrote the whole astral trip down.

Comment: The most common cases of UFOs I was encountering around the Moon were disk shaped and in the shape of the letter T. I had rarely encountered flying crafts in the shape of a black triangle with three strong lights, visible only from one side. It is interesting to mention that although I was seeing black triangles rarely, every time I had seen such a craft it had always had the same destination - one crater on the dark side of the Moon. It is my belief that humans pilot these black triangle crafts, and these are the ones tested in the Area 51.

To the best of my knowledge, Russians and Americans are present on one base on the dark side of the Moon (which is never visible from the Earth), despite the major bases of the Grays. It is a part of the exchanging technology program and it is one of the top-secret projects hidden from the public knowledge.

As far as Mars is concerned, in contrast to public opinions I can say that when you come closer to the surface you find it mysteriously alive. Even on my first visit to the red planet, I noticed huge underground activity. It became clear to me that many old bases existed under the surface and some of them were old maybe more than 500000 years and still active for that matter. However, it seems to be the same technological signature as the one that can be found on the Jupiter satellites: Europe and Io, but that is a completely different story. When we look at the sphinx face of Mars, it is obvious that in 1976, it presented a strong and unbreakable proof of life on other planets.

In my opinion, the M 12 have ordered the human face with the teardrop on one of the cheeks to be distorted so that it would leave the impression of a natural anomaly. Thus, it is quite possible that they have done it with alien assistance or even with their own star crafts, which they have recovered from UFO crashed-sites or with those, which have been part of the exchanging technology program.

Subchapter 4.18
WALKING THROUGH PLANES

Date: August 28, 1998. My beloved wife Svetlana was deeply asleep for more than an hour and probably dreaming. I thought it would not be bad to go on some astral excursion. To pull that off was easy for me, because before I went to sleep I did short zener training, which increased the strength of my mind that on the other hand allowed me a quick jump into the astral plane. I brought my physical body into the state of Trance and blocked the whole thinking process in my mind. Almost instantly, astral reflections in the form of psychic pictures started to appear on my mental screen and I projected my consciousness in one of the first that came along.

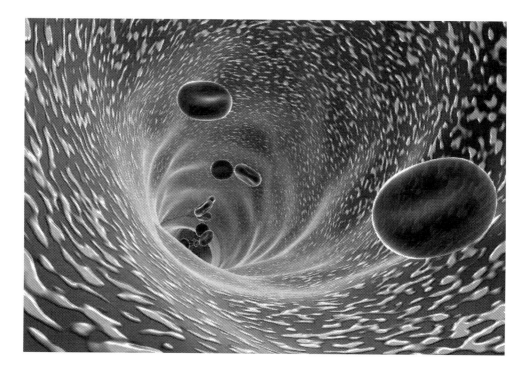

A moment after the astral projection took place I found myself in the lower dimensions of the area known to the public by the name - Lower astral. This is the area where the ambient is not so pleasant for describing and it is an astral settlement of many negative forces. I was perfectly aware that I arrived in the part of the astral plane where the dark power ruled and my whole astral body was experiencing an unpleasant feeling. No matter how long you have been present on the astral plane, every time you come here, you can rarely remain indifferent.

A huge, at least 100 meters wide cavern started to open in front of me, which could mean just one thing: dark zone, filled with wide abysses, caves, dark astral structures with tunnel character, large variety of negative forces and all kinds of dark astral creatures.

I was not afraid and slowly went in. The ambient was dark and it did not promise anything nice. I did not fly very fast but I was alert all the time. After a while, a contact came from nowhere. A giant disgusting transparent face appeared in front of me with evil eyes shining with a strong red light. "The face of a demon" - a thought flashed in my consciousness. His thoughts were dark and the next moment a strong echo appeared in my consciousness: "Who allowed you to come here?"

I remained calm and I simply ignored his question. I did not stop but I increased my speed and continued to go deeper into the cavern. The face was moving alongside and it stopped at the same distance in front of me. Deep down I knew the potential dialog with the demon would make me vulnerable and it would not bring anything good. Therefore, I did not let a single atom of the two-sided astral energy to stream between us. I knew it would allow him to use it as a bridge and attack me with all his strength.

Still, he attacked anyway. Haragei was screaming deep inside me. The first thing I felt was a high density of negative astral substance around the eyes of the demon's transparent face and a moment later I felt a strong wave of energy coming my way. I felt my consciousness very powerful and pure and at the same time, I felt it getting ready for the fight somehow in its natural way. My astral body flashed instantly bright light and a feeling of strong charge of cosmic love passed through me.

A few moments later, I lost my human contours and became a blue-white fireball that moved relatively fast. The vibrations of my astral body were altered by mental vibrations, which resulted with my new outfit – my mental body. Although I was moving in my mental body now, a natural process of teleportation started to appear to take my consciousness into the higher planes because of the improper vibrations, but I did not allow that and simply blocked the teleportation process.

I had felt the astral world belonged to everyone since long ago, and in this particular moment, I wanted to explore the dark zone. Because of my mental form, the demon could not hurt me, so I did not feel any fear nor I had even paid any attention to the incredible strong mental waves coming from his eyes. He focused his energy waves directly to hit me but instead, they just went through me and they were starting to vaporize somewhere behind me. My consciousness was in deep harmony with my blue-white burning flame body and it did not feel a single slight emotion of anger or even hate toward the giant transparent face.

There are not many words to describe the experience but the closest I can come up with is like I had melted in some strange light which was a part of the infinite net of lights that flow along the whole Universe. I increased my speed rapidly and just when I was passing through the giant face, I addressed him in a strong mental voice: "It is irrelevant to me if you try to stop me. I will pass through you anyway!"
In that same moment, I heard an angry but painful roar throughout the whole cave. The face of the demon stayed behind me and I continued further in the dark zone. While I was flying at high speed, I noticed that some of the caves I was passing through were very wide and some were less wide. Most of them were with the skeleton character and very similar to some scenes in horror movies. It was a very unpleasant sight because those skeleton caves actually had the head of a bull and the body of a human and most of them had long tails.

The smallest of the skeleton caves were about 30 meters long and 20 meters wide and the bigger ones were more than 200 meters long and wide almost the same. I increased my speed to the point where I could still follow where I was flying through. The sites that started to open in front of me were incredible. The skeleton caves were not visible any more and now I was flying in the caves with dark walls. In contrast to the skeleton caves, the walls of these caves were not transparent and the only light was coming from my mental body. Many inscriptions were there on the walls, probably written in some ancient language dating from the time when myths and legends were reality.

"Unbelievable sight" – I thought. As I was going deeper and deeper, disgusting creatures of all kinds started to appear. Most of them were the gatekeepers of their part of the dark zone and I ignored them all. I was very deep into the dark zone, which was only an outside shell of Hell, when I felt the Haragei alarming me to a critical point. A feeling of strong evil power everywhere around me started to affect my mental body and I decided that it was deep enough and if I went any deeper there was a possibility not to be able to get out.

I did not want to find out the answer to that question, so I gave a strong command to myself for leaving the dark zone. The moment the command was given, I felt my mental body forcing its way up as if catapulted. Luckily, I did not encounter any problems on the way up, which surprised me because I was very deep in the lower astral levels. The ambient around me started to fade away rapidly and I passed through the hard ground at such a speed as if running away from Hell. Huh, and I was.

I came out into daylight. In less than a second I passed through the clouds in the sky and continued to climb up. I saw my mental body retreating and my astral human contours returning. A feeling of great power, which allowed me incredible fast moving through the space, overwhelmed me.

A few seconds later, I passed the blue atmosphere of our planet and reached space. Earth radiated such beautiful light into space and it never seized to amaze me every time I was leaving or returning to the planet. I stopped and started to observe Earth more closely. "It is wonderful"- I said to myself. Interested, I followed some group of smaller clouds passing above a part of Europe. After a few minutes of enjoying myself in the pretty sights, I decided to perform a free fall towards the Atlantic Ocean.

I moved at high speed and when I reached altitude of about 30 kilometers I started to fall in free style. Wow, try to describe that sensational feeling. I was falling for so long with a great feeling of complete freedom. The only thing I can say to every one capable of astral traveling is: " go and try this".

As seconds went by, I was falling faster and faster and the culmination happened when 2 meters above the water I stopped and froze. I was hovering with my head down towards the water and I knew I would never forget this experience. Down ahead of me I was watching the shiny sky and up I was observing the ocean surface. I turned myself upside down and took a normal position. I was in the mood for quick maneuvers, so I jumped about 1000 meters higher and stopped again. I was above high sea somewhere in the middle of the South American and African continent. I spotted the beautiful morning rays, which gave the ocean surface even more wonderful look. The weather was mostly sunny and clear and smaller groups of clouds were visible in some places.

That gave me a funny idea and I went towards the group of clouds. I started having fun flying above and beneath them but most of the fun I had was when I was moving through the holes in the clouds pulling all kinds of maneuvers. I increased my speed to the East rapidly and very soon, I encountered another group of clouds. I repeated the same fun on them, too but this time at a higher speed. After I had passed them, I continued my flight to the East.

The morning Sun was so beautiful from that perspective. I was flying at the same altitude as the Sun was in the sky. I stopped instantly and froze.

Again, as during the free fall I had pulled earlier, I did not feel a millimeter of inertia from the sudden stop despite the fact that I was moving very fast. A smile lit up my astral face because I was satisfied with myself since it cleared up to me that I had reached a very promising point of understanding the astral science. I looked towards the horizon and again, from the zero point I moved myself with strong power. I dropped my altitude and after a few moments I was flying 30 meters above the water. I accelerated to a certain point where I did not know if I was moving further above the water or the ocean was moving towards me. Soon I noticed the land approaching rapidly and I reduced speed. The west coast of Africa looked phenomenal. In less than a second I pulled strong sides maneuver and continued with a parallel flight above the African coast. I was moving fast, at least 700 Km/h and that also felt very powerful. Soon I dropped my speed to a normal of about 300 Km/h. I assumed I was somewhere over Angola judging by the coastline. The ambient beneath me was very interesting but I enjoyed mostly the wonderful sandy beaches untouched by people. From time to time, I flew above some small settlements but the dominant characteristic of most of the places close to the coast, were the uninhabited forest regions.

After a while, I spotted a big tourist cruiser anchored near a beautiful reef. Although the reef was not so wide, the water was obviously deep enough for a ship with those proportions to anchor. The moment I turned left and directed myself towards the ship, I felt that something had changed in the environment around my physical body. I was fully aware that if Svetlana tried to wake me up it could cause many problems to my astral body especially during the returning process.

Note: *The astral body forced to return into the physical body from many reasons like physical shaking etc., can cause anomaly in the energy balance of the chakras while the joining process is going on. In such cases the aura rapidly tightens itself and a moment later it stretches itself out of the normal dimensions and in the end, it is pulled back to the normal dimensions. In practice, this process has shown as tremendously unpleasant experience for every astral traveler. It is a rare case, but sometimes can cause the energy strike, which can hit some chakra and cause even physical consequences.*

However, I did not want to risk a non-regular return to my physical body, so I concentrated on my room. The next moment, I found myself elevating above the bed in the bedroom. Svetlana turned to my side intending to hug me. While her arm was moving over my physical body, I quickly joint with it. I opened my physical eyes just in time to see my wife's arm hugging me. Just in time – I said to myself. I was staring at the ceiling and wondered if anybody would ever believe my words that all this was possible and completely real as everything else in the physical reality. "In any case, a good astral trip" – I concluded.

Subchapter 4.19
A WORD OR TWO ABOUT MY ASTRAL TRIPS

In contrast to many authors of the related subject, I decided to present the astral plane through my own life experience as best as I could. I tried to cover most of the topics how does it feel to be there, the way the abilities of the astral body are used, what kind of life forms are present there, what kind of danger can one encounter there and how to deal with it, etc.

Anyway, no matter how hard I have tried to simplify the human ability to astrally project and walk through the astral plane, it will be a hard task to understand how all that can be possible to achieve for a human who does not have at least one similar experience. Therefore, for many of my astral trips I have mentioned in this book, I have also given a comment where from the reader can understand more easily how is it possible.

Still, I have to mention that the astral experiences I have put in this book are only a part of my early stage of astral traveling and I have classified them as weaker ones. In many of them, my contacts with alien forms dominate, but that is my reality and it does not mean that every one of you will meet them on the astral plane. In fact, if you reach high level of astral development and still you do not meet them, you do not have the slightest idea of how lucky you are. However, if that happens to be your case, always be aware that it does not mean we are alone on this planet. From my point of view, we have never been alone. So, the only question remains – What shall we do about it?

Anyway, I have put my weaker astral trips in the book on purpose because if I had put the ones that are more recent, many of you would not believe such things were possible to be performed in the astral world. Nevertheless, believe my words when I say that those astral trips are only a child's playing in the backyard compared to other things that a human can perform with his or her astral body. Still, the truth is that the top achievements of the astral science are reachable only for the most persistent and determined candidates. I have been honest with you throughout the whole book, so my obligation is to tell you that for developing the middle abilities of the astral body 5 years are needed, maybe more or little less, but for the top abilities it takes much longer. There are exceptions to this non-written rule but in average, the picture looks like that.

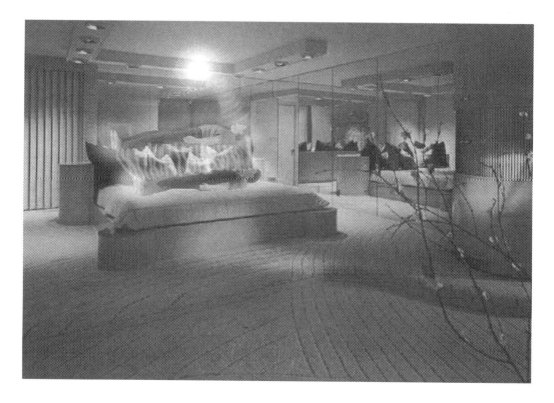

Thus, for a true candidate, practicing astral projection means his/her constant activity on the physical and the astral plane. Sometimes people say - you cannot live in two worlds, or you cannot sit on two chairs at the same time. Well, I disagree with that point of view, because it can be done and in fact, I am a living proof of that. With the right discipline you can join those two worlds and live both physically and astrally.

Knowing this truth by my own experience, I am always saying to my students that with the right effort and strong will there is time for the two worlds. Anyway, a well-trained astral traveler is in a much better position than the others, because while the rest sleep only a little aware of themselves, (in a form of a dream experience), the astral traveler travels with his/her subtle bodies across the immaterial worlds fully aware of him/herself. Therefore, for every one of you, who feels the same

I do, I can only say this: the astral projection offers you to live night and day in a way you cannot imagine.

It is a portal that leads you so deep into the structure of your deepest essence and in the same time it allows you to travel to places, which can reveal to you the ultimate secrets of the Universe. The truth is, as your life goes on and you continue to live both physically and astrally, it unavoidably leads you to a point where you will no longer lose consciousness. You will become fully conscious night and day and this will change you completely. You will gain freedom, and that is one of the most important things in your life. The major mosaic called Universe will start to become visible for you and that will change you irreversibly, too. You will find the purpose and the cause for your presence here.

Anyway, despite my best efforts to present many of the things related to the astral projection in details, I have touched many of them just on the surface. That is completely normal because you cannot put the whole astral science in one book and proudly say – Yes! That is the whole thing!

Billions of things still need to be mentioned about the astral science. The astral world is so rich with life and it is a home for many of the life forms that do not have any crossing points with humans. All kinds of natural and artificial spirits, gnomes, fairies, salamanders, mermaids, angel creatures sometimes present in the higher parts of the astral plane and many more are among them.

They all share the same astral space with humans, but they usually build invisible borders around their territories usually invisible for a normal astral vision and very often not accessible for an average astral visitor. Nevertheless, it is important to understand that the astral world is not a territory as large as a continent but that it is space even larger than the physical part of the Universe.

Just for the record, there is a plane closest to the physical matter below the astral plane and it is known under the esoteric term etheric plane. It is a plane full of vital energy known as prana, so it is often used by many astral parasites that are in need of energy. The truth is that the etheric plane is also a major topic to be covered, so I will briefly say that in most cases the etheric plane is used by humans who possess a remote viewing ability or ones who can observe aura helped by their third eye.

It is also useful to know that a major area known as mental plane exists above the astral plane. It possesses much higher vibrations than the astral plane but it does not represent the highest point of spiritual evolution. I know of four other planes above the mental plane, but that does not necessarily mean that there is no possibility of other dimensions of existence above them. I have managed to touch the cosmic plane more known to you as a nirvanic plane just a few times in my life through the Kundalini rising process and only for a very short time. Thus, I cannot speak of how large it is, nor does it have an end.

Anyway, if we consider for a moment that the seventh so called cosmic plane is the highest and we are at the first and the lowest called physical plane, we come up with the picture how low we stand on the scale of the evolution. On the other hand, it gives us a clear perspective of how hard we should work on our self-realization to move up the stairs of the spiritual evolution. Anyhow, one day we will have to start climbing, so why not start today?

Still, those who have mastered their subtle bodies are quite capable of unlimited out of the body traveling beyond any physical limits in space and time, so their chances for the spiritual improvement are infinite.

Finally, despite the fact that many of the mysteries about my life were revealed on my astral trips, many will have to remain secrets. As far as Shambala is concerned, I can only say that I went physically to the desert Goby twice. The first time was in 1996 and the second in 1998. However, I am not allowed to speak about what I have seen there. The only thing I can say about Shambala is: "It exists. It is there. It is major. It is unbelievable."

Chapter 5
REMOTE VIEWING

Remote viewing is a term in parapsychology that describes a process in which the psychically gifted person is watching some kind of astral television based on a program that he/she has chosen on his/her own. This process enables a well-trained remote viewer to focus on his/her mental screen where psychic visions start to appear and the viewer uses mental efforts to catch those psychic pictures, which in fact are astral reflections of places that he/she wants to observe.

This ability is actually related to the human's third eye that makes it possible for the mind to see things that are not visible to physical eyes. Therefore, the simple definition of remote viewing would be - *observing the physical, etheric and the astral area without leaving the physical body.* However, many anomalies that can distort much of the results of the remote viewing might appear in the early stages of the development of this extraordinary ability. That's because a beginner strongly focusing on scanning some area is unable to hold his/her mind unattached longer, and often becomes emotionally attached to his/her individual feelings and opinions concerning the things he or she is watching. Those individual feelings and opinions will have major influence on the already very weak astral reflections of the chosen area, and it will distort them or even trigger observation of some other area, which suits mostly his/her suppressed desires.

Therefore, a student on the start line must learn to shut down his/her own personal feelings and attitudes first if he/she wants to succeed mastering the remote viewing ability. One should become an empty receiver to be able to absorb major amount of data, classify them, filter or analyze them. In other words, once one succeeds to catch the astral radiation of the target area, he/she has to remember them and analyze them later. Later the student will learn another approach to the analysis.

All this etheric and astral radiation that streams through the mental screen is provided by the third eye and projected directly to the mind. Any invisible physical place becomes visible for the third eye if the mind succeeds to dive deep into the etheric or the astral matter and remains there long enough. Nevertheless, as I mentioned before, the etheric and the astral plane are almost infinite areas full of infinite radiation. Thus, in the beginning, the mental screen of the remote viewer is flooded with hundreds of other reflections coming from those planes in the shape of psychic pictures or visions. Anyway, practice has shown that as far as the radiation that appears on the remote viewer's mental screen is concerned, I am positive that mostly it has its origin in the astral plane and much rarely in the etheric plane. I know it sounds contradictory, and logically it should be the other way around, but the fact is, it is the truth. It is simple, because our third eye absorbs the sensitive images that come from the astral plane filled with thoughts better than the ones that come from the etheric plane mostly filled with vital energy.

However, every student must understand clearly that remote viewing is ability hard to achieve and that it will take some time before one is capable of selecting the target astral reflection from the infinite number of other astral reflections appearing on the mental screen. Thus, in the beginning, one's mind must become a clear mental surface open to all the astral radiation coming from the astral area.

Then, by using the third eye one must learn how to focus the mind on chosen targets and block all other images visible to him/her. This is a hard period for every student, but in time and with practice it can be achieved. Long ago, I personally had some difficult time mastering it and I will try to explain how the whole thing works:

Before the student even tries to achieve the remote viewing, first of all he/she must learn to create mental shapes, forms and images of the places in the mind helped by the ability of visualization and concentration. Then, the student must learn how to keep them frozen for as long as he/she wants to, not letting them disappear from the mental screen.

Therefore, at the very beginning of the mental creation process, the observer must become capable of holding the selected target in his/her imagination. To achieve that, drawing the place on a sheet of paper for at least 30 times, and practicing the visualization of the place for at least 7 days for about 10-15 minutes would help a lot. That would help the observer to "imprint" the picture of the selected area deep in the etheric matter below the astral plane.

Anyway, after a few days of previous visualization exercises, the student should sit in some comfortable half lying or lying position, in some quiet place where he/she can work in peace and silence. The potential remote viewer should close the eyes and start to observe the mental screen. At this stage, the viewer does not have to imagine or force a mental creation of some kind, but to become a passive observer. The effect that will follow will be very similar to watching a movie in the cinema. The only difference is that this time the screen will be in his/her head.

The secret lies in becoming a silent witness, without getting emotionally attached to things that will start appearing on the mental screen. In time, the astral reflections will start to enter the mind and the remote viewer has to put some mental effort to remember them. The training with the zener cards (which will be mentioned further on in this book) can also help the student activate the mental screen. Besides the zener training, a constant focus on looking straight up with eyes closed can also trigger the awakening of the third eye (Ajna chakra), and because of that, the mental screen will become more visible.

In the beginning, in front of the student's eyes only total blackness will be visible, which in time will become foggy, and then as the third eye becomes more and more awaken, it will become an open mental screen where the astral pictures will be coming. It is interesting to mention that the third eye is the one doing all the work and the mind is only the boss in the whole process.

Anyway, it is not necessary for the student to visualize the third eye becoming shiny or to take some shape like circle, triangle, etc., only to remain a passive witness of the astral visions streaming into his/her mind.

Here how the blackness is altered by the open mental screen:

From the depth of the blackness of the mental screen slowly but surely, some unclear figures and contours will start to appear. In time, the student will notice an unclear picture appearing and it will be gone in a split of a second. Then, if the student's mind remains calm and only focused on the mental screen without any emotional attachment other pictures will come. The color of the pictures will be unclear and mostly black and white in the beginning, and as the time passes by, images will become clearer and somewhat colorful. The duration of these astral pictures will vary and it will be determined by the student's will to hold them or reject them on the mental screen.

Later, when the remote viewer reaches an advanced level of psychic observation, the pictures will have clear colors. When the student reaches this level of development, he/she will start to hear sounds in the mind connected to the related astral vision almost instantly. Eventually, the pictures and the sounds will become perfectly clear to the observer. When that starts to happen, the student will know he/she has reached the point where from he/she can try to find the selected target of the carefully chosen place.

The whole process at this stage will appear as somebody presenting the student infinite series of pictures of people, animals, close and distant places, houses, buildings, space images, underwater images, pictures from another time, etc.

In time and with practice, those pictures will become motion pictures. Thus, the remote viewer faces another task and he/she has to learn how to freeze the chosen picture, and analyze it without vanishing from the mental screen. The analyzing process should be done strictly mentally and without using words in the thoughts and with no emotional response towards the astral picture; otherwise, the picture will vanish from the mental screen. It is not advisable to even think in pictures because that will surely influence the sensitive mental screen.

If the remote viewer is capable of reaching this point of observation, I suggest a further try for observing the astral radiation by using a higher level of consciousness. By a higher level of consciousness, I mean consciousness of the consciousness itself. One consciousness exists in the average consciousness, and observes filters and analyzes all the data coming and leaving the remote viewer's mental screen. In other words, the remote viewer adapts to this new part of the consciousness and when this is achieved, the viewer can easily think and make choices in a higher and subtler way not touching the sensitive astral pictures. Then, all that needs to be done is to focus on the selected area and in a few seconds, it will become visible for the remote viewer. Once the viewer catches the astral radiation of the target area, he/she can easily move and observe everywhere and everything just by using a small mental effort. Here is one example of how the remote viewing process is done:

Let us assume that a picture of a large apartment appears on the mental screen of the student. To succeed with the remote observation of the apartment, the student should use some mental efforts to partly enter the mental screen by pulling the picture towards the third eye.

While this process is on, the remote viewer's mind must remain maximally calm and under no circumstances to become emotionally attached to the picture, because if it does, the picture will be altered by another one more suitable to his/her emotional charge.

The next step is to locate the astral reflection of the target and to "freeze" the picture on the mental screen. Once the student succeeds that, he/she has to pull the picture closer to the third eye using strong mental efforts to slip into the picture at the same time. In other words, the student has to magnetically pull the picture in and to use mental efforts to push him/herself out and walk through the picture at the same time.

The whole secret at this stage is in the balance of these two forces – the outer, which one pulls towards him/herself and the inner, which he/she forces out. In this particular case, one has to pull the picture of the entrance room of the selected apartment towards the dot between the physical eyes, and walk through the entrance of the apartment visible on the mental screen at the same time. Once the student succeeds to pull that off, he/she is free to observe the other rooms in the apartment.

In the beginning, the remote viewer will face certain problems moving in some direction. In most cases, if the moving procedure is not done correctly, it will transport the observation to a completely new place. The trick is, the student who has chosen to move (*for example*) to the right in the apartment has to start pulling the appropriate movement towards the third eye and simultaneously push the consciousness to move right. That will surely lead to the biolocation of the consciousness, and that is why the remote viewer has to stay in the middle point between the apartment and the mental screen.

If the biolocation is too weak, it will not be perceived as it should be and if it is too strong, it will induce an astral projection in the apartment. Because of the fact that the main purpose of the remote viewing is to observe distant places without leaving the physical body, the student must be capable of holding the mind helped by the third eye no further than the mental screen. The mind of the remote viewer must be neither too shallow nor too deep. The perfect location of the mind would be very little out of the surface line of the mental screen towards the apartment, and constantly on alert not to go deeper. However, if that is too difficult for a student, he/she can simply lock the mind on the surface line of the mental screen, and the observation will be just fine.

The remote viewing process will run smoothly, but the ability of moving will be little reduced.

All the experiences that the remote viewer manages to collect from the selected area should be put in a diary. That has many purposes, but one of them is adapting the consciousness to the etheric and astral vibrations, which will allow the remote viewer to be constantly aware of the other planes while still on the physical plane. In time, a well-trained remote viewer will be capable of observing distant places on the mental screen with small mental efforts with unbelievable accuracy and precision.

What is most interesting, after a few years of remote viewing practice, one will be able to observe the physical, etheric and astral area just by closing his/her eyes while enjoying a ride on the bus, resting, drinking coffee or doing some everyday job. That will surely bring a complete expansion of the remote viewer's consciousness in which he/she will be constantly sensitive to an even tiniest radiation coming from the etheric or the astral world. From this point of psychic development on, there are no real limits for the human consciousness.

By using this method of achieving the extraordinary ability known as remote viewing, very soon you will become capable of observing distant places helped by your third eye with major precision without leaving your physical body. Please, use your new ability wisely and do not ever use it for selfish reasons.

Chapter 6
CLAIRVOYANCE

Clairvoyance is a paranormal ability closely tied with the remote viewing. The human's third eye has the leading role since it enables the mind to see through the mental screen. There are many methods to develop the third eye. I have chosen to present the method I have mastered a long time ago and am completely sure it works.

The method is universal and most of the psychic abilities can be developed through it. This method, which in fact is a system of exercises, consists of seven stages starting with the zener cards and as each stage is completed, the training gets harder and harder. However, before I go any deeper into the subject of the psychic training, it is better to clear up some things first concerning the zener cards. The zener cards, also known as ESP cards, are the basis of the modern parapsychology. Although most people consider them just a useful tool for ESP testing, they are much more than that. The use of the zener cards is also a powerful tool through which individuals can awake and develop their third eye with a special training. One deck of the zener cards consists of five symbols multiplied five times - star, waves, plus, circle and square.

All of the 25 cards are totally black on one side and on the other side there is white background with bolded black colored symbol. In the beginning, the task of the student helped by an inner sense is to feel or see the symbol on the card. Because during the training the student is blindfold, while the sense of the student's physical sight is off, the other senses increase and sharpen more. However, the purpose of this universal method is not to sharpen the other senses, but to awake and develop a (figuratively speaking) "new sense", which contains the other five senses in it and much more.

It is completely irrelevant how you call this new sense – third eye, sixth sense or Ajna chakra. You will not make a mistake, because it is the same thing. Once this new sense starts to awake, most of the psychic powers can be achieved, cultivated and made ready for everyday use. The system of exercises to follow will lead you to a point where you will become the master or your mental potentials.

The universal method is so complete that each of you willing to sacrifice about two or three years of your life can achieve higher mental powers and develop your psychic abilities beyond words. Nevertheless, although some authors promise you that you will develop your psychic powers in weeks by some specific method, I will not give promises like that and I will give you only the time that took me to develop them. It must become perfectly clear to every true student that it takes major self-discipline, top determination and persistence to keep up with the everyday hard training.

Subchapter 6.1
STAGE ONE

As for almost everything else in psychic practice, the student must find a quiet and isolated place to be able to work undisturbed with an assistant. It must be done in pairs because the student must be blindfold all the time during the training, and will need somebody to put the zener cards behind him/her and inform the student about the accuracy of the answers. The whole process in this stage works like this:

The blindfold student must sit on a chair and the assistant should sit two meters behind him and put the cards one by one on a smaller table. In the beginning, there must be some clear space between the student and the table where the zener cards with the symbol up will be put.

Since it is going to take about two to three hours of practicing, some instrumental music cannot do any harm to the training process and it will provide a smoother training. However, it is important that the music is with relatively slow rhythm and pleasant for hearing. Some sounds from the ambient or New Age music enjoyable to both of them will do just fine. However, the quiet and slow instrumental music can bring only benefit to the training and if somebody likes to practice in silence, it is perfectly OK, and can work in silence. The assistant should reshuffle the deck well, and put the cards one by one. The table, except for the only one card, which has to be put in the middle point, must be completely clear of any other objects. For now, the side with the symbol of the card should be up because it will allow the student to feel or see it more easily. If during the process of practicing, the assistant forgets to remove the deck from the table, it will be a major mistake. The rest of the cards in the deck, though turned on the side with the black background up, will surely influence the student's efforts to locate the symbol of the target card, which is in the middle of the table. For that reason, the assistant who can seat on a comfortable sofa should split the deck in three piles. All those parts should be put on the sofa and by no excuse on the table where the target card is. The first pile should contain the wrong answers, the second the correct answers and the third one normally, the cards which remain to be put on the table.

When the mental scan of all cards of the deck is over, the assistant informs the student of the correct answers and notes the result in a notebook, which can be used for monitoring the student's progress. Then, the assistant has to reshuffle the deck well and when that is done, the process goes on with the next deck of cards. The student is allowed only one answer, and the assistant (at least in this stage of the training) should confirm the result of the student's answer with a simple Yes/No, or True/False.

The black fold around the student's eyes should be neither too tight, nor too feeble. Student's clothes should be comfortable like tracksuit or so, to be able to sit in the chair for hours without feeling uncomfortably. Before the training starts, it is advisable to try to sit in one position on the chair that mostly suits the student's body and to "freeze" in that position. The student can put his/her arms on the knees or thighs, but he/she should try to hold the head, neck and spine in straight line as much as possible.

Until now, I have explained the basic rules of the training, and now I will explain the inner procedure to be performed in the mind. The inner process, which will be performed in the student's mind, requires great ability of visualization, concentration, and focus on the inner psychic force and by all means great ability of the consciousness to move out of the physical body.

Before the start with the first deck of zener cards, the student must calm the mind by entering the meditative state similar to the one I have mentioned in the "deep peace meditation". After having calmed his/her thoughts and reached inner peace, the student should concentrate on the inner energy, which flows through his/her body. When the student feels the streaming of pleasant bioenergy, he/she is ready for the training and can give the assistant a sign to put the first card on the table.

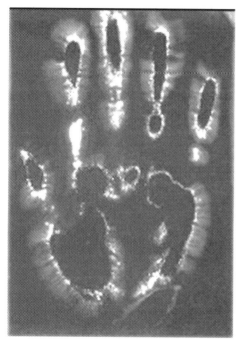

Then, the student must completely free his/her mind and to try to pull out the inner sense, which lies deep down in him/her to feel the objects that are around. The first thing the student must concentrate on is the streaming of the energy between him/her and the chair. The student has to feel the chair as a part of him/her the way a driver feels the car while driving it. Then, he/she should redirect the psychic feeling following the pattern: – between him/her and the carpet (if there is any); between him and the legs of the table; the whole table; the target card; and at the end between him/her and the card's symbol.

The secret lies in establishing some kind of emotional bridge between one's self and the symbol of the target card. The rest will come by itself. The establishing of this kind of an emotional bridge should be done very slowly and with no rush because it will produce contra effect if done otherwise. In other words, the student should not keep a feeling of impatience within since it will surely lead to a wrong answer. On the contrary, the correct answer comes as a result of patient psychic touch between the student and the symbol of the card.

In time and with practice, the student will surely reach the level of being capable to easily move his/her psychic touch onto the objects that are around. The inner feeling will develop greatly and it will become so sharp that sometimes the student will feel almost equal as a physical touch with the card. After the student reaches 70% of accuracy in the answers, he/she should repeat this score with the next five decks.

Note: *Under no condition, no matter how well the training goes, it is not advisable for the student at this stage to start working with two cards at the same time. That would be a big mistake, which will cost the student much more than he/she can imagine. If the student tries to feel two or more cards in the*

same time, he/she will soon lose the psychic touch and will have to work very hard again to reach the same point of development. In other words, the student will lose two months of training just in a few minutes and will have to practice even longer to reach the same level of accuracy. Please, believe my words, because I have passed the whole training myself and encountered the same problem. The practice with more cards will follow in the next stages when the student is ready for it. Thus, the discipline of practicing is one of the primary objectives that will lead the student to progress.

When the student succeeds to reach the result of 70% accuracy in the previous five decks only by using the psychic touch, which usually takes two or three months to complete, he/she is ready for the next stage. Still, this is only the weaker manifestation of the third eye and now the student must work on the visual part of it, which is much harder to achieve.

Subchapter 6.2
STAGE TWO

In the second stage, training should be extended from three to four hours a day. After the completion of the first stage, average time to complete the second stage varies from four to six months.

The training starts exactly the same way like in the first stage, with the student's achievement of 70% accuracy only by using the inner sense of psychic touch. A new element, which the student has to add to the training, is focusing on the mental screen in a similar way previously described in the remote viewing process. The student should become a passive observer and wait for the mental screen to become visible. When the level of concentration is reached and the mental screen is visible, the student has to change its location.

That can be done by using mental efforts to pull the mental screen from the location in front of the student's closed eyes to the back of the head. Perhaps, in the beginning, the student will encounter some difficulty to achieve that, but with practice, he/she will succeed to hold the mental screen on the back of the head. The best way is to visualize that the mental screen has become transparent, to look for the counters of the table and to try to catch the rectangle form of the zener card, which is in the middle of it.

The most important thing for a student is not to forget to lose the psychic touch with the table behind even for a second. Both processes should be done in parallel mode, and the mental screen should be frozen in the right direction by the guidance of the psychic touch. Next thing that the student should do is to try to observe through the mental screen towards the table where the card is. At the same time, the student has to free him/herself from all the other thoughts or emotions and to concentrate on the observation as best as possible.

With the intensive concentration, the contours of the table and the card, which is on it, will start to emerge from the depths of the student's mental screen. The student's mind must be completely stable and frozen on those very weak counters appearing on the mental screen on the back of his head. The primary process in this stage will be similar to making a hole in the back of one's head. The stronger the mental pressure on the back of the head becomes the stronger and more visible the mental screen becomes. By mental pressure, I do not mean physical grip of the neck or the head. I mean psychic pressure which is psychical 100 %, and which is a natural result of the strength of the mind reached by previous training with the zener cards.

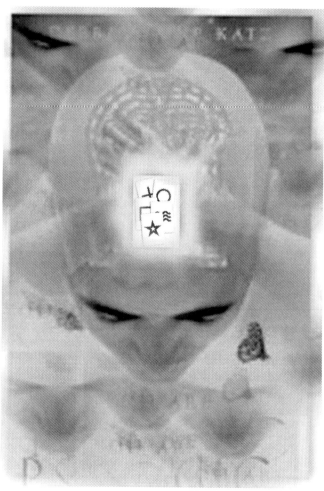

In other words, the student guided by the psychical bridge between him/her and the table behind must force the mind with enormous amount of mental strength to make a psychic fissure in the back of the head. The appearance of this psychic fissure is the first sign that the third eye of the student has started awakening. This period of training is very important because the actual thing that is happening is creation of the fissure in the etheric matter and the third eye will be learning to observe through it. Anyway, the student will know when this fissure is present if he/she experiences these effects in the mind:

Because of the major mental effort during focusing on observation through the mental screen in the direction of the table where the zener card is with the symbol up, one will soon feel that something has changed in his/her inner sight. The darkness of the mental screen will be altered by some illumination. Then, as the mental pressure on the zener card starts to hit stronger, it will become gray. Next, the gray color of the mental screen will start to express some foggy characteristics. Stronger concentration with the mental force through this foggy background will make the dot with less density visible on the mental screen. Finally, in this small dot something similar to a small fissure will start to appear. Everything around this small fissure will remain foggy, but some light will start to appear in it. If the student continues pushing the mental force through this small fissure, he/she will realize that he/she is seeing something. At first, one will see unclear contours but in time and with practice he/she will develop his/her psychic observation.

Once the psychic fissure appears, the mind of the student must not become weaker not even for a second, but to keep the fissure open all the time. The fissure can also appear in some other direction like table legs or so, and the student should put some mental efforts to relocate the fissure directly above the surface of the zener card. It is very important not to become over-exited from the newborn situation but to remain perfectly calm, stable and focused on the training. In case the student becomes overwhelmed with excitement, starts to fool or jump around, the psychic fissure will close instantly, and the student will have to work twice harder to achieve the same level of development.

Very soon after the student freezes the fissure above the zener card, the symbol on it will start to become visible. However, in the beginning the images will be only black and white. With further concentration on observing through the fissure on the mental screen, the color will start to appear. It will be coming slowly, but it will come. The moment the color starts accompanying the psychic sight of the student is a good point from which it will not take long before the student manages to scan all of the 25 cards correctly. Perhaps, in the beginning through the fissure, some anomalies will be visible like seeing a square, which in reality is a circle, but they will vanish in time. Under no circumstance, the student should try to extend the psychic fissure until he/she has reached the score of 25 correct answers with five decks in a row. If the result is 24, it is not good enough and one has to work until he/she reaches the top score of 25.

Note: Jumping into the next stage of the third's eye development, without previously achieved perfection is a major mistake. Because of that, the student must be patient and wait until the result shows full readiness for the next level.

Subchapter 6.3
STAGE THREE

This stage covers the gradual extension of the psychic fissure and observation improvement. The training time extends from four to five hours a day. It is very important for the student not to miss a single day of training because the painstakingly achieved level of development is still very sensitive and it can easily retreat. Average time for completing the third stage varies but usually it takes two weeks to a month.

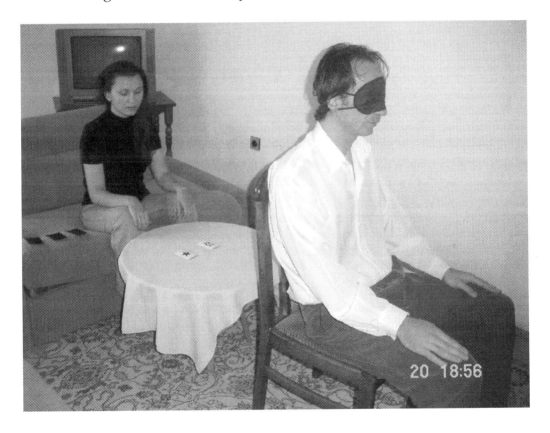

Stage 3a

After the student has achieved the result of 100% of accuracy in minimum five decks watching through the tiny fissure, the assistant is allowed to put two cards at the same time in the middle of the table. As before, perfection is top priority and the student has a chance to no more than just a single answer.

Now, the assistant puts two cards on the table and the student has to put strong mental efforts to extend the psychic fissure for at least as much as to have both cards in his/her psychic sight. Soon, though maybe not at once, after the student succeeds to extend and freeze the psychic fissure, he/she will reach the result of 100% accuracy with two cards at the same time. Because his/her inner sight will be constantly frozen on the surface of the table, the student will soon notice that from time to time he/she is able to catch the movement of the hands of the assistant.

In contrast to the previous experience, now the student can watch strictly in color. At this level, the fissure will allow the student to feel and watch in more subtle way. Although the third eye is developing very fast and the student is capable of feeling and seeing the next cards in the deck, it is advisable (at least in this stage) to concentrate only on the two target cards. Sometimes, the psychic fissure will get foggy but with the right mental pressure, it will get clear again. When the student has managed to perfectly see the five decks with two cards, the assistant can add a card more and now the student has to observe three cards at the same time. As before, one has to use mental efforts to extend the psychic fissure even more, at least as much as to be able to have all three cards in the psychic sight.

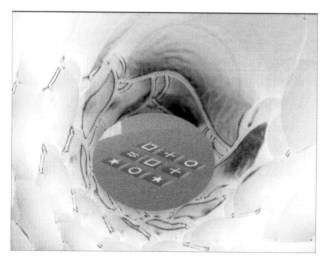

Usually, this is the part of the stage the student achieves very easy, because now his/her third eye has become very active and the mind has only to use just some small mental effort to focus on the task and to solve it. The rule of five-deck accuracy with 100% applies here as well, and before achieving this result, one cannot go any further. The moment the student has reached the needed result he/she is ready for nine cards at the same time. Now, the assistant has to put nine cards on the table in a formation of three rows with three cards. Both the student and the assistant have to agree and clearly determine the rules of the next task. Whether it is going to be from left to right of the row or the opposite, or the first row is going to be the row closest to the student or to the assistant is completely up to them.

Again, using some mental effort, the student has to extend the psychic fissure, for at least as much as to have all nine cards in his/her psychic sight. At this level of the stage, the student has made a larger psychic hole and is no longer experiencing an observation through the mental screen, which is on the back of his/her head, but is experiencing an experience as if watching directly above the table. In a way, the student's consciousness has departed very close to the border side of the psychic fissure and the student is watching through it. Once the part with the nine cards is over, the student is ready for the fourth stage.

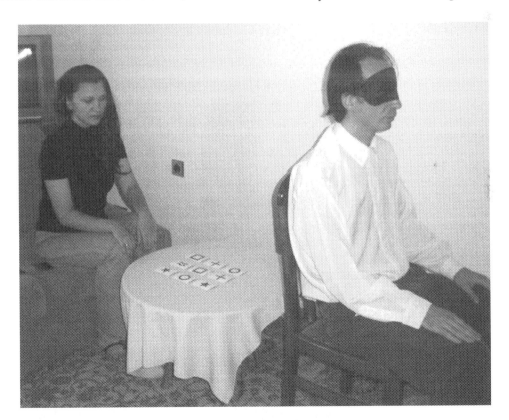

Stage 3b

Subchapter 6.4
STAGE FOUR

When the student is done with the nine cards at the same time, put in a formation of three rows with three cards, the assistant has to put all cards on the table. It has to be in a formation of five rows with five cards. Logically, bigger extension of the psychic fissure is required for the student to be able to see all of the 25 cards. It is different now, since the student now gains the ability to move the psychic fissure on his/her own will. In this stage, the psychic fissure does not retreat and because of that, the student is capable to freeze or unfreeze it wherever he/she likes in the room.

Soon, other effects will appear in the student's consciousness like hearing the assistant's thoughts, feeling of floating, all sorts of astral visions coming from the astral plane, etc. All these effects in this stage of development have to be put aside and the student has to focus only on the observation through the expanded psychic fissure.

When the student has finished with all of the 25 cards in a formation of five rows with five cards with at least five decks, the next task is three rows, which contain 10 cards in the outer rows and 5 in the inner one. To test the student's ability to perfectly see with his/her inner vision, the assistant should turn a few cards in different rows upside down. The student has to locate the cards turned onto the other side and to tell which cards in which rows are with the black background up, with their symbols, of course. It will be a good checkpoint for both of them to get the real picture of the accomplished so far.

Watching through the black background of the zener card will not be difficult for the student at this stage. However, if it is, the student can solve the task only by using stronger mental pressure on the black surface of the card and the symbol will immediately become visible for him/her.

As the training advances, the assistant should test the student's clairvoyance more often by putting harder and harder combinations in the rows like five circles in one group in the same row, or lots of cards turned upside down, etc., and to ask the student: "What do you see now?"

In other words, the assistant has to put the hardest combination of all of the 25 cards, but now, the student can do amazing stuff and probably, he/she will solve every task that the assistant assigns very easy and very fast. Once they are done with the testing and the student does not miss any more, the assistant should go in another room and put all the zener cards on the floor. To achieve the observation in the other room, the student has to move the psychic fissure through the wall, which separates the rooms and to freeze it above the floor where the zener cards are. When he/she successfully solves all 25 cards, the assistant should take a pen and point to different cards. Now, the student has to see in which row the card is, and normally, what is the symbol touched by the peak of the assistant's pen.

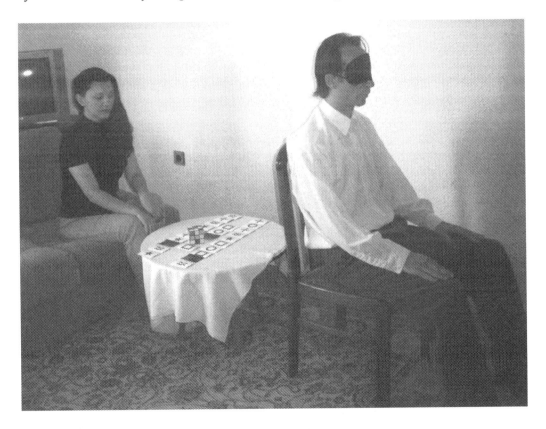

Stage 4

When all this is achieved, the student is ready for the next stage of the training. The time necessary for completion of the fifth stage varies from one to three weeks.

Subchapter 6.5
STAGE FIVE

In this stage of the training, the student continues to further develop the inner sight, and if everything goes, as it should, eventually, he/she will be capable to read with the physical eyes closed. To complete this stage it usually takes 7 to 9 days. Before one begins with this stage, he/she has to repeat all of the previous stages. Since the student is now in great shape, he/she will finish them incredibly fast. I assume this so, because having reached this level of clairvoyance to repeat all of the four previous stages it will take the student less than 20 minutes. When that is done, the assistant should bring other deck of cards, which will contain all the letters of the alphabet. By size and shape, they have to be the same with the zener cards with the only difference that where the symbols of the zener cards have been, the letters stand on the letter cards now.

Just the same, as with the zener cards, the assistant has to reshuffle the letter cards well and to put one letter card in the middle of the table. The task of the student is to try to see the letter helped by the psychic fissure. The procedure is just the same, as with the zener cards. When the student finishes with 100% accuracy with one letter card in minimum five decks, the assistant can put two cards and when that also is completed, they can start with 3 letter cards at the same time. When they reach this level of the fifth stage the assistant can combine some shorter words like day, sun, one, car, etc. The student should not have any problems with the reading now, because his/her third eye is very active and the inner sight is very close to the clearness of the physical eyes.

Then, the assistant has to combine some four or five lettered words and when that is done as well, to start with more complex and longer words. It is amazing for both of them to participate in live in this kind of event, and it is an unbreakable proof for presence of the pure mental power in the room. The training continues with long and complex sentences, which will require other decks with letter cards because sometimes (for example) the letter E will repeat itself in the sentence more than 7 times. Very important to be mentioned is that the student's consciousness will surely be exposed to all sorts of phenomenal effects like direct hearing of every assistant's thought, many astral visions that come and go incredibly fast, the loss of the physical feeling, etc. The student will have to restrain from exploring those effects, which come because of the high level of the third's eye function.

Also, the student will experience a strong spinning feeling around the chair to the level that it will look like he/she is going to lose consciousness and fall into a complete blackness. The above normal mental power awaken by the third eye produces that effect and the student has to get used to it and to learn to control it. Now the student's mind is very strong and the student will soon discover awareness of the processes that are running through his/her physical body never dreamed of before as possible to be sensed.

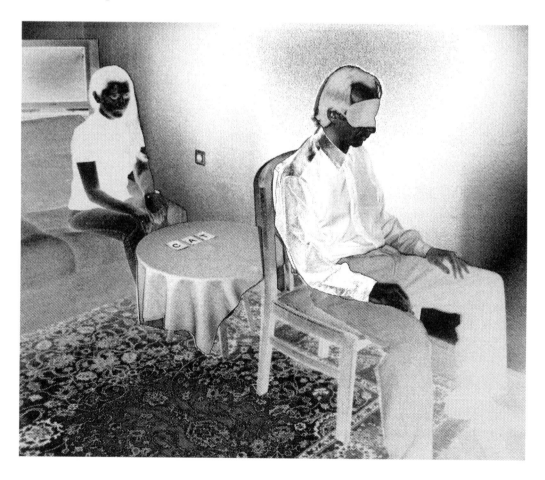

Stage 5

After the student manages to perfectly solve all the tasks assigned in the form of sentences to be read, the assistant should mix the two decks, the one with the zener cards and the one with the letter cards and put them on the table in many rows. This time all the cards have to be closed or with the black background up, and the next task for the student will be to see them all. The assistant now has to take the notebook and record all the data the student tells. The successfully solved task of this kind points clearly that the student is ready for the next stage.

Subchapter 6.6
STAGE SIX

In the sixth stage, the student will experience something as never before. He/she will be able to see exactly the same as with his/her physical eyes and much more. The student will achieve what most people consider impossible in this very advanced stage. However, before the student becomes capable of doing far greater extraordinary things, he/she will have to develop the inner sight even more by learning to observe deeper into the physical matter.

The stage begins with the assistant reshuffling the whole zener deck and putting it in the middle of the table. Now, the student is assigned another task and will have to see all of the 25 of the zener cards at the same time penetrating through the whole deck. To achieve that, the student will have to change the frequency of the inner sight and to visualize all 25 cards placed in the astral space one above  another. When the vision of the whole deck levitating in the dark astral space in front of him/her appears in the consciousness, the student will have to use some strong mental effort to deeply penetrate through the whole deck. He/she will have to tell the assistant the answers for all of the 25 cards starting from the first to the last one and the assistant should not touch the deck, not even once. The assistant will have to record the student's answers in the notebook and when all the 25 answers are given check the results.

It is relevant to be mentioned that this is a difficult task and in the beginning, the student will surely encounter some errors. That is because the student does not use psychic fissure but uses another frequency of perception instead. A little patience will enable the student to get used to this new way of seeing and he/she will surely learn how to do it. He/she can achieve the deeper scanning visualizing his/her astral hands removing and seeing one by one all the cards on the astral reflection of

284

the physical deck, which is in the middle of the table behind. In other words, the student will have to visualize him/herself astrally picking one card from the deck visible on the dark astral space in his/her consciousness. Then, turning it upside down the student has to try to see the symbol if it is not already illuminated and to throw the card away. Then, he/she has to repeat the same procedure with the remaining 24 cards.

When the student reaches the level with 100% accuracy with the deep scanning in minimum five decks one after another, he/she is ready for the next thing to be mastered. Now, the assistant will have to reshuffle the deck again and to ask the student to tell which card is (for example) 19th, counting from the top or from the bottom card. To solve this task the student will have to reach again within his/her consciousness and to find the whole deck, which will be levitating in the astral space. Then, the only remaining thing to do is to count and when he/she reaches the 19th card, the student will have to remove it from the deck and to see the symbol on it. It is as simple as that and there is no other secret for this task. The assistant will have to ask the student then about the symbols of the rest of the cards in the deck and when that is nicely done, the training continues with 2-5 cards at the same time. For example, the assistant can assign the student to tell the symbols on the 5th, 11th, 18th, 21st and the 23rd card.

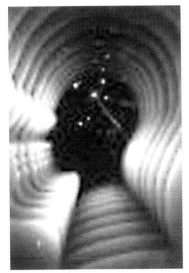

Usually, when the student reaches this level of the sixth stage, the astral light will illuminate the symbols of the target cards and he/she will not have to count them one by one to solve the tasks. I have mentioned the way the procedure can be done anyway. The next step in this stage is deep scanning through the deck of letter cards. The procedure is the same as with the deep scanning of the deck with the zener cards. Once this is also accomplished, the assistant mixes those two decks into one and the student has to see them all starting from the top to the bottom card. This is a very good exercise or should I better say test, and when it is completed the student is in a real good psychic shape.

The next level of the sixth stage is mastering the zoom ability of the student's inner sight. Including a book into the training should do the trick, so the assistant should put it in the middle of the table and open it on some page. Then, the assistant will have to choose one sentence from the page and to encircle it with a pen. The task of the student is to move the inner sight through the psychic fissure above the surface of the book and to start to zoom it until he/she reaches clearness to read from the page. To pull this off, the student will have to work and train hard because maximum concentration and full control of the psychic fissure is required. The student will have to find out the number of the page of the book and to read the sentence circled with the pen.

When the student achieves this, he/she is capable of seeing so much clearer and better even to pull this off when the task of reading is in other rooms. In this stage, the student has to tear apart the psychic fissure by using the maximum strength of the mind. In other words, to do that, the student will have to use ultimate mental efforts to extend the psychic fissure to infinity until he/she experiences that the psychic fissure is starting to tear apart. Furthermore, he/she has to put final pressure until the fissure is torn apart completely and until the student gains an ability of seeing exactly the same as with his/her physical eyes. Once the psychic fissure is torn apart, the student will see completely normal no matter to where the student points his/her head. It is an amazing experience and only by using certain mental efforts, this new inner sight will be accompanied with other supernatural abilities.

This is a very high achievement of the student and his/her third eye is awake. From now on, the real effects of the astral force will start to appear and the student will have to learn to master them all.

Subchapter 6.7
STAGE SEVEN

The seventh stage is the most interesting. Further, the training continues with the student's practice to project him/herself into his/her astral body and to perform an observation in other locations. In this stage, the student needs two assistants to give the assignments, one to stay in the same room with him/her and one situated in another apartment.

The first thing that the assistant in the other apartment should do is to take one photo and put it on a table with the image up. Now that the psychic fissure is torn apart and the student watches with the mind just the same he/she would observe with physical eyes the student faces another task. He/she has to leave the physical body and to take a short astral trip to the other apartment with the purpose to see the photo that is on the table. Then, he/she has to return to the physical body and to tell the first assistant all the data collected from the out of the body experience. Both assistants should be in touch by cell-phone all the time during the seventh stage to exchange the data and clarify the accuracy of the student's observations.

The best part is that the time has come for the student to explore all of the psychic effects that have been coming into his/her consciousness a long time. Because of the great strength of his/her consciousness, the student is capable of leaving the physical body in less than five seconds. It is enough for him or her to use some mental effort to astrally project at least two meters up front. Then if one turns around he/she will find him/herself sitting on the chair blindfold. As soon as the student does that, the perspective of the inner observation changes, he/she will lose the physical sense and will find him/herself in a new body standing two meters in front of him/herself. If he/she looks upon him/herself, the student will see that he/she is in a transparent body, which is a complete copy of the physical carrier. The student will also notice the tiny white line, which is representing the human contour and some smaller or larger blue illumination around it. The whole room will be perfectly visible to his/her astral vision and he/she will soon discover that he/she can see much better and deeper than being ever able with his/her physical eyes, of course if that is what the individual wants. Perhaps in the beginning, the student will experience biolocation because of not being experienced enough to hold his/her consciousness on the astral plane but in time one will learn to control the new, immaterial body.

Now is the right time for the student to learn to use the astral body, starting with a strong command to leave the apartment. As soon as he/she does that, the student will realize that his/her astral body reacts on even tiniest wish or command. To reach the apartment where the second assistant is, the student can concentrate to find him/herself directly in front of the table where the task is and his/her astral body will teleport there immediately. It is also possible to do the same by the standard way of penetrating through walls, entering into other apartments, going out and flying until reaching the target apartment, etc.

However, after the student has reached the target apartment, he/she has to look around and walk to the table where the photo has been placed. It is appropriate to try to remember as many details as he/she can about the apartment and all the things seen on the way there and back, before he/she returns to the physical body. After the student regains the physical feeling of sitting on the chair again, he/she has to describe the photo to the first assistant with all the data noticed during the astral excursion.

Then, the assistants have to compare all the data from the student's statement by their mobile phones. When the second assistant confirms the accuracy of the data in the student's statement, the first assistant is writing down the result in the notebook or a laptop. The student has to repeat the same procedure by reading a sentence from some book, which will be put on the table of another apartment. The reading should not be difficult for the astral vision of the student because of the previous experience with it.

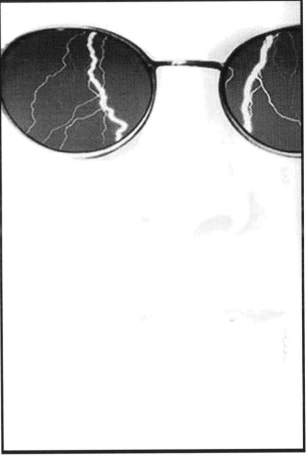

However, it can take some time to master this to perfection. Then, the tasks will become increasingly difficult and chosen on the second assistant's free choice. For example, the assistant can put some thing in a closed box somewhere in the apartment and the student using the astral body has to find where the box is and what is in it. All the results will have to be constantly monitored. A good exercise for the astral development of the student would be to work with both assistants at the same time. Reading 10 digit numbers, one that will be in the same room in front of the first assistant and one that will be written on a sheet of paper in front of the second assistant is the content of this exercise. The best test for the limits of the student's power will be to solve tasks that are very distant from his/her physical body by taking astral trips to other countries if he/she has some friend to assist him/her with the training.

Note: When the student has reached the level to read with his/her physical eyes closed and by using only the inner eye, the student will have to develop his/her mental skills more and more. In time and with practice these abilities will increase and the effects of the mental power will be beyond average human understanding. As far as clairvoyance is concerned, I will have to note that it is not complete until the third eye is fully open and active. However, now the very advanced student who has mastered all these seven stages has also made tremendous step forward, but a long and unknown path still has to be walked ahead. I have presented all seven stages designed for the awakening and developing of the third eye. In this particular case it is the clairvoyance ability through the step by step opening of the psychic eye from which the sixth and the seventh are the most appropriate for developing many other psychic abilities like telepathy, psychometry, psychokinesis, etc.

Chapter 7
TELEPATHY

Telepathy is a process of mental communication between two or more minds, in which the exchange of mental messages takes place like some kind of natural psychic bridge between them.

We all are constantly exposed to the attack of infinite psychic vibrations, which influence us in many ways. For example, when we contact a certain person, we can experience a peaceful and pleasant feeling, while with some other person we get an intense and very unpleasant feeling. That is simple to understand because we use the same psychic frequency with people who feel the same about many things in life as we do, and the other way around.

However, not just people, houses, buildings and streets, public places, etc., have their own "psychic atmosphere" as well. Even whole cities possess psychic atmosphere around them, atmosphere that contains all sorts of psychic vibrations, which living forms who live there radiate from their minds. As far as I managed to discover, the ability of telepathy was a standard tool of communication in ancient times. However, after the Earth's global flood, which as I said before, was a consequence of a global war, most of the human survivors caught on the surface were abducted by aliens and genetically altered. Fortunately, the ability for telepathic communication was not entirely erased because the aliens have not damaged the centers of the human's brain responsible for telepathy, but they have only cut off their bioelectrical power supply.

Thus, if somehow the bioelectrical impulses can reach those centers in our brain, the ability will become functional again. In fact, to the best of my knowledge, some of the top scientists working underground in top-secret facilities have been well aware of this fact. They have made a tremendous progress working with some of the best  psychics in the world, but they still keep the results of their research hidden from the public. However, some people are born naturally gifted to read or transmit thoughts while others have to work hard to develop them. Thus, the good part is, the telepathy can be developed because anyone capable of thinking is also capable of telepathic conversation.

Anyway, with the right method employed, telepathy can still be developed and used as a standard communication tool. The true strength of telepathy is far beyond the level that most of the people believe is possible. Thus, I am completely sure that even today, only one in a million possesses the potential to reach a stadium of psychic development in which he/she can use this wonderful ability the same way it was used thousands of years ago. All this is tightly connected with the Meta gene inside the DNA, which in fact provides the extraordinary psychic abilities in the first place. Yet, though the Meta gene is present inside the human's DNA a great deal, it remains in the latent state without proper development.

However, before someone learns how to use telepathy he/she has to understand this simple truth: "Each thought that invades our consciousness does not vanish instantly but goes to the natural thought plane that exists across the whole Universe. This thought plane contains infinite thoughts, which come from all spheres of the existence."

Anyhow, each thought being transmitted away by and from us possesses certain mental energy, which determines the duration of those thoughts in the thought plane. Furthermore, if those thoughts are very strong and focused they can be transmitted throughout the thought plane directly into another mind. On the other hand, helped by the Ajna chakra, the mind can receive those thoughts, which come in many forms but mostly in the form of hearing the thoughts.

Nevertheless, for the telepathy to function smoothly an active third eye is necessary. From my point of view, I believe that the best way to develop telepathy is by using the same universal training for clairvoyance mentioned in the previous chapter, which in fact is universal training for developing the human's third eye. Thus, for a student to start experimenting with telepathy the completion of the sixth stage is required. To be patient and to restrain from exploring one's telepathic abilities until one reaches the proper stage is very important, although the student feels the telepathic effects long before he/she reaches the sixth stage.

When the student has the sixth stage accomplished already, he/she can start developing telepathy by trying to read the assistant's thoughts. In the beginning, the assistant should think of some word and helped by the ability of visualization to write the same word somewhere in the surrounding space. I am completely sure that the student who has come this far will see the word instantly. Then, telepathy has to be further developed with harder tasks for the student. The assistant should visualize whole sentences next around the student's space (the student sits blindfold in a chair with his/her back towards the assistant).

When the student achieves that too, the assistant has to visualize geometric shapes like transparent or colored sphere, pyramid or cube and slowly and step by step to go further to more complicated geometric shapes to be further modified in the assistant's imagination. Next step is much harder. The assistant now has to remember some event from his/her own distant past and to constantly hold that memory in his/her mind. For example, a summer holiday that he/she had experienced some 10 years ago can serve the cause well. The student's task is to catch those thoughts of the assistant and to tell the whole event seen telepathically.

Note: *I have to note that the student should be very careful while scanning the assistant's mind, because if too much pressure is put on him/her, it can cause some undesired injury. The problem usually appears in the sixth stage because the student feels strong mental power and once he/she focuses his/her maximum strength, it can hardly stop if something goes wrong.*

The same problem happened to me long time ago while I was still a disciple trying to awake my mental forces. My trainer was Velibor Rabljenovich and I was repeating the sixth stage when things got out of control. He wanted me to scan him completely and to find out what he was hiding deeply in his mind. Although I was sitting in a chair two meters away from him blindfold, I was seeing him and the whole room perfectly with my mind like I had my physical eyes open. I remember that he started to block my mental efforts to scan his mind by building many unbreakable mental walls around him with the purpose to prevent me from finding out what he was hiding.

However, my third eye was in great shape and I spotted the mental walls in his mind momentarily and when I tried to break them or bypass them I found out that my mental waves were reflecting away from them. Velibor started to

293

laugh and was joking with me about how week I was and that I would never enter his mind. Although he was laughing at me and telling jokes on my account his mind did not weaken a bit, this in fact, was a sign of a well-trained consciousness. His jokes became offensive and though I was always trying to maintain my mental control and inner peace, he made me very angry. In one moment, I became so angry that I felt a psi-wave coming from deep down. When I released it, it broke all Velibor's mental walls. Seen from the physical aspect, I felt my whole body contracting and shaking. From the spiritual aspect, I felt like I had lost my human shape and become pure energy accompanied by the feeling of indescribable heat, which I had never felt before.

My trainer stopped laughing at me and became silent. All the walls in his mind broke down and I had clearly seen my target. It was a transparent cube with a five-digit number written on one of the sides. The moment I wanted to withdraw my mental force from his mind I found that it did not want to withdraw. I got frightened when I felt that instead of withdrawing it was growing stronger. No matter how hard I tried to back off, it seemed to me like the power had taken control of its own. The power was focused directly on Velibor's head and after a few seconds he started yelling at me that his head was starting to burn from the inside and that he felt it would explode if I did not stop what I was doing. Yet, I could not stop and the force became even more powerful. Although I was blindfold and had my back turned on him, I clearly saw as the veins on his neck and head were starting to puff up and I spotted blood running from his nose. Real panic went through me and I was aware that if I did not stop the force, it would kill him. I reached deep down in myself to the source of my power and gave a strong command – "BACK OFF IMMEDIATELY!"

Luckily, the psychic energy obeyed and stopped instantly. I heard Velibor falling down on the floor the same moment the force backed off. Quickly, I removed the binder around my eyes and got up from the chair as fast as I could to help my friend. Despite all the pain Velibor had gone through, he remained with the smile on his face and told me: "Pane, the training is finished because you are starting to scare me. You possess now the same power I do and please, be ware of hurting somebody!" His veins became normal and his whole appearance stabilized. Silently, not a single word uttered, we cleaned the blood from the carpet and then he looked at me, smiled for the last time and left my apartment. Since then, we never trained together, and our life paths took different courses.

He moved to Belgrade and I never saw him again, not even on the astral plane. However, I knew that he was not angry with me - he taught me everything he thought he should have.

Anyway, the usage of telepathy sometimes considers scanning somebody. To avoid the negative effects that I mentioned above, everyday meditation is needed. That way, the mind will be purified and the great mental strength will be stable and under control. If the circumstances allow it, at least once a month, for such a developed psychic person it would be good to visit some place surrounded with beautiful nature where he/she would be able to release his/her mental powers.

That way one will be able to release his/her mental forces and will not be a potential danger for anybody. Joining with the nature will also bring peace and only creative relationship with everything around into his/her mind. This is very important for the student that has just developed a higher level of mental power. As he/she will notice him/herself, the force will be constantly changing and when it reaches certain level of fulfillment, it will be difficult to control it because it will force its way out anyway.

It often happens that such a student encounters some telepathic effects, which can be called difficulties, when surrounded by many people. For example, if the student enters a public bus he/she will hear the thoughts of all the people that are in it. This could be very annoying experience if it starts happening all the time. In the beginning, the student has to get used to such experiences and in time, has to learn how to block this ability to hear other people's thoughts. The blocking will bring psychic relief and it will have refreshing effects on one's mind. A simple way to achieve that if necessary is to put an unbreakable barrier around the third eye, which will isolate his/her mind from the telepathic influences of the environment. Just in case, here is how the blocking method works:

The student's mind has to create a transparent ball in his/her head. With his/her inner vision, one has to absorb all the light coming from the third eye into the ball. Once the ball is filled with light, the mind has put a protective black shield around the ball. However, in the beginning, it will require strong mental efforts from the student, which will have to be present all the time, while the light from the Ajna chakra is trapped inside the etheric ball. In time, the student will learn how to do this with minimum mental efforts and by using a simple mantra – a special word that has certain sound vibration that gives mental power. For example, it could be the mantra "Om". It is very important to remember that when the mantra is spoken it has to be spoken mentally, but at the same time to be visualized graphically. The combination of these two forces will provide the maximum effect the mantra brings and if one is missing it will not work.

Once the student has mentally spoken the mantra in his/her mind, the light that is trapped inside the ball will turn off. When the psychic wants to turn the psychic powers on again, he/she will have to look for the same ball, which is around the third eye and to use the same mantra to turn the light on again. Then, with the strength of his/her thoughts one has to destroy the transparent ball and to allow the light to come again from the place where the Ajna chakra is situated.

Chapter 8
AURA

Around every living thing there is an energy field known as aura. Radiance emanates from the energy field that surrounds all life forms. Generally, the existence of the aura has been proven with the Kirlian photography and today, many scientists work on sophistication of the aura observation technology. However, from a technical aspect, as I previously explained, a Kirlian photography involves the transferring of a high frequency charge through a metal plate attached to a Polaroid film camera base. The fingertips are lightly placed on the film encased in a light-tight bag, and an electric exposure is made. Sixty seconds later, after the film develops, the Kirlian photograph is complete and the subject's energy field is revealed. In those times when the Kirlian photography was officially presented to the public, some para-psychologists came up with the statement that actually, it was the astral body of the human recorded with a camera, which extends the physical

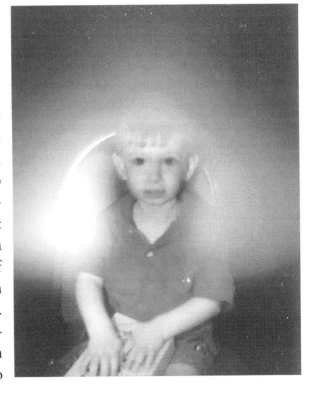

life and continues to live after the physical death appears. While the scientists work on their advanced technology, in Tibet for thousands of years a secret teaching about psychic aura observation by using the third eye is passed on from generation to generation to special gifted lamas. Carefully chosen lamas starting at the age of seven or even younger, with a strong sign of paranormal are trained with special training methods. Those lamas, who are considered incarnations of a higher rank, are initiated into the metaphysical secrets, which have roots from long ago in very ancient times. In time, a fully trained lama can scan the radiance that emanates from the energy field of a complete stranger, and tell the stranger's past, present and future. Reading from one's aura the lama can easily read one's intentions, desires and fears. With the strength of his brain waves the lama can influence one's aura and make healing changes, block one's movements and completely control one's behavior.

This ability today is a secret and out of reach for the public. It is a subject of many research projects concerning utilization for different purposes like humanitarian ones for everyone's better life as well as for destructive purposes. It is sad though true that the military is the most interested in the destructive powers of these abilities.

Anyway, there is an energy shield around every life form, which provides protection from all environmental psychic influences and besides of the physical body, it provides a vitalization of all other subtle bodies that the life form possesses as well. For the record, the word aura comes from the Greek word "avra" which can be translated as "soft wind". As under some circumstances in the Earth's atmosphere magnetic fields are created, in exactly the same way during a person's intensive concentration, inspiration and meditation energy that emanates through one's aura field is created. The more spiritual this energy is the more beautiful colors of light it produces on human aura. In some conditions, the aura extends itself, and in other, it assembles itself to the point of total closure. If our thoughts are focused on love and friendship our aura extends itself and shares its energy with other life forms. On the other hand, if our thoughts are defensive and there is presence of fear or rejection in them, it assembles itself to a total closure. In that particular case, our aura will remain closed until the danger or the unpleasant situation has passed.

Furthermore, the aura science is a major one. From another perspective, if there is something wrong with the health of a human, it is surely visible on his/her aura in the form of a shadow or a dark spot. I believe all of you will agree that it is very important for everybody to maintain one's own psychophysical health and for that reason I have chosen to present one method in this book, which will provide an easy detection of those energetic anomalies inside the aura. Helped by this method each of you willing to try it can learn how to clean the entire dirt from his/her aura.

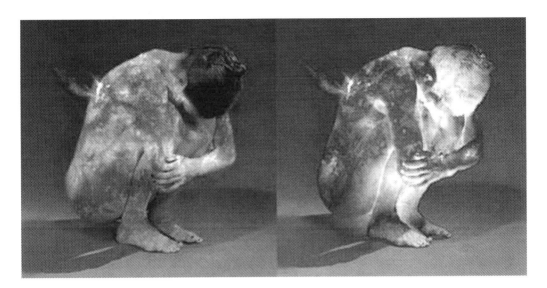

Subchapter 8.1
AURA CLEANING METHOD

Sit in some meditative position and relax your physical body. Start with deep and controlled breathing, and after a while, leave the breathing process to take its own natural rhythm. Open yourself to your inner self and feel your natural bio-potential. Concentrate hard and once you discover it deep inside you, allow it to come to the surface of your energy field. The warmth in your body will be the first sign that your inner energy has started to awake. Try to release it increasingly. For all this to have the right effect, you have to believe in what you are doing with all your heart and mind. Otherwise, you will not feel anything and you are just wasting your time. It must become clear to each of you that all the paranormal powers are mainly possible only if one thing is present – faith in yourself.

Create a white-blue energy ball as explained in the energy absorbing meditation. Let the psi-ball grow until your physical body becomes the center of the ball. Then just empty your consciousness from everything else and focus yourself only on the radiation that emanates from the ball. When you reach this point, start to visualize a strong light illuminating you from the inner wall of the energy ball. The light has to be so strong that it has to run through your whole physical body, which will create some visual effect that will become half transparent.

Then, just try to notice if the light is leaving some shadows on your physical body. If there isn't any, OK, but if there is one or more shadows, be sure that there are some energy anomalies on your aura, which are or will result with bad health in the future. Still, to be completely sure of the presence of certain anomaly, move the hand where you feel the energy streaming is stronger towards the location where you have spotted the dark mark.

Your hand has to be at least two centimeters above the selected zone of your physical body. If the streaming of the energy that comes from that location is different from the other zones of your physical body and if it is accompanied by certain coldness on that spot you can be completely sure that the energy anomaly is there. The heat difference combined with the inner vision of your aura is always reliable evidence of a weakened or damaged spot on the surface level of your aura if some illness is present. I hope not, but if you have discovered any zones like that, move your hand back to your normal meditative position, close your eyes again and concentrate on the energy ball. With your inner

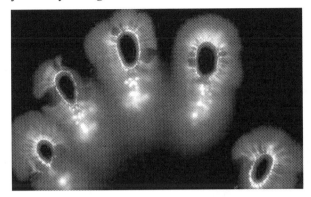

vision, focus all the light beams coming from the inner wall of the psi-ball directly on the zone where the dark spot or shadow has been detected. Then, radiate the shadow until it becomes illuminated. When it reaches the normal color with the other zones of your half transparent physical body in your inner vision, cut off the light beams. Then, move your hand again to the zone you have just exposed on radiation with the etheric particles and try to feel if there is any heat difference again on that spot. If the heat is the same with that of the other zones of your physical body, you have succeeded to remove the energy anomaly from your aura but if it is not the same, repeat the same procedure again.

Sometimes the illness is much more serious, so it requires longer time to eliminate the energetic anomaly, but with the right desire to help yourself and faith in your natural healing forces the results will be easy to detect.

In case you have found more than one energy anomaly, start to eliminate them one by one. When there are not left any, stretch your hands in front of you in slow motion and feel the way you are absorbing the whole energy from the ball back to you. In the end, return all the energy from the ball back to you shut down the psi-ball and finish the meditation. With no strong moves stand up and do not forget to take a warm shower.

Why washing with water is so important? – Everybody is constantly in touch with all sorts of outer energies through the environmental bio-field and a tiny part of them stays in the aura. When a person uses the energy of his/her aura, he/she should be aware that there is presence of particles of outer energies at the same time. I believe it is not

necessary to explain that every place and every living creature possesses its own energy, which comes in touch with the environmental bio-field through the aura and mixes there. When an individual goes to different places and has contacts with different life forms, the energy that he/she can collect from there can be positive, negative or both. If the aura shield of the person is weak, which from the physical aspect manifests as weak immunity, the individual can easily attach energies that can badly influence his/her health. It is completely natural because the energy flows everywhere, all around us and through us. It connects us and provides life for us.

That is why before and after we work on our aura or manipulate with the bioenergy in our energy shield it is necessary for us to wash ourselves. Water is a natural filter that purifies all our inner energies. Even in great health, it is good to perform this aura cleaning method at least once in three months, which can enable an easy detection of some eventual energetic anomaly that can cause some health problems in the future.

Subchapter 8.2
AURA OBSERVATION

As I mentioned before, Tibetan lamas possess very old but effective system for developing the ability of psychic observation of human aura. Still, their system is based mainly on opening the third eye of the talented lama (which is performed with specific surgery in the area between the eyebrows) and on the education about what specific color in the aura means.

A part of the bone of the forehead is removed on the spot between the eyebrows and replaced with a small object made of special tiny wood. The implanted object is in the shape of the letter "U" and it is polished with some special etheric oils combined with liquids extracted from specially chosen plants. Only traditional Tibetan lama surgeons know the recipe. These etheric oils combined with secret liquids that have some oil characteristics too prevent the tissue from infections and putrefaction.

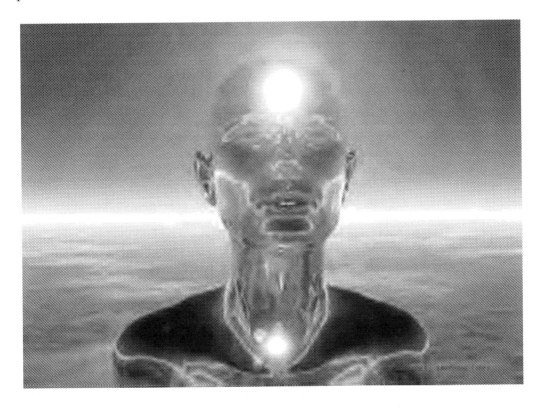

After the surgery is finished, the gifted lama has to remain blindfold for about three weeks. Then, the lama surgeons remove the object from the disciple's head and he stays with the opening in his forehead forever. In time, skin covers up the opening and only a tiny scar in the form of the letter U remains. Lamas responsible for the disciple's condition and progress, slowly and day by day increase the light in the room with a purpose to expose the disciple to daylight one step at a time. If they expose the disciple directly on full daylight, there is a great danger for the disciple to become physically blind forever.

The whole purpose of this surgical operation is the awakening of the third eye because they think the bone on the forehead of the lama is a barrier and weakens the influence of the pineal gland on the environment. As time passes by, the lama learns to use his third eye for many purposes, aura observation being only one of them.

Still, this surgical operation is a privilege for specially chosen lamas. No matter how opposite the public opinion is, it is an effective way of opening the third eye. Luckily, it is not the only way, and there are many other ways of opening the third eye but they last much longer and are far more difficult to accomplish. Anyway, the effects are quite similar eventually.

One of the other ways I have mentioned above includes the universal training of a slow and one step at a time system of opening the third eye. As I said before, the system is split in seven stages. Thus, once the student reaches the seventh stage, he/she will be certainly capable of seeing aura not just around all life forms but around every object as well. This other frequency of perception will allow him/her to see the whole spectrum of the colors the aura possesses. It will be enough to focus his/her consciousness to see the aura and it will become visible for him/her. In contrast to the energy field that exists around life forms, the aura that surrounds objects will usually not be in many colors but mostly with dark blue radiation.

If some object is surrounded by many colors it is because some life form has left a strong energetic signature on it and it practically means that some person has left a part of his/her aura on that object. It usually happens with some object we are very fond of and carry it all our life on us considering it priceless treasure.

Speaking of the subject of aura around objects, diamonds or some other precious stones possess aura full of wonderful colors, but I personally consider them different life forms and they are totally other subjects for analyzing. The more the life form becomes spiritually developed the more beautiful and shiny the colors of the aura become and vice versa. Sometimes, the astral traveler can encounter so highly developed life forms on the astral plane, which in the esoteric terms is known as "Devas", with an aura much larger than human's. The surrounding light around Devas is so shiny and strong that average human astral traveler usually can not see in their direction or can not even stand their presence. That is because their aura causes a burning process in the aura of a lower or average developed human being and the contact is usually very short. However, those highly evolved life forms rarely come down to the astral plane but they can often be found on the mental and higher planes.

Often, one with an opened third eye has to employ big efforts to get used to all sorts or lights that can be found on all kinds of astral creatures. The individual will have to learn the meaning of colors. The confusion usually comes in an untrained human sight when colors start to mix and separate in a split of a second, which is completely normal and represents only the momentary conscious state of the life form.

In the process of analyzing the aura seen from another angle, the protective shield is a quite extraordinary part of the spiritual science. It can sense the environment in so many ways. For example, speaking from my own experience, if you find yourself in complete darkness walking through some house or apartment helped by the protective shield you can sense where walls, doors, table, chairs, etc., are. It is sufficient for you to just pass more or less close to them. The best I can describe it, it is like the sphere barrier around is cutting the edges of walls, doors, chairs, etc., and you can feel the shape of the object and the distance from you. It is an amazing ability. Besides all that, it can sense movement. A long time ago, I was experimenting with this protective shield a lot. Two assistants of mine using long sticks were pointing at my back without touching me, normally while I was blindfold. They were about 2 meters away from me and the ends of the sticks were about 1 meter away from me. It was amazing because I was able to feel the exact locations where the two end-points of the sticks were penetrating my protective sphere without using my inner vision, just pure sense of my aura. To the best of my knowledge, some dolphin and shark species are real masters of using this sense when they are after other smaller fish to feed themselves. Though they feel the movement of the fish around them they also have complete sense about the shape of the bottom to the level of feeling the tiniest rocks they pass above. However, although I have said the energy field is of etheric substance in order to be better understood in that particular moment, the truth is that it is made of all substances, which can be

found on all planes of existence in the Universe. Furthermore, it is difficult to be explained to perfection, because as I said before, the aura is a major science and the student has to learn it, step by step, which takes long time of experimenting on this and other planes. Thus, for the record, the human aura possesses seven layers, all of them different by their depth inside the whole energy field and their connection with certain things. The first three layers are the most easily detected and are usually visible for most psychics capable of using their third eye. However, for the deepest layers of aura, a special training is required from a top master difficult to find these days. Now let us take a look what some of the basic colors in human aura mean:

RED

Its interpretation depends upon the shade and as with all colors in question, upon the relationship with the rest of the colors. Permanent dark red indicates high temper while temporary sparks of the same color symbolize only a momentary state of mind filled with anger or even hatred. A human who carries a strong dark red light in his/her aura usually is one who has suffered a great emotional loss in the past and still has not gotten over it. On the other hand, a human who caries permanent strong light red color in his/her aura usually represents a person attached to sexual experiences, while temporary sparks of the same color can indicate a momentary state of the mind filled with sexual charge or need for sexual experience. However, such a person can often be apt to be domineering and quick acting. Generally, the red light in the aura symbolizes a nervous, impulsive, very active person, one who is probably self-centered. It mainly symbolizes a materialistic person and if the scarlet tone is present, it indicates an overdose of ego.

GREEN

Basically, a permanent presence of the green colored light in the aura indicates a person who is generous and compassionate. Such a person tries to help everyone and everything because he/she is driven by the force and thinks he/she can make a difference and make a better world for everybody to live in. Still, temporary green sparkles usually indicate a state of mind filled with friendship or deep compassion with some event that has happened recently to someone dear. Generally, the presence of green indicates a positive person always willing to help.

YELLOW

In most cases, a yellow colored light in someone's aura represents the person's freedom and non-attachment. It can be also a momentary state of mind filled with happiness and joy. Nevertheless, it also indicates a person's strong intellectual power, hunger for new exciting ideas that will make his/her life funnier and more interesting. It is a rare case, but if the yellow halo around somebody's head is present in the aura, that certainly means a true spiritual oriented person.

<u>BLUE</u>

Blue indicates personal growth, and walking along some spiritual path. If there is a sky blue light in the aura it mostly means a clear and constructive oriented consciousness, which is a candidate for the highest spiritual achievements. When it is mixed with white, it indicates that the person possesses paranormal abilities above the average level. A presence of dark blue can sometimes indicate deep sadness about not being able to change many things in life. Besides purity of heart, it can symbolize a very serious embodied spirit with a special task to achieve here on Earth.

WHITE

It is the color of purity and rarely happens to be found in the auras of average people. It indicates a spirit that does not live only on the physical plane, but walks along other planes of existence. However, it is the color of a spiritual leader and if there is at least some small presence of golden light, it is certainly a case of most highly developed life form.

ORANGE

It usually indicates a person willing to control others. If orange light is a permanent part in the aura, it is a self-centered person who thinks he/she knows everything and that everything around him/her exists for his/her pleasure and happiness only. On the other hand, if only rare sparkles of light of the same color are present in the aura it actually indicates temporary mood to take advantage of some situation.

GRAY

Presence of gray color in the aura indicates pain and hatred. Stay away from those persons who emanate this colored light inside their aura. Most of the people who have problems with mental health possess gray color in their aura. It can be a murder-oriented person, so as I said before stay away from such a person.

Chapter 9
PSYCHOMETRY

The psychic impressions that can be sensed from people, objects, places, etc. are put in the ESP (Extra Sensory Perception) category known as psychometry. We all leave invisible energetic traces on objects we touch, people we communicate, etc. Those traces invisible with a naked eye stay in the aura of people, objects, etc. Consequently, it is quite possible for a human with psychometric ability to easily sense which object belongs to somebody, what happened to the object in the past, what will happen to it in the future and many more amazing things.

In practice, this ability can be achieved only if one's consciousness is focused on an object's aura where all energy signatures exist. Furthermore, from the object's aura a gifted person can even read and analyze energies that will come in the future. The psychic simply connects with the object through some kind of psychic channel and absorbs the whole astral data about it.

You can rarely find a person that possesses psychometric ability only without some other paranormal powers like telepathy, the ability to astrally project, psychokinesis, etc., because they are all part of the same source – human's third eye.

To a spiritual student who wants to develop the psychometric ability I recommend the same universal system of training. When the sixth stage is complete, the student is ready to start experimenting with his/her inner force in the direction of psychometry. The assistant should bring some unknown object to the student who has to be blindfold and deeply concentrated. Among the first things that the student has to do in the process of developing psychometry are to take the object the assistant has brought in his/her hands, and to start focusing on the object. Although the student is blindfold, the object will be perfectly visible to his/her inner vision. When the connection between him/her and the object is established, the student has to change the frequency of his/her inner sight.

In other words, the student has to detect the object's aura, which is usually a dark blue light. When the aura becomes visible for the student, he/she has to slip his/her consciousness directly into the light of the object's aura. One will pull that off very easily if he/she feels the object with all his/her being in order to get to know it better. If the student succeeds to feel the object to the atomic level, it will not be long until visions start to appear in the student's consciousness, which in common cases represent the past of the object.

However, I have to mention that sometimes the student will feel or see things that are not nice, so if that happens, the best would be to withdraw his/her mental contact from the object. As soon as he/she has sensed something negative is covering the object, with the withdrawal of the mental contact from the object's aura, the student will protect him/herself by not allowing an overflow of the negative energy from the object's aura to his/her own.

Since this happens rarely, those should be simple common objects, which have been in contact with average people, objects like pens, books, toys, etc. The accuracy of the student's answer should be noted in the notebook or the laptop. Anyway, this ability has been used in the past and as far as I know even today by gifted psychics usually hired by the police to solve some cases, which have reached dead-end with the standard procedures.

Note: The student has to discover as much as possible about the object from all the flashes and visions that appear in his/her consciousness. In exactly the same way as in remote viewing process, one has to block all individual feelings and opinions about the object and to become an empty and clear surface of consciousness, capable of receiving the radiation, which the object radiates. In time, those sensitive astral pictures attached to the astral matter of the object will crystallize and the student will generate a great amount of data about the object itself. After every séance in which the student will use his/her psychometric abilities, it is advisable to take a shower. The pure water will wash and eliminate all those tiny etheric particles, which can slip undetected into the student's aura.

Chapter 10
PSYCHOKINESIS

Through the process of psychokinesis, one generates the maximum level of concentration of his/her physical and mental forces. The pulse is speeding up to 200 and the activity of the cerebellum with the whole area of the brain around the top of the head is four times bigger than normally.

It has been scientifically proven that during the séance of psychokinesis the individual who demonstrates his/her psychokinetic ability loses weight, although he/she does not sweat too much. Practically, the whole muscular structure experiences tension and the muscles cramp because of the sending of the amplified bio-electrical impulses directly to the brain, which amplifies them even more and sends them out of the physical body.

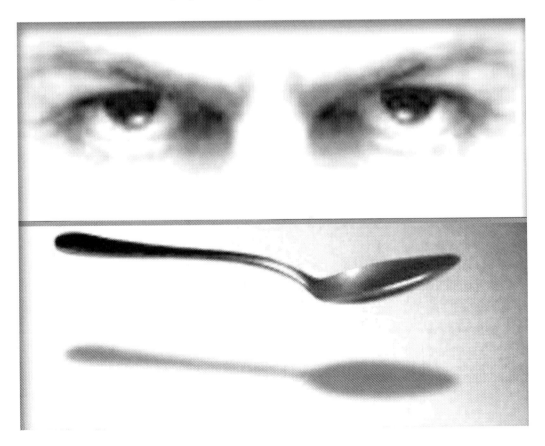

I believe that all of you have heard many definitions of what psychokinesis is all about but the simplest one and the most understandable is probably this one: "Mind over matter."

This mental influence over matter is a product of an extraordinary strong mind, which helped by the brain, sends psychic waves towards the object and causes movement. Depending on the strength of the psychokinetic force, the physical object can be moved, deformed, levitated, etc. Inducing self-levitation or neutralizing one's own gravity happens rarely but it is quite possible with people who possess far above the average psychokinetic force.

Like with most of the extraordinary powers, my experience with psychokinesis is also by the universal training, which starts with zener cards. For the psychokinetic tests to begin, the student is being required to complete the whole system of exercises divided in seven stages first. Then, for a student who has made it this far, the psychokinetic practice starts with one match from the matchbox.

The student no longer needs to be blindfold, so he/she can take off the bind around his/her eyes and take a seat beside the table where minutes before the zener cards, letter cards, different pictures and drawings, books, etc., have been put. For the psychokinetic practice, they are not needed anymore, and all the student needs is a simple match in the middle of the table to move it only by using the mental force of his/her mind.

When the match is on the place, the student has to establish maximum concentration of his/her mental and physical forces. In other words, one has to reach deep down in him/herself with the intention to release a major mental force to overcome the matter. To achieve that, it will help a lot to try to establish strong psychic contact with the match first as described in the first stage.

In those moments, it must become perfectly clear to the student that the success of moving the object with only his/her mind will depend primarily on his/her strong will, concentration and visualization. One has to be strongly self-confident of being completely capable to move the match. Concentration is crucial and the student has to focus on the object with maximum mental force as if his/her life were depending on it. If one has any doubts in him/herself even for a second while focusing his/her mental strength on the object, he/she will fail. The traditional Japanese saying perfectly fits here: "If you believe something is impossible to be achieved, you admit your defeat and failure before even trying!"

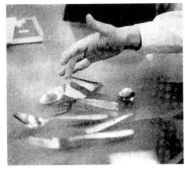

Because of that, the student has to approach the match strongly and aggressively. By aggressively, I mean exactly that, because in the beginning before the student succeeds to overcome the physical matter at least once – this is very important. For the record, the real psychokinetic strength lies in a calm and focused mind and not in aggressively oriented one, still for a beginner, presence of anger can help a lot for the success of the attempt and I will explain why. Thus, the student has to become very angry with the match and to start scanning the small object to the atomic level. In the next step, as the little object starts to move in the desired direction, he/she has to include clear visualization. In other words, one has to desire that movement from the bottom of his/her soul, and to be completely self-confident in positive outcome, i.e. that the object is going to move.

Before we go any further, let us get something straight here. Two things are relevant for the mental power to overcome the matter – love and hatred. Both of these feelings are charged with mental power and can influence the physical environment. A peaceful mind leads to love and anger leads to hatred. You can use them both to move the object. Speaking of psychokinesis, the beginner has to generate psychic power sufficient to move the small object, so one needs some of those two opposite natural forces. In my personal opinion, the student who is on the start line with psychokinesis can use the anger as the best generator of his/her inner mental potentials, but with only one rule - not to let the hatred prevail over. One can be angry with the match emotionally but he must prevent starting to hate it.

However, if the student has done everything right, because of the highly developed mental force due to the previous training, the match will slowly start to move on the table. In the beginning, it will be only for a few millimeters, but it will be sufficient for the student to gain strong self-confidence of being capable to move the object by only the strength of the mind. Once the student succeeds this, next time it will go faster and smoother.

Having mastered the seventh stage does not mean fixed time to achieve psychokinetic movement of the object. It varies from student to student. For some, success will come in an instant, for some it will come in a month or so, and some students will never succeed. The secret of psychokinesis lies in these three things:

1. Strength of the mind (psychic force)
2. Ultimate faith in success
3. Ultimate will to succeed

If only one of these components is missing, the success of the student's psychokinetic attempt to overcome the physical matter is condemned to fail. However, for those students who possess extraordinary psychic strength, who deeply believe in themselves and possess unbreakable will (that resulted as success) to move the match with their minds, even greater achievement follows.

In the next level of developing psychokinesis, the student is asked to lift the match and to hold it in a vertical position. Again, one has to establish hard psychic contact with the match and has to lift it vertically in his/her mind. The procedure is always the same – visualizing the movement, the thing is done astrally and then the same is manifested physically. Once the student has seen the match in his/her mind lifted by the strength of his/her mental force and does not have any doubts that he/she is capable of accomplishing that, it will not be long until it starts happening in the physical reality.

If the student has pulled that off, too, he/she is completely ready to attempt curving some metal wire. To accomplish that, one has to physically take the wire in one of his/her hands and bring it close to his/her eyes. When the wire is in horizontal position the student has to focus his/her look on some middle point of the wire with a purpose to burn that spot in his/her mind. The stronger the mental pressure on that spot of the wire becomes, the faster the wire will curve. As before, if all of the three components are present in the student's mind, he/she will complete this task smoothly. If not, the student will have to work it out until doing it right. If the individual focuses his/her look on the middle spot of the wire for at least ten minutes thinking of nothing else, just visualizing the wire curving, eventually it will surely happen.

When this has been achieved as well, the student is ready to attempt to bend some spoon or fork or even to try to levitate some smaller object like a table tennis ball. To be a direct participant or even a witness of such demonstration is an unforgettable experience; still, those are the lower effects of the psychokinetic power that humans once possessed.

For example, in the Potala palace in Lhasa, ancient scripts written in Sanskrit exist, describing that for thousands of years, once in 50 years the most talented lamas, yogis, shamans and Shaolin monks have been gathering to compete in the ability of levitation.

Twenty chosen ones sit in the lotus position in one row and the lamas that do not participate in the tournament tie them with a heavy chain, which ends with big stones. Then, on the mark of the lama in charge, they neutralize Earth's gravity and lift themselves up to the altitude of 100 meters in the same order they have been sitting on the ground. The heavy stones help them not to lift themselves up too high. However, in my opinion, they are more part of the tradition than of real use because if somebody possesses such mental power with a total control over it, it would not make any difference whether one is chained with stones or not.

Anyway, the scripts say that after the chosen ones are ready and in one line 100 meters above the ground, the lama in charge gives a sign again and they have to depart themselves 20 kilometers further to where another group of lamas wait for them. They pass this distance in long jumps at a record time. In the end, the winner gets special title and permission to visit the underground city of Shambala.

Rare witnesses of this event speak of it as of something unforgettable and as of unbelievable sight. The fliers levitating in the position of lotus simply slide through thin air as if bounding from the hard surface similar to a smooth stone bounding on the water surface when properly thrown.

Witnesses say this jump is sometime longer than 200 meters, and the whole event looks more like a dream to which no eyewitness can stay indifferent. Throughout the secret scripts I have mentioned before, it is also written that the ability of the physical levitation can be achieved after 12 years of long meditation combined with special rhythms of pranayama.

I am aware this sounds unbelievable, but Tibet is covered with many mysteries and legends based on true events. I remember that only a decade and a half ago the west became interested in those spiritual skills of the east through the chi energy demonstration of Chinese Shaolin monks, who demonstrated extraordinary skills.

If we consider the fact that the greatest masters of the Shaolin temples say that those demonstrations are only the lowest effects of the power of chi, a logical question appears – if those amazing things are the lowest effects of the inner energy, then what are the highest ones?

Chapter 11
THE FINAL RISING OF THE KUNDALINI ENERGY

Besides the many awakened and cultivated psychic powers, accomplished by hard psychic training the latent power of Kundalini is still not fully released and realized. Now, a very advanced disciple who can easily enter the astral plane, see through closed eyes, who is able to communicate telepathically or can move smaller objects with his/her mind, etc., is ready to face his/her true nature where his/her true power lies. Thus, the best way of Kundalini awakening can be achieved if the disciple leaves his/her home for seven days and goes somewhere quiet and isolated where he/she can be in harmony with the nature. That should be somewhere, where he/she would feel completely safe and secure.

For example, it could be a nice cabin on some lake's shore, a mountain cabin or some quiet and isolated small cabin by the ocean. One of the most important things for the person that has reached this level of development is to feel safe and secure in that place and not to be disturbed by anyone while the spiritual awakening takes place. From one point of view, the awakening of the mighty Kundalini means the return of the human to the nature. That is because all natural astral elements will come in touch with the true and worthy disciple during his/her transformation into a higher spiritual being. Once the human makes his/her first steps on that road, there will be no return for him/her. At least, not in the way one was used to, because he/she will understand the purpose of one's own presence in time and space. At the end of the road, one becomes a part of everything and reaches enlightenment. The process, which takes seven days, should start every day before sunrise, when the pranic energy is very strong and the whole nature is awakening for the new day. Seated in the lotus position the disciple will have to turn on a different chakra each day in a way he/she has never done before.

DAY ONE

During the first day, one determined to reach the top spiritual heights has to turn the Muladhara chakra on and to face its manifestations. He/she has to be seated in lotus position, and in very deep meditative state from which he/she will easily accomplish astral projection. Once one finds him/herself in his/her astral body, he/she has to remain so close to his/her physical one. If the disciple has passed the whole training system I have recommended, he/she will have no problem at all to stay in the astral body so close to his/her physical without being stuck in the immaterial body.

When the astral projection is successfully done, the disciple has to change the frequency of the astral vision with a purpose to see the aura, which radiates around his/her own physical body. A beautiful sight appears in front of the disciple and he/she will enjoy the dancing colorful light with the colors changing in certain rhythms. The next thing the disciple has to do is to concentrate to the light of the aura of the whole surrounding nature. The disciple simply has to focus strong to see the true face of nature and the infinite dancing lights will become visible to his/her astral sight.

Note: *The event is so amazing that it sounds like a science fiction or fairy tale, but believe me, it is real if the spirit is ready. Our very existence does not include only physical, but includes far beyond that. We are all part of the same beautiful natural force that flows everywhere and in everyone. I can only say that it is a sight of the creation itself. Life comes from this creation and we all share it in a special way. The Buddha, the awoken one has seen the same amazing thing and each of you can see it too if you are willing to reach it. Every living thing possesses soul; so do not forget that each of you is capable of seeing this if you want it strong enough. So, please do not surrender to the limits of the material world. Instead, allow your soul to be free.*

The dance of light will stretch everywhere, and the disciple will soon realize that the lights are coming and leaving the aura of his/her physical body. The aura around his/her astral body will no longer be only a tiny dark blue emanation but much bigger and in so many

321

beautiful colors. Next thing the disciple has to do is to move closer to his/her physical body and to put his/her right transparent hand above the location where the Muladhara chakra is located. Then, he/she has to do circles with the hand in clockwise direction and that will soon result with the undulation effect of the aura above the location where the lowest chakra is. The spinning has to continue above the Muladhara until a whirlpool appears. Once the whirlpool becomes visible as a result of the spinning movement of the disciple's hand, the disciple has to try to establish telepathic contact with the natural elements. If the disciple's thoughts are pure and noble, the nature will accept him/her as a part of it and it will allow the communication.

Then the disciple has to ask the natural elements for help, in a pleading manner: "Mighty forces of nature, please, light the fire of Muladhara"! As soon as the friendly request of the humble disciple has been expressed, the astral elements of the nature will turn the Muladhara on. In that moment, the basic chakra will start to shine with strong light. Then the disciple has to send regards to the forces of the nature with the thought: "Om! It is done!"

The next moment the disciple has to join with his/her physical body to experience the manifestations that Muladhara will bring next. As soon as the astral body of the disciple returns to his/her physical carrier, the consciousness will notice a strong bright light coming from the location where the basic chakra is. A few moments later the consciousness will start to gain the characteristic of liquid because Muladhara is still the lowest chakra in the evolution of humans and it manifests mostly the lower forces of the human's nature like fear, anger, lust, hatred and jealousy. His/her consciousness will be brimming with thousands of visions of lower character and most of the repressed emotions will reach the shortest way to the surface. Still, for a disciple that has already disciplined his/her mind, all those manifestations will look like theater. In his/her mind, the dominant components are the deep peace and wisdom, so any of those manifestations will not reach him/her deeply because he/she has already known it would come and has been fully prepared for them. The truth is that his/her spirit does not attach to things anymore, does not see only in black and white, good or bad but sees above those two opposite sides. Those manifestations last depending on the individual but in average, they last for about four hours.

Once the storm of visions and repressed desires and emotions (which all together will be mostly of the sexual nature) calms down, his/her consciousness will become an empty surface. The Muladhara will then shine even brighter because of the purification, and the disciple can retreat to the premises he stays at because the purpose for the first day has been completed.

DAY TWO

On the second day, it is Svadhisthana's chakra turn. Again, like any other day during the rising week, the disciple has to be seated in the lotus position and to reach a state of deep Trance from which he/she will be able to achieve an astral projection easily. The procedure is the same with all the chakras to follow and as soon as he/she finds him/herself out of the physical body, the disciple has to change the frequency of his/her astral sight. When the aura around his/her physical body becomes visible for him/her, the disciple will notice the Muladhara chakra still shining. Now the disciple has to come closer to his/her physical body and to start spinning clockwise his/her transparent right hand around the location where the Svadhisthana is located the same way he has done with Muladhara. Once the undulation appears above the Svadhisthana location, the disciple will have to continue with the spinning movement until the whirlpool appears.

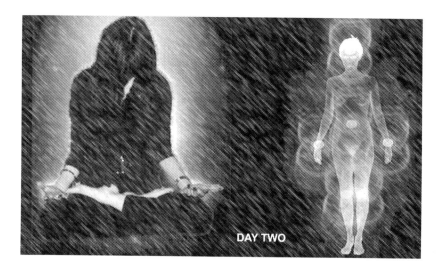

DAY TWO

Then, as with any other to be awaken and turned functional he/she has to connect with the natural forces and to ask for help with this humble request: "Mighty forces of nature, please, light the fire of Svadhisthana"! Again, if everything done, as it should have been, the powerful natural forces will concentrate their mighty powers on Svadhisthana and they will do a fluctuation on the location where the disciple has made a whirlpool. The Svadhisthana will then start to shine with all its glory and the disciple who is still in his/her astral body has to address the nature with this thought: "Om. It is done"!

When that is done he/she has to return to his/her physical body to face the manifestations that will soon rise as a result of the already awaken Svadhisthana chakra. Here things become dangerous for the whole process of rising because at the same time the Svadhisthana represents a limbo through which the human spirit will not be able to pass if it is not ready yet. The latent dark nature that lies in every human will attack the disciple's spirit with such powerful strength that if he/she is not worthy the fight will be over soon. The worst is that the negative side of the individual will not choose tools to create great illusion with a purpose of deception. Thus, for the disciple's mind not to be overtaken by this negative side, he/she has to possess the virtues of extra bravery, a will strong as steel and the most important- pure heart to succeed in overcoming all the tests the evil force will be imposing upon him/her. Not a single spark of jealousy has to be there in the disciple's mind on his/her spiritual path and he/she has to be completely sure about the task to reach Nirvana. Only then, the disciple will be safe from this negative force, which will test him/her with his/her own most repressed feelings and most wanted desires.

Thus, the disciple has to ignore the illusion no matter how real the illusion looks and his/her consciousness will have to be constantly focused on the task without letting anything else to enter. In other words, the disciple has to understand that this dark force is a part of him/her and he/she must not break concentration now. If he/she does that for just a moment, the Svadhisthana will shut down itself and the attempt for reopening the second energetic center soon will be equal to zero. Thus, if the individual has understood the truth within that desires can never be fulfilled completely, not for thousands of incarnations and that the truth lays in the subtlest level of existence, the dark force will be beaten and nature will let the disciple pass the second chakra. Once the disciple focuses on this simple truth all illusions attacking his/her mind will stop in an instant and his/her consciousness will become an empty surface. Then the consciousness will calm down and the goal for the second day will be achieved.

DAY THREE

The third day is for the awakening of the Manipura chakra. The procedure of the opening is the same as in the two previous energetic centers. Once the procedure is done, the disciple returns to his/her physical body and faces the manifestations that Manipura brings. Among the first things visible for the disciple after joining with his/her physical carrier, it will be a strong blue-white light coming from the Manipura.

The name of this energetic center in Sanskrit means the "The city of jewels" and this is not given just like that. The Manipura chakra shines so strong that it seems the source of the light comes from other thousands of lights. Here the lower nature of the disciple is temporary beaten, but there will be other tests to pass in the higher chakras. Still, the Manipura does not hold any traps for the disciple, but his/her consciousness will transcendent itself.

The transcendental consciousness will experience the manifestations of Manipura, which will be accompanied by many spiritual effects. All the visions following it will only make the disciple's spirit even richer with greater wisdom and knowledge.

DAY FOUR

This day is planned for the Anahata chakra. The disciple's consciousness will experience the indescribable floating of life natural force in the shape of cosmic love when the manifestations of this energetic center appear. When this has been reached, the individual will affiliate the cosmic love deep down in his/her spirit to remain there forever. Here is where the Sanskrit word "Anahata" comes from. It means incessant, which symbolizes the cosmic love coming from the higher realms and its incessant connection with one's spiritual heart.

Author - long time ago

DAY FIVE

The time before sunrise on the fifth day belongs to Vishuddha chakra. The consciousness has experienced its final purification and all those small anomalies that have remained in the disciple's energetic system will vanish. The visions that will start appearing in the disciple's consciousness will be of even greater character and from the physical aspect the Vishuddha will start to extract nectar, which will have astonishing effects on his/her whole physical body. Once the disciple feels that the nectar is extracting from the throat energetic center, it will be appropriate to address the natural elements by the thought: "Om"!

DAY SIX

The next day the disciple is ready to face a real explosion of psychic powers, which Ajna chakra possesses. Here lies another test for the disciple. The moment when the mighty natural forces open the Ajna chakra, the disciple will return to his/her physical body where another task awaits. The above normal strength of the mind will come forward and the disciple will have the feeling like every psychic power that he/she has been developing for years had joint in one mighty unity so difficult to bear.

The problem will be that the powers no matter whether it is telepathy, psychokinesis, seeing aura, psychometria, astral projection, super hearing or something else will want to dominate. The most difficult part is that in the disciple's mind it will look like each of those psychic powers has its own consciousness and grips to conquer the others.

In other words, the miracles will start happening in one's mind. In one moment, he/she will find him/herself standing beside his/her physical body and in a second he/she will start hearing the thoughts of hundreds of people, animals and plants away from him/her. In another moment the effect of the poltergeist will appear around his/her physical body – the rocks will start to move or levitate on their own, etc. Anyway, the disciple will encounter a great extension of his/her consciousness in which the events will be changing in seconds. If his/her mind is not strong enough or is not ready for those effects, the experience can cause serious psychic consequences.

To avoid all those negative consequences the disciple must not attach his/her consciousness on any of those psychic powers but to see them only as subsidiary holdbacks to be overcome. Despite the storm caused by the psychic experiences, the disciple has to maintain his/her completeness and concentration, and to allow none of those attractive powers to deceive him/her. The whole secret for passing this test is in producing a super conscious state of consciousness called "Samadhi".

Some people say that the Samadhi comes in Sahasrara chakra but that is not true. Without the Samadhi the human will be beaten shortly after a deluge of powers appears as a result of the awaken Ajna chakra.

The Samadhi itself will allow the disciple's consciousness to take a parallel consciousness, which will flow together with the existing one. Once that is done, because of the parallel conscious command "Stop!" the storm will come down within the disciple who is reaching for the highest spiritual achievement in this lifetime that only the worthiest disciples can reach. If the thought's strength is extremely powerful, the storm of the psychic powers will stop instantly. The Samadhi will encircle all the powers in the existing consciousness. Once it is done, the powers will calm down and will be fully under the parallel consciousness control. It is interesting to be mentioned that this is why the Ajna chakra is called "The control center". The Ajna chakra really is a control center of all those supernatural powers.

Once the strong manifestations of the psychic powers disappear, and the storm is altered by the complete emptiness of Samadhi, the test is passed and the Nirvana is very close.

DAY SEVEN

The seventh and the last day of the process, is the day when one consciousness now divided in two parallel ones will vanish and a new consciousness will be born. This is the day to awake and release the mighty Kundalini and when upon the worthy spirit, the Nirvana will come.

The Sahasrara chakra will not be awoken the similar way the previous ones have been, because the Kundalini itself will turn the highest energetic center on and will leave the etheric body of the disciple through it. The super consciousness known as Samadhi, helped by the universal inner sight will notice the six chakras shining in full glory. Now, it is the Kundalini energy's turn to be awoken. Thus, before the very advanced disciple that has reached this point of spiritual evolution awakes the Kundalini, I would advise him/her to first imprint the mantra *"Om mani padme hum"* with the Samadhi on the substance of the etheric plane on all sides of the world. It will be a signature of his/her self-realization and it will give the respect to the nature.

When that is done, the disciple has to reach deep down in him/herself and to see in which of the three lowest chakras the three times assembled energy exists. In most cases, the spiral energy lies in the Muladhara chakra, but sometimes because of hard spiritual efforts made in the previous incarnations it can be in some other chakra. Once the Samadhi locates the Kundalini energy in some chakra, one has to generate the full capacity of the mental, energetic and physical forces directly on the location in the spine. Then the true disciple has to address him/herself to his/her own Kundalini with this thought: "Mighty Kundalini, you, who exists from the beginning of time and in everything that breathes, awake and join with me"!

If the disciple's request is free of selfishness and comes directly from his/her purified heart, Kundalini will awake. That individual is considered blessed. The disciple will feel the major bioelectrical heat in the chakra where the three and half times assembled energy has been sleeping since the last incarnation awakening it and a thunder sound will appear in his/her ears. The spiral energy three and half times assembled will unroll and it will start its journey up through the Sushumna nadi.

The physical body of the disciple will grip hard and in the next few seconds, it will become so calcified almost like a stone. In the spinal cord, the disciple will feel the spinal brain fluid rising in great speed towards his/her brain.

The moment when Kundalini reaches Ajna chakra, it will stop. Now, it is time for the final battle, which will be the hardest one, because the disciple's ego will attempt to enter inside the Samadhi. The ego will do that in the trickiest way, so the disciple has to be very careful now that he/she is in front the Nirvana's gate not to lose the battle. His/her ego will take its own appearance and it will materialize in front of his/her physical body. Then, his/her own ego will start telling him/her sweet words of the disciple's greatness and that his/her spirit is going where nobody else is going. Then the ego will ask the Samadhi to join the journey, but the disciple's spirit has to see above all illusions in space and time. Knowing this, the Samadhi must not allow the ego to regain the control of the spirit by entering the Samadhi with a purpose to manifest again. The disciple's spirit should not succumb to the ego's sweet words because it is saying those words with only one purpose – to distant him/her from the right path. Therefore, to avoid the ego's efforts to defeat him/her, the first thing that Samadhi should do is to recognize that the ego exists in the parallel consciousness that lies in the same spirit.

That simple truth of the ego's location has potential to defeat the ego. In fact, it is the only way to defeat it in the final battle. The normal consciousness has to die and only the Samadhi has to survive. Only if this is done the Kundalini will go further on its path. If this is not done, the ego will take the control of the Samadhi and the super consciousness will vanish. Only the normal consciousness will remain and the illusion will rule again.

Still, if the spirit of the human does not allow to be driven by the illusion of his/her own ego and humbly remains the course to the final goal, the victory above the material and the lower forces of the nature will be achieved. The moment when the ego is being destroyed, the Kundalini force will hit the Sahasrara with the maximum strength. It will enlighten the top chakra and it will leave the human through the Sahasrara's gate. In the Samadhi, the person will experience it starting to burn with millions of little sparkles illuminating the whole area of his/her physical brain.

The straight line of the strong light will leave the individual's etheric body and he/she will feel his/her aura burning by the heat of the

Kundalini. Then the Samadhi will break in million pieces and in a few long minutes, which to the disciple will look like eternity, the spirit will experience the highest plane of existence. The physical world will disappear from his/her vision and he/she will find him/herself in the Nirvana's plane where the will of God is known. His/her spirit will be as large as a Vast Ocean, which stretches in space with no shores. The goal is achieved.

The worthy spirit has touched the Nirvana and it will be free from being born in the physical body again. God's purpose and intention will become visible for him/her in those long minutes while he/she is present on the Nirvanic plane and in the future the spirit will act only in accordance with His will. However, while the spirit will be present on the nirvanic plane just for short, the Samadhi will also disappear and a new enlightened consciousness will be born.

All the forces of the nature will bow to him/her and he/she will understand the purpose of his/her presence in time and space and the reason of his/her physical incarnation. The individual will reach his/her self-realization and will never be the same.

The ecstasy of one's spirit will be infinite and when one returns home to the civilization, he/she will see only one vision in his/her heart: "To help every living creature to recognize its true nature and to understand the purpose of all creation."

CONCLUDING REMARKS

Generally, *"Extraordinary Powers in Humans"*, has accomplished to cover a huge variety of topics in one great unity, in a way that is so clear and easy to follow. The author remembers making tremendous effort writing the book because sometimes it looked an impossible task to achieve. In his mind, it looked like he was trying to put a major area in just one box, which has to have room for other areas. Still, following the vision in his mind about what the spiritual manual should look like he succeeded and finished the book.

However, trough the *"Extraordinary Powers in Humans"* the author has given away a part of his soul – energy that has been part of him and now belongs to everyone who reads the book. It may sound strange, but the author feels some kind of relief. It resembles the situation when somebody keeping something locked deep inside for so long finally finds someone to share it with and feels relieved afterwards. The heavy burden is not so heavy anymore because the knowledge that the author has been patiently generating for years is now free and can belong to every one who feels ready to accept it.

Finally, the author will present once more the simple truth that he has been taught while still a young boy:

"There are two realities in life. The first one is the reality we take as normal and where everything is defined and explained and the other one is the one that has a hidden dimension, where nothing is clearly defined and fully explained. The first one is called physical reality and everything in it starts and ends in the dimensions of the physical world. The second one, known as spiritual reality, has no such limits because it goes beyond the physical world."

Everybody has to choose among the options which reality he/she likes to live in. The author's final question is: "Which reality are you going to choose?"

- THE END –

Many Thanks to:

- My dear wife Svetlana Andova and my children Leon and Sara.
  Without them, the creation of this book would have never been possible.

- Illustrators:

  3D Studio – "Beyond visible"- Skopje
  Digital design – "Inner Light"- Skopje
  3D Digital Art Studio – "Solar dust"- Skopje

- Editor:

  Mrs. Suzana Goceva Zdravkovska

-And to everyone else, who have helped in any possible way in
  the realization of *"Extraordinary Powers in Humans"*.

  Author's contact: astral@mt.net.mk

TABLE OF CONTENTS

GLOSSARY

Astral Plane: An intermediate level of reality between the Physical plane and the higher, more divine realms of the Universe.

Astral Projection: A process where the consciousness in the astral body separates from the physical body by one's own will and projects on an astral plane.

Astral Body: A subtle body that consist of astral substance, which is soul carrier for the astral plane.

Akasha records: A hidden layer of the astral plane where the past, present and the future of all life forms and civilizations is recorded in a form of holograms.

Asana: Specific poses or postures that are developed to bring many benefits to a yogi and most of them a great balance between one's physical, mental and spiritual forces.

Aura: Energy field that surrounds every living thing.

Kundalini Shakti: The most powerful spiritual force, which exists from the beginning of time in everything that breathes.

Prana: A life force (free vital energy) that floats everywhere across the etheric plane and provides life to all living forms.

Etheric plane: A level of energy and existence between the Astral Plane and the Physical plane.

Pranayama: Science of controlling prana through breathing techniques, which dictate the lengths of inhalation, retention and exhalation; prepares the mind for deep meditation and develops psychic abilities.

Yoga: Extraordinary science created to lead the yogi to a complete harmony of the mind, body and spirit where the self-realization is reachable.

Bioenergy: Pranic energy, which can be used for many purposes but mostly for inducing healing changes.

Etheric body: A vehicle or body whose density lies between that of the astral and physical bodies.

Mental plane: A level of existence, which exists above the Astral Plane.

Chakra: Whirlpool of prana energy or etheric energetic centre, which is connected with all other centres through vast net of energetic channels.

Nadi: Energetic channel within etheric body.

Sushumna nadi: Primary energy channel within etheric body.

Pingala nadi: Secondary energy channel within etheric body.

Ida nadi: Secondary energy channel within etheric body.

Nirvana: State of self-realization, when one has achieved full liberation and freedom from the cycle of death and rebirth.

Nirvanic plane: Highest level of existence reachable in this Universe.

Meditation: A process in which the mind is diving deep inside its own essence.

Samadhi: Super conscious state in which one is very close to achieving the highest spiritual goal.

Karma: Natural law that runs all things. It is a result of moral acting or moral consequence of some act done for selfish reasons.

Telepathy: A process of mental communication between two or more minds, in which the exchange of mental messages takes place like some kind of natural psychic bridge between them.

Psychometry: Psychic impressions that can be sensed of people, objects, places, etc.

Psychokinesis: Mind over matter.

Remote viewing: A process in which the psychically gifted person is watching some kind of astral television based on a program that he/she has chosen on his/her own.

Clairvoyance: Astral vision.

Zener cards: Also known as ESP cards. One deck consists of 25 cards (5 symbols multiplied 5 times – star, square, circle, plus and waves).

Visualization: Ability of the consciousness to construct mental shapes and form and hold them as long as it wants to.

Levitation: Ability of the human being to neutralize Earth's gravity only by the power of the mind.

BIBLIOGRAPHY

Kundalini Tantra - Swami Satyananda Saraswati

Kundalini Yoga - Shakta Kaur Khalsa

Bioenergy: Vision for the New Millennium - Indo-Us Workshop on "Eco-Friendly Technologies for Biomass Conversion (Corporate Author),

Energy Medicine: The Scientific Basis of Bioenergy Therapies - Candace, Ph.D. Pert

The Heart of Meditation: Pathways to a Deeper Experience - Swami Durgananda, Sally Kempton

Silent Power - Stuart Wilde

Astral Plane: Its Scenery, Inhabitants and Phenomena - C. W. Leadbeater

The Tibetan Book of the Dead (Mystical Classics of the World) - Robert Thurman (Translator), Huston Smith (Introduction);

Third Eye - T. Lobsang Rampa

Astral Dynamics: A New Approach to Out-of-Body Experiences - Robert Bruce

Astral Projection and Psychic Empowerment: Techniques for Mastering the Out-Of-Body Experience - Joe H. Slate

Limitless Mind: A Guide to Remote Viewing and Transformation of Consciousness -- Russell Targ

Remote Viewing: What It Is, Who Uses It and How To Do It - Tim Rifat

The Voice of the Silence: Being Chosen Fragments from the "Book of the Golden Precepts" - Helena Petrovna Blavatsky

Telepathy: How to Use Your Power of ESP- Tom Pearson

The Pk Man: A True Story of Mind over Matter - Jeffrey, Ph.D. Mishlove, John E. Mack;

Clairvoyance: How to Develop Your Psychic Powers - Joules Taylor, Ken Taylor

The Human Aura: How to Achieve and Energize Your Aura and Chakras - Djwal and Kul, Kuthumi Kul

The Human Aura- Swami Panchadasi

Practical Psychometry - Hashnu O. Hara

Psychometry: The science of touch - Beverly Jaegers

Sixth Sense: Including the Secrets of the Etheric Subtle Body - Stuart Wilde

The Etheric Body of Man (Quest Book) - Lawrence J. Bendit

The Astral Body: And Other Astral Phenomena (Classics Series) - Arthur Powell

Printed in the United States
213753BV00003B/1/A